Finance in an Age of Austerity

For Peter, Lucy and Ty

Finance in an Age of Austerity

The Power of Customer-owned Banks

Johnston Birchall

Professor of Social Policy at Stirling University, UK

Edward Elgar

Cheltenham, UK • Northampton, MA, USA

Published by
Edward Elgar Publishing Limited
The Lypiatts
15 Lansdown Road
Cheltenham
Glos GL50 2JA
UK

Edward Elgar Publishing, Inc.
William Pratt House
9 Dewey Court
Northampton
Massachusetts 01060
USA

A catalogue record for this book
is available from the British Library

Library of Congress Control Number: 2012951768

This book is available electronically in the ElgarOnline.com
Business Subject Collection, E-ISBN 978 1 78195 184 2

ISBN 978 1 78195 183 5 (cased)

Typeset by Servis Filmsetting Ltd, Stockport, Cheshire
Printed by MPG PRINTGROUP, UK

Contents

Abbreviations   vii
Acknowledgements   ix

1   Introduction   1
2   The evolution of cooperative banks   7
3   The evolution of credit unions   34
4   The evolution of mutual building societies   64
5   The evolution of banks owned by other types of cooperative   88
6   The performance of customer-owned banks during the crisis   94
7   The comparative advantages of customer-owned banks   116
8   Some alternatives: savings banks and micro-finance
    institutions   135
9   Regulation, governance and the need for member participation   149
10 What motivates members to participate?   164
11 Customer-owned businesses – the wider picture   182
12 Conclusion: a cooperative counter-narrative   210

Appendix – a note on terminology   213
Bibliography   215
Index   229

Abbreviations

ABACUS	Association of Building Societies and Credit Unions
ABCUL	Association of British Credit Unions Ltd
ACDI/VOCA	Agricultural Cooperative Development International/Volunteers in Overseas Cooperative Assistance
ATM	automatic teller machine
BC	banche popolari
BCC	banche di credito cooperative
BP	Banques populaires
CA	Credit Agricole
CBRC	China Banking Regulatory Commission
CCA	Canadian Co-operative Association
CE	Caisses d'Epargne
CFI	cooperative financial institution
CM	Credit Mutuel
CUNA	Credit Union National Association
CWS	Co-operative Wholesale Society
DID	Developpement International Desjardins
EACB	European Association of Co-operative Banks
ESS	evolutionarily stable strategy
EU	European Union
FCB	farm credit bank
FHLB	Federal home loan bank
FHLBB	Federal Home Loan Bank Board
GDP	gross domestic product
ICBA	International Co-operative Banking Association
ICMIF	International Co-operative and Mutual Insurance Federation
IIFC	Islamic investment and finance cooperative
IMF	International Monetary Fund
MIT	Mutual Incentives Theory
MPCS	multi-purpose cooperative society
NABARD	National Bank for Agriculture and Rural Development
NACSCU	National Association of Co-operative Savings and Credit Unions

NAFCUB	National Federation of Urban Co-operative Banks and Credit Societies
NAFSCOB	National Federation of State Co-operative Banks
NCUA	National Credit Union Authority
NGO	non-governmental organisation
NPL	non-performing loan
PCF	people's credit fund
PD	prisoners' dilemma
RBI	Reserve Bank of India
RCC	rural credit cooperative
RCCU	rural credit cooperative union
RCS	rural credit society
SACCO	savings and credit cooperative
S&L	savings and loan
SME	small and medium enterprise
SPPE	State Shareholding Corporation
TSB	Trustee Savings Bank
UCB	urban cooperative bank
USAID	United States Agency for International Development
WOCCU	World Council of Credit Unions
WSBI	World Savings Banks Institute

Acknowledgements

First I want to reverse the usual order and thank my wife Bernadette for being so supportive. She has been patient not just with the usual long absences in my study, but also with the long absences that occur inside my head when I am supposed to be paying attention. Our frequent discussions have helped unravel mental knots that were stopping me from progressing with the book. Thanks are also due to our grandson Ty for understanding why we have not been able to go on some of our weekly adventures.

A special thank you goes to those people who supported the idea of the book: Stefano Zamagni, Carlo Borzaga, an unnamed referee, and Francine O'Sullivan at Edward Elgar.

I want to thank all the academic colleagues who have been a great help (in alphabetical order):

Bridget Carroll, Suleman Chambo, Jean-Pierre Girard, Lou Hammond Ketilson, Henry Hansmann, Hagen Henry, Seungkwon Jang, Paul Jones, Akira Kurimoto, Angus Laing, David Llewellyn, Alastair Milne, Hans Munckner and Yuichiro Nakagawa.

I also want to mention my old friend and colleague, John Burnett, who died five years ago, but whose voice I hear every time I write social history.

Several colleagues from various national and international organisations have also been a great help: Alban d'Amours, Bouka de Vries, Maria Elena Chavez, Armando Costa Pinto, Pete Crear, Charles Gould, Pauline Green, Paul Hazen, P.A. Kiriwandeniya, Felice Llamas, Iain MacDonald, Ed Mayo and Andy Poprawa.

I am fortunate in having a congenial group of colleagues in the cooperatives research group at Stirling University: Eric Calderwood, Keri Davies, Silvia Sacchetti, Richard Simmons and Ermanno Tortia.

Finally, I have to thank the Leverhulme Trust for awarding the Fellowship that enabled me to take a year to write the book.

1. Introduction

Books do not usually start with an appendix, but perversely this one does. The appendix provides a rather dull explanation of all the different terms used to describe the alternative to the 'capitalist' banks that have let us down so badly over the last few years. The problem is that we have become so conditioned to seeing investor-owned banks as the norm that when we try to describe an alternative words fail us; we do not know how to describe it. This book will show that there is an alternative banking system that has a long and distinguished history, and in many countries already is a serious competitor to other kinds of banks. However, because of historical accidents and misunderstandings it now comes in several guises: cooperative banks, credit unions, savings and credit cooperatives, building societies, mutual savings and loans, and so on. In order to *see* the alternative we first have to name it. We need an umbrella term, and so this book is about *customer-owned banks*.

The idea of *customer-ownership* is simple. Some banks avoid the need for a group of investors who take ownership rights over the business. They turn their customers into owners instead. There are all sorts of consequences to this decision that will be explored in the book. On the one hand, they are not all that different from investor-owned banks; they do the same kind of business, relying on managers and boards of directors to take decisions, using the same technology and providing similar products, but they have different motivations and their definition of business success is very different. Crucially, they do not have the incentive to take the kind of risks that have brought so many investor-owned banks to ruin and required the need for massive government bailouts.

The idea of a *bank* is also simple. It comes either from the Italian word for bench (*banco*), where moneylenders would sit, or from the other meaning of bank, as a mound or heap of money. For children it is a 'piggy bank', a box to put their coins into until they need to take them out again to buy something. This was true for adults as well in the days before banks evolved into businesses; in eighteenth-century Britain there were 'box societies' where people saved their money by putting it into a box kept in a local public house. They would elect trusted members to be the keyholders, and would share out the money according to rules agreed by the group. As we shall see, there is a direct line of descent from these box societies to customer-owned banks such as building societies.

Some readers may object to the use of the term *'customer-owned* banks' because they do not like the idea of reducing members of a social movement to the status of customer. They may feel this is too commercial an image, but this is exactly why we should use the term. Traditionally, the promoters of credit unions among low-income people have seen them as members of a community who have a common bond, rather than as individual consumers, or small business people, or employees. We, on the other hand, are customers who expect banks to provide us with the services that we need regardless of what community we may belong to. Why should we treat poor people differently? Some readers will object to the use of the term 'customer-owned *banks*' because only some financial cooperatives have the right to use the term 'bank'. This is because, in each country, regulatory authorities have reserved for themselves the power to call a particular financial business a bank. Generally the test is whether it offers its customers current accounts, and takes part in the clearing system. Those who fail the test are then called 'non-bank financial institutions'. This is clumsy, and also inconsistent; savings banks are still called banks even if they do not provide current accounts, simply because they have always been called banks!

What do we mean by customer-owned banks? The essential elements are ownership, control and benefit. The customers own the bank, with each person having one member-share. Nobody can sell it without their agreement. This does not mean that they should be able to demutualise it; the bank does not belong just to the current cohort of members but is an intergenerational endowment held by the cooperative for the benefit of current and future members. Membership is not transferable, and so there is no market for shares. The customers also control the bank. As members, they are an integral part of the governance structure, with powers derived from personal membership; they have one person, one vote, regardless of the amount of capital they have invested.

The customers are also the main beneficiaries. The main purpose of the bank is to benefit the members rather than to maximise profit. They can expect some of the profits to be distributed to them as a dividend, but this is proportional to the use they make of the bank rather than to their investment. Because of the intergenerational endowment, some of the profits also have to go towards strengthening the bank's reserves.

There are some operating principles that follow from these distinctive features of ownership, control and benefits. The main source of capital for the bank is retained profits added to reserves. The main source of money for lending to members is member savings. The banks are often part of a network with powerful apex bodies that provide them with mutual financial services. This enables them to remain local while benefitting from economies of scale and scope. Their focus is on long-term relationships with their customer-owners, not on making profits for shareholders.

It follows from these distinctive features that customer-owned banks should be stable and risk-averse. The banking crisis of 2008 was a great test of this hypothesis. With a few exceptions, the banks we have identified as customer-owned confirmed it to be true. They came through it without needing any government bailouts, without ceasing to lend to individuals and businesses, and with the admiration of a growing number of people disillusioned with 'casino capitalism'. They really are an alternative to the investor-owned banks that may be too big to fail but are also too corrupt to be trusted.

The book begins with four chapters exploring the different types of customer-owned bank: how they began, why they became so popular and grew so fast, and how they have survived all the financial crises of the last 100 years. Chapter 2 begins by telling the story of the invention of cooperative banking in the 1860s by two German social entrepreneurs, Schulze-Delitzsch and Raiffeisen. It compares their two systems and then shows how their ideas took off all over Germany, with primary societies and then apex bodies being created that proved mutual savings and credit could be provided by people who would otherwise be unbankable. It then describes the way their systems were copied all around continental Europe until there were thriving cooperative banking sectors in nearly every country. Surprisingly, the contours of these social movements are still clear. Their recent history is told, and then a detailed analysis is made of the current situation, providing statistics on the size and extent of the sector and its relative importance in different countries. This shows just how large and important the cooperative banking sector is, with a 45 per cent share of the market in France, 40 per cent in the Netherlands, and so on.

Chapter 3 provides the same treatment for the credit union sector throughout the world, beginning with the work of two more social entrepreneurs, Desjardins in Canada and Filene in the USA. This is a continuation of the same story, as it was the German system that was adopted under a different name. The chapter shows how the idea spread from one continent to another, but also how promotion by colonial and then nationalist governments in some countries in Africa and Asia led to government-controlled sectors that paid little attention to the idea of membership. It then provides a detailed recent history and analysis of the current situation in each world region. It shows that again, in some countries such as the USA, Canada and Ireland, the sector has become a strong competitor with other banking sectors. It has also become a major player in the micro-finance sectors of low-income countries.

Chapter 4 introduces another type of customer-owned bank, the building society (known in the USA as a thrift, or 'savings and loan' (S&L)) that specialises in savings and lending for house purchase. This type has its own distinct history, which stretches back even further than that of the cooperative banks into eighteenth-century Britain. The transition from terminating to permanent societies is explained, and then the story is told of the rapid development of the movement in Britain and the USA. Having become pre-eminent in their field, in both countries they suffered from demutualisation. The consequences of this are discussed: the failure of converted S&Ls in the USA in the 1980s, and the failure of converted building societies in Britain in the recent banking crisis. One result is that the benefits of mutuality have become more obvious; customer-ownership creates a stable, low-risk system for recycling savings into loans.

Chapter 5 provides a short introduction to yet another type of customer-ownership, though this time in an indirect form. Banks owned by other types of cooperative – in particular consumer, agricultural and worker cooperatives – have become very significant in some countries. The UK Co-operative Bank is the best example; the distinctive history of this bank, with its policy of ethical lending and vigorous championing of consumer interests, is then explored.

Chapter 6 assesses the performance of the three main types of customer-owned bank: cooperative banks, credit unions and building societies. It compares their performance to that of other types of bank in the period before the crisis, then estimates the impact of the crisis of 2007–08 on the banks, and describes losses made by particular central banks in the USA, Japan and Germany. It analyses the performance of the three types after the immediate banking crisis up to 2011, and asks how they will perform in the future. The conclusion is clear; before the crisis, customer-owned banks were competing successfully against investor-owned banks, during the crisis they were almost completely unaffected (except in the area where the crisis originated – the USA), and the losses incurred have been made up very quickly. The chapter concludes that there must be something about the customer-owned business model that makes it so strong.

Chapter 7 then takes up the challenge of making the advantages and disadvantages of these banks more systematic for their customer-members and the wider society. It provides a framework for understanding business advantage in terms of types of ownership. Then, as in the author's previous work on other types of cooperative (Birchall, 2012d), it discusses the advantages and disadvantages to members under three dimensions of ownership, control and benefit. In relation to cooperative banking, it adds in a fourth dimension – federation. Then it discusses the benefits of the cooperative ownership model to the banking system, finding that customer-owned banks provide diversity and stability. It identifies several benefits to local economies: the banks mobilise savings so as to provide loans to local businesses, they organise the sending of remittances from migrant workers, and generally have a pro-growth impact.

Chapter 8 discusses alternative types of bank that might provide similar advantages. It provides a short history of the savings bank, and describes its current spread worldwide. Then it analyses the sector's performance during and after the banking crisis. Ayadi et al.'s (2009) 'stakeholder banking' model is evaluated as an alternative to the 'customer-owned' banking model. Savings banks are found to have some important similarities with customer-owned banks, but their vague ownership and control structures may lead to instability, as has recently been shown in Spain and Korea. The chapter then discusses the similarities and differences between credit unions and the Grameen bank model of micro-finance. Other types of micro-finance institution are also considered as an alternative; they suffer from too much reliance on donor support, are difficult to scale up and are not as sustainable as credit unions.

Chapter 9 introduces the concepts of regulation, supervision, governance and member participation, identifying the main issues facing customer-owned banks. It cross-references different types of customer-owned banking system by type of regulation, supervision and governance. Then it identifies four current issues: the need to deal with the tightening of government regulations in the aftermath of the banking crisis; problems caused by supervision of subsidiaries and the growth of hybrid forms of ownership; the difficulty of effective supervision and governance in developing countries; and the need to reform government-controlled credit cooperatives.

Chapter 10 tackles the issue of human motivation, providing evidence from a wide range of behavioural sciences concerning the ways in which members, boards of directors and managers are incentivised. First it draws on theories of cooperation from evolutionary biology, developmental psychology and game theory. These provide broad generalisations about the conditions under which people will be prepared to cooperate with each other. These generalisations are then applied to the current situation in customer-owned banks. The chapter then draws on the author's mutual incentives theory to explain the circumstances under which members will participate. It then presents findings from studies carried out by the author on member participation in cooperatives, applying insights from these to customer-owned banks.

Chapter 11 provides a wider picture of other types of customer-owned businesses in retailing, insurance, utilities, agricultural supply and small business consortia. A short history is provided that shows how often they have intersected with the history of cooperative banks and credit unions. Their current situation is described, and interesting comparisons are made with the banking sector. The chapter then makes clear the advantages and disadvantages of each type, and the way mutual insurance in particular complements customer-owned banking.

The conclusion argues that customer-owned banks have proved they are a viable alternative to the investor-owned banks that have so far failed to serve the 'real economy'. They help us to move from an 'anti-narrative' in which we are paralysed by disillusion, to a 'counter-narrative' in which we regain the power to act. If this sounds enigmatic, it will become clear to those who trouble to read the book . . .

2. The evolution of cooperative banks

When economic historians study the development of a particular type of business organisation, they can draw on two distinct ideas: evolution and design. First, consider *evolution*. Businesses are founded, and then they grow larger, sometimes changing or expanding their purposes, and then they may enter into a period of decline, eventually being wound up. The analysis can be taken to a higher level, and we can see how a group of businesses in a particular sector evolve together through collaboration and competition, growing and declining under the impact of new technologies, changes in consumer demand and competition from other ownership types. At the top level we can distinguish a 'community ecology' of organisations that make up a whole industry, such as food retailing, cotton production or banking (Hannan and Freeman, 1989). In the next four chapters we want to understand the evolution of different types of customer-owned bank and so have to analyse developments at all three levels: individual banks that have managed to survive and replicate themselves; groups of banks that have established a distinct customer-owned sector within the wider banking industry; and the banking industry as a whole. However, the emphasis will be mostly be on the middle level – a customer-owned sector within the larger banking industry.

In order to provide an organising framework for the complicated story that history presents us with, it is tempting to theorise about the life cycle of individual businesses and sectors. In a recent book on member-owned businesses (Birchall, 2010), I suggested five stages: a founding period, a period of growth, period of consolidation, period of decline and death. However, organisations are not living creatures and so their death is not inevitable. They may change their shape through conversion to a different type of ownership structure, or they may experience renewal rather than death as new people take over. They are not so much creatures as institutions – sets of values, taken for granted understandings and routines held together by legal status – that human beings flow through as they live out their working lives (Birchall, 2010, pp. 39–40).

The metaphor of evolution can be taken too far. It suggests that organisations are subject to forces beyond our control, and that the current business environment is the result of an impersonal process in which the logic of random mutations and natural selection work themselves out. Our species evolves more through cultural evolution, and this includes mutual learning, conscious design and experimentation, and copying of successful organisations. We learn from our successes and failures, and through language are able to spread this knowledge far and fast. When we look at the early history of the different types of customer-owned bank we find individual people, whose names and biographies are known, designing new types of business organisation and trying them out to see if they work. We find other known individuals taking these designs to other countries and modifying them consciously to make them work under different conditions. However, the rapid replication of such organisations depends more on social movements that, while they also contain individual leaders, invite us to theorise about groups and classes as they struggle to make a living under conditions that are not of their own making. Here the idea of evolution becomes more than metaphor; people were actually trying to find ways of surviving and helping their children to survive.

THE INVENTION OF COOPERATIVE BANKING

We begin in the mid nineteenth century in Germany, or rather in that loose collection of kingdoms, grand duchies and principalities that we now know as Germany (they were not unified until 1871). Compared to Britain it was an economically retarded region that only grew into a great industrial nation late in the nineteenth century. While Britain was in the throes of the industrial revolution, the German states were, as one economic historian described it, 'nearer to Tsarist Russia' in their economic development (Kemp, 1985, p. 79), though a customs union and a network of new railways were beginning to encourage free trade between them. In the early part of the century serfdom had been abolished and a new class of independent farmers was being established, who were becoming more and more dependent on a market system with a monetised economy. In the towns, the slow rate of industrialisation meant that artisan industry still predominated, producing mainly for the surrounding countryside. Unlike in Britain, where workers were by this time mainly working in factories for capitalist employers, German workers were still protected by their guild system, so craft industry still survived. However, as in Britain, both the rural areas and the towns were suffering the stress of rapid population growth; in 1820 the population was 25 million, but at unification in 1871 it had doubled.

In 1846 and 1847 there was a famine throughout Europe caused by poor wheat harvests and a blight on the potato crop. In Ireland a million people

died and another million emigrated. In Scotland the famine gave landowners the excuse to clear the Highlands of people and introduce sheep
farming. Everywhere in Europe the common people were suffering – in
the rural areas directly through lack of food and in the towns through high
food prices caused by the shortages. At the same time, liberal intellectuals
were leading a campaign among the middle and working classes to limit
the power of monarchs and install democratic constitutions, sometimes as
part of a wider project of building new nations such as Italy and Germany.
The revolutions of 1848 were not well coordinated, and they failed almost
everywhere, with reactionary forces regaining control and allowing only
limited democratic rights, but with hindsight we can see how, out of the
old feudal, monarchical system, a modern society that we can recognise was 'struggling to be born' (MacPherson, 1999, p. 3). Cooperative
banking was one of these modernising elements.

Hermann Schulze was born in Delitzsch, a town in Saxony that we place
in East Germany but that at the time was in Prussia. This was the largest,
most populous and most powerful German state. With its flat land and
rich soil it was known as the breadbasket of Western Europe and, though
the peasantry had been released from serfdom, a 'Junker' class of powerful
landowners dominated the economy. Prussia was the dominant power in
the federation that loosely made up what is now modern Germany, and it
was not afraid to use it, going to war against Austria in 1866 and France
in 1870 before completing the unification of Germany. Schulze studied
law at Leipzig and Halle Universities before becoming a lawyer and then
in 1841 being appointed the 'patrimonial judge' of his home town. It is
difficult to say precisely what this job entailed. It was patrimonial because
he was standing in as a paid official for a job officially carried out by a
local squire. There was little in the way of local government at the time,
and so he could have been somewhere between a town clerk and a public
prosecutor. This position enabled him to observe at first hand the poverty
and distress caused by the famines of 1846–47.

Schulze played a prominent part in the liberal movement in Prussia,
and during the revolution of 1848 was elected a member of the Prussian
National Assembly. He joined the 'left-centre' grouping; he was a liberal,
a moderniser, but not a revolutionary. At this time, he added the name
'Delitzsch' to his surname to distinguish himself from other Schulzes in
the assembly. He presided over a commission of enquiry into the condition
of the labouring and artisan classes, and as an early commentator put it,
'became impressed with the necessity of co-operation to enable the smaller
tradespeople to hold their own against the capitalists' (Encyclopedia
Britannica, 1911). In 1849 the King imposed a new assembly that was
much less democratic, and Schulze began to get into trouble with higher

legal officials; in 1851 he withdrew from the assembly, not re-entering it until 1861.

Before he retired (temporarily) from political life, Schulze had already set up his first cooperative bank, naturally in his home town of Delitzsch. Where did he get the idea from? He was influenced by the British friendly societies that showed how collective self-help by working people could enable them to provide mutual insurance against sickness and unemployment. More directly, he was able to draw on the idea of cooperative banks that at the time was being promoted by Victor Aime Huber. Huber was an interesting character; a graduate in medicine, he never got round to practising as a doctor but preferred a career as a writer, academic and social reformer. He wrote several travel books on different regions in Europe, and a two-volume study of the English universities, and held posts as a professor of history and modern languages. His facility with languages and extensive travels gave him an overview of one of the burning issues of the day: how to avoid class struggle by reintegrating an alienated working class into society. He saw the potential in the Rochdale model of a consumer cooperative that had been formed in 1844, and also studied the French model of worker cooperatives. In a series of pamphlets published in German, he advocated the idea of cooperative banking (Kanther and Petzina, 2000).

In 1849, in response to the distress caused by the famines of 1846–48, Schulze founded a friendly society. He also set up an association of shoemakers for the purchase of raw materials; this is what we would now call a producers' supply cooperative, and it is an effective means by which self-employed artisans can increase their incomes. In 1850 he founded his first credit association. Although it relied initially on capital supplied by rich founder members, it had ten members who were all artisans, and so was a hybrid of a philanthropic society and a cooperative. At the same time, a colleague, Dr Bernhardi, set up a bank in the nearby town of Eilenburg that was more genuinely cooperative and so in 1852 Schulze modified his own bank to become self-supporting, with the members contributing share capital.

What attracted him to the idea of cooperative banking? In Germany at this time, one of the main problems that was retarding economic growth was lack of capital (Kemp, 1985). Unlike in Britain, here a market society had developed before large-scale industrialisation, and small business people, artisans and farmers needed access to capital if they were to survive. They needed to take advantage of new markets; yet the commercial banks, set up to service richer customers, were unwilling to provide for their needs. Philanthropic banks set up by the rich to lend to working people were unpopular because they seemed more like charity than self-help. As Henry Wolff put it, capital was not equal to the demands made on it. People remained poor through lack of capital, and lacked capital because they were poor (Wolff, 1893, p. 20). There was a need to find a way to give credit to those who had no security to offer in exchange. Luigi Luzzatti, the great Italian promoter of cooperative banks, talked of the need to find a moral guarantee, a means for the 'capitalisation of honesty' (Wolff, 1893, p. 23). Leon Say, another promoter, summed up the task as 'the democratisation of credit'. There was an urgent need to find a way of releasing all the productive power that lay latent in the working people for want of capital. For this to happen reformers had to find a way, as Luzzatti put it, of 'aspiring to descend'.

Schulze's system demanded that members subscribe for a single share, the value of which was fixed as high as people could afford so as to provide working capital for the bank, but which could be paid in instalments. Liability would be unlimited, which meant every member effectively stood as surety for the debts of all the others. Profits, after paying a dividend of at least 20 per cent into reserves, would be distributed to members as a dividend on share capital. The banks would provide share accounts for members' savings, deposit accounts for larger amounts of money held on shorter notice, and drawing accounts (a forerunner of the modern current account). They granted loans to members with security given in the form of a personal pledge by a relative or friend. Set up on such a complex basis, they were meant to be run professionally, and with a salaried executive elected for three years by a general assembly, overseen by a supervisory board.

Schulze was a great organiser and propagandist, and he travelled round the country expounding his system. The number of banks organised on his model grew rapidly. In 1856 he published a book, and in 1859 organised the first congress of more than 200 banks that resulted in a General Union of German Industrial Co-operative Societies, of which he became director. In 1861 he re-entered the Prussian parliament and became a prominent member of the Progressive Party. In 1865 he set up a central cooperative bank, and then in 1867 secured the first cooperative law in Prussia, and then four years later a wider German law. He then published guidelines that ensured uniformity in legislation throughout the German states. However, he did not have an easy time of it; Wolff comments that, being a liberal, he was harassed by the government and deliberately excluded by Bismarck in drafting the law on cooperation. He single-mindedly stuck to his programme and by the time of his death in 1883 he had organised 1900 societies with 466 000 members (MacPherson, 1999). Because many banks did not join his union, Wolff gives a higher estimate of 4000 associations organised on his rules, with 1.2 million members (1893). A contemporary

observer, C.R. Fay, noted that 'in practically every town of any importance there is a Popular Bank' (1907, p. 33).

Friedrich Raiffeisen was born ten years after Schulze in 1818 in the
village of Hamm in the Westerwald, on the right bank of the Rhine in
the far west of Germany. The environment was quite different from that
experienced by Schulze; instead of the flat lands, large wheat farms and
towns of Prussia, it was a mountainous area of forests and small farms
and villages. It had one thing in common, though; it was in a region that
was owned by Prussia and so here it was the Prussian military that sup-
pressed the revolution of 1848. He was of humbler origins than Schulze,
being the son of a farmer, but his father was for a time mayor of the village
they lived in and this gave him a role model. At the age of 17 Raiffeisen
embarked on a military career, but eight years later an eye disease forced
him to give this up and go into public service instead. He was mayor
of two villages north of Nuewied: Weyerbusch and then Flammersfeld.
Then he became mayor of Heddesdorf, a village next to Neuwied that
would later be incorporated into it (Encyclopedia Americana, 1920).
In 1865, ill health forced him to resign as mayor of Heddersdorf and he
began a third career in business, first as a cigar manufacturer and then a
wine merchant.

Again it was the terrible famines of 1846–48 that were the catalyst for
action. He began by distributing bread and potatoes to the poor, but knew
this was not enough, so he tackled the problem head on by setting up a
Society for Bread and Grain Supply. With the help of private donations
he bought flour and established a cooperative bakery that succeeded in
halving the price of bread. He set up a cattle purchase association for the
farmers; what we would call an agricultural supply cooperative. He then
began to tackle what he saw as the underlying problem of usury. In 1849,
with £300 raised from rich supporters, he set up his first loan bank at
Flammersfeld, and then in 1854 a second bank at Heddesdorf. However,
like Schulze he began to see the disadvantages of a bank that relied on
philanthropy. As in many such banks before and since they had problems
with repayments; borrowers did not see it as their bank but as a means for
distributing charity. They were reluctant to pay back the loans and the
wealthy patrons lost interest. As we shall see in Chapter 8, philanthropic
savings banks were more successful but they did not dispense loans, and
the wealthy patrons simply oversaw the investment of people's savings.
In 1862 Raiffeisen set up a third society at Anhausen and made the same
transition that Schulze had made from philanthropy to cooperation; here
the farmers themselves became the members (Fay, 1938).

Raiffeisen's model differed from Schulze's in one fundamental respect;
it did not require share capital. This was because he was aiming his banks

at poor farmers, not the more affluent artisans and tradesmen of the town. Members had unlimited liability. Raiffeisen insisted on this, even when by law limited liability became available, because he wanted the farmers to rely on each other; while they could put up their farms and equipment as collateral, the main guarantee of commitment to pay off a loan was the involvement of all in the debts of each. His strategy for developing the banks was to rely on leadership by the local village priest and to limit each society to one village. He stressed the moral and communal character of the enterprise as well as its financial aims. Profits were not distributed but held in reserves, and loan capital was made up from small savings and deposits. As the societies were so small, they only needed one salaried official, a part-time accountant.

Like Schulze, Raiffeisen was a tireless propagandist for the cause. He wrote a book expounding his system, and in 1877 set up a General Union of Rural Co-operative Societies. By the time he died in 1888 he had helped to found 423 local banks. After his death the movement grew even more quickly; by 1905 Fay reported there were over 13 000 rural credit banks under his system. They outnumbered the town banks by ten to one and had twice the number of members, but gave out only a sixth of the credit. Over half the small farmers were members, while another 10 per cent, mainly the larger farmers, were members of the town banks (Fay, 1907). Taken together, both movements were an astonishing achievement that got the urban and rural workers out of debt to moneylenders and enabled them to survive in the new market society. Contrast Britain, where the peasantry had been destroyed and a combination of large tenant farmers and aristocratic landlords had enclosed and depopulated the countryside. The artisans had been destroyed by the factory system, and the large capitalists had transformed the towns into industrial slums. In Germany, the cooperative banks contributed to the survival of both farmers and artisans well into the twentieth century.

The genius of Schulze and Raiffeisen was to solve persistent problems in banking for people on low incomes. Knowledge of the credit-worthiness of one's neighbours meant loans were safer. Unlimited liability meant members had a keen interest in monitoring each other. The homogeneous membership base meant peer pressure to repay. But there was also a strong sense of communal solidarity. These overcame the potential conflicts of interest between borrower and saver, and shareholder and manager. The Raiffeisen system was better at this than the Schulze system, but both were much more successful than any other type of business model (we will test this for savings banks in Chapter 8). As we shall see in Chapter 3, this is still true for credit unions in developing countries; they are strong among low-income people, with a bias towards rural areas, and with personal

Table 2.1　Differences between the Schulze-Delitzsch and Raiffeisen systems

	Schulze-Delitzsch system	Raiffeisen system
Entry conditions	Membership share, set at high level, paid in instalments	No member share, or if forced by law, a nominal one
Dividend on share capital	Yes, sometimes high %	No, all surpluses go to reserve
Voting rights and governance structure	One vote per member, with management committee and supervisory committee	The same
Remuneration to committee members/ managers?	Yes, and also commissions to managers for business gained	No, except for cashier/ bookkeeper
Type of lending	Short, three months as norm (to meet needs of traders, artisans). High interest rates	Long, up to 10 years (to meet needs of farmers). Interest rates as low as possible
Attitude to growth of association	Based on one town but with large catchment area. Otherwise unlimited growth	Parish, minimum 400 population. Limited growth
Type of guarantee	Commercial – mortgages, bills, guarantors and so on	Reputation, unlimited liability
Type of liability	Unlimited at first, until limited liability allowed	Unlimited, later limited in Hungary and Italy

relationships making sustainable, low-risk banking possible for people on low incomes.

THE SCHULZE AND RAIFFEISEN SYSTEMS COMPARED

At the time, the differences between the two systems were the source of intense debate, even controversy. Table 2.1 summarises the similarities and differences in their systems.[1]

In Schulze's system, every member took up one share that was set at a high level but payable by instalments, which committed a member to a long course of saving (Wolff said the share could be between £10 and £30, and Fay said at least £6). It is no wonder his banks appealed to small tradesmen, clerks and artisans but tended to exclude the poor. Raiffeisen had no joining fee or share capital, so the poor could afford to join and he avoided the risk of a bank being run for the benefit of a few non-borrowing shareholders. In a law of 1889, the German Chancellor Bismarck overruled him and insisted shares be issued, so from then on Raiffeisen's banks asked for a nominal share. Schulze saw the need to allow dividends on share capital, though he wanted it to reduce over time. He was well aware that big dividends could divert the association from its proper purpose (as Wolff tersely commented, they should be fighting usury not practising it). He was right to be concerned; some of his banks pursued high dividends and then demutualised into joint stock companies so the shareholders could profit even more. Raiffeisen's rules made all the surpluses go to the bank's reserve; this was the backbone of the whole system, meeting any losses and making lending cheaper, though surpluses could also be passed on to members in higher interest rates on deposits and lower interest on loans. In order to make sure there was no incentive to demutualise, Raiffeisen's rules prevented the share out of reserves to members even if a society was dissolved; all the assets would have to go to a good cause.

Both systems had one person, one vote and a two-tier system of management and supervisory boards. However, Schulze decided the directors should be paid salaries and commissions. His critics thought this would give an incentive to unsound lending and would prove costly (a concern echoed in recent arguments over whether bankers should receive high bonuses). They had a point; in 1885 the salaries and commissions in the town banks averaged 12 per cent of turnover (Wolff, 1893). Raiffeisen called for unpaid volunteers and in his societies only the cashier-bookkeeper was paid. The type of lending was also very different. Schulze's banks gave short-term loans of three months, which meant they were good for urban businesses but useless for small farmers, who needed credit over longer seasonal cycles. In Raiffeisen's banks long lending for up to ten years was the rule, which meant farmers could plan for long-term investments that improved the quality of their land and stock. Schulze's banks were based on a whole town and so could grow bigger whereas Raiffeisen's, being strictly confined to one parish, could not. This affected their attitude to risk; the urban banks asked no questions as to the purpose of the loan and they took all kinds of collateral as security (Fay, 1938). Critics said this effectively ruled out the poor who only had their reputation to offer. In the rural banks there was a sense of common obligation that meant mutual knowledge was their only form of credit.

Both systems began with unlimited liability among the members, and gradually moved to limited liability as their central banks and large reserves began to make lending less risky. It was a German tradition not to limit liability, and unlimited liability had two clear advantages: it made sure that new members were carefully vetted before being admitted, and ensured a high level of member participation. The law of 1889 allowed limited liability but there was no rush to convert; by 1905 only 284 of the rural 913 banks had made the change (Fay, 1938). In contrast, in other countries cooperative banks could not get going at all unless liability was limited; promoters in Italy and Hungary limited it right from the start.

Which system was better? Raiffeisen's was popular with social reformers, because although it raised much less money it had a firmer moral base and was much less risky. It was a purer form of cooperation in banking and, above all, it reached down to the poor. Yet as Fay pointed out, the controversy was unnecessary, because 'neither realised that their differences of method were due to, and justified by, differences of environment' (1938, p. 20). Each promoter was right in his own way. Yet the controversy will not go away. We will be encountering similar arguments about the nature of credit unions in Chapter 3.

GROWTH OF A MOVEMENT

In Germany the urban cooperative banks grew steadily until by 1892 there were 1044 of them in Schulze's union plus a large number organised along same lines not belonging to the union, making a total of around 4500 with 1.5 million members. However, this type was not entirely stable. Conversion to investor-owned banks was frequent; for instance, in Saxony in 1889 there were 115 credit associations, but two years later 12 of them had converted (Wolff, 1893, p. 55). Between 1875 and 1886, 36 associations went bankrupt, and 174 more went into liquidation. In 1892, one authority estimated that there had been 184 failures out of 1910 banks, an attrition rate of nearly 10 per cent. Wolff said the cause was greed and carelessness; they had taken doubtful bills and lent freely to outsiders (until a law of 1889 compelled them to stop), and had lent carelessly on mortgages. He blamed the way in which Schulze's system had put temptation in their way by setting a premium on risky management (1893, p. 62). Experience had exposed the defects of the system, yet Schulze's followers continued to adhere to it, keeping the rules stationary when they should have been improved. The banks failed to provide enough security, and the temptation of high dividends, salaries and commissions were one-sided benefits that in the long run undermined them. The Schulze-Delitzsch associations declined while their rivals grew.

Still, by 1905 the economist C.R. Fay could report that there were 1020 banks with 585 000 members and they were established in nearly every town of any importance. We know a few details about the members of the banks. Around 60 per cent of them took credit, while the rest just used the bank for savings. A wide range of trades was represented but the percentage of hand workers was declining – the banks were becoming more middle class. However, Fay maintained that this was because they had succeeded in making their members better off rather than because they discriminated against working-class people (Fay, 1938).

The Raiffeisen banks made a slow start, with growth only beginning in the 1880s. Perhaps they reflected Raiffeisen's own character in the unassuming and modest way they proclaimed their advantages. By 1893 there were over 1000 of them (but again that number could be doubled with societies that were not in the Raiffeisen union). Then the movement really took off: by 1905 there were over 13 000 rural banks with nearly a million members, a staggering increase of nearly 800 per cent.

Both movements were good at developing regional and national unions, central banks and commercial subsidiaries. The Raiffeisen movement set up a central bank and a trading firm supplying machinery, feed, manures, seeds and coals to farmer-members. Supply associations were also set up in each district, but they were kept independent of the local banks so their business would not become mixed up. A cooperative insurance department was set up to insure cattle, and marketing co-ops followed in dairying, hops and wine. Credit from the banks meant that these could develop the now familiar system whereby farmers were paid in two stages for their produce, one payment on delivery of the produce and another when it had been marketed. The banks proved more stable than their urban cousins. Wolff was able to report in 1893 that in 43 years there had only been ten cases of fraud; in every case losses were made up out of reserves or sureties, and there had been no temptation to convert to joint stock company status.

From Germany the idea spread to Austria, Italy, Switzerland, Belgium, the Netherlands, Spain and France. Germans living in Central Europe took it to Poland, while in the south-east Serbs and Bulgarians created strong movements (MacPherson, 1999). There was great progress in Russia among the serfs, and the idea was also tried out in Egypt, Japan and China. By the 1890s Austria had nearly 1500 credit associations, Hungary 576 and Switzerland 900. In *Italy*, the outstanding leadership of Luigi Luzzatti (who was later to become Prime Minister) led to the establishment of 900 urban banks with a third of the banking market. Luzzatti was not afraid to adapt the form to Italian conditions, making the societies more democratic (with a large supervisory board and a specialised risks committee), limiting liability, giving preference to smaller loans, creating links with friendly societies and providing loans to worker co-ops. In parallel with Luzzatti, another promoter, Dr Wollemborg, founded rural banks along Raiffeisen lines; by 1906 there were 1461 of them, mostly associated with the Catholic Church. In *Ireland* the rural bank found a ready audience, despite as Fay put it 'the intense hopelessness of a nation distracted by political and religious quarrels' (1938, p. 74). As in most countries, it arose on the back of agricultural cooperation. By 1905 there were 200 banks, the majority in the poorer west of Ireland. Because of the dire poverty of their members they were not able to develop as savings banks but lent money on from government and from private banks.

In the *Netherlands*, it was Raiffeisen's system that was promoted in the late nineteenth century rather than the Volksbank model. However, the movement was organised in two farmers' groups split along religious lines and served by two central banks. In *Finland* the government was involved right from the start, because the reorganisation of the credit system was necessary before land reform could be started. The great Finnish reformer, Gebhard was acquainted with Raiffeisen system, and adopted it, but there was no hope of self-financing so a central Okobank was set up that channelled loans from the government and received a yearly subsidy. Farmers received a comprehensive training programme in the fundamental principles of banking, and by the end of the 1930s they had acquired the majority of shares. In 1903 there were eight credit cooperatives, but by 1928 there were 1416; they dominated the market in agricultural credits for small farmers (Kuustera, 1999). Together with Okobank they played a decisive role in carrying out the land reforms of the 1920s.

Despite this rapid growth throughout Europe, there were natural limits to this type of business model. In *France* and *Belgium* the movement got off to a slow start because of competition from savings banks that the government was subsidising with high interest rates, and because the first 'credit mutuels' were swept away in the war of 1870. By 1906 there were only 17 in France and 18 in Belgium (Fay, 1907). In *Britain* the industrial revolution was more complete, and because of the conversion of most working people to a wage-earning class there was much less need for credit. Private banking reached lower down, meeting the needs of farmers and urban business people, while working-class people could deposit their savings in consumer cooperative share accounts, savings banks and building societies. In *Denmark* farmers were mainly livestock growers, so had no need for credit to tide them over to the next harvest. Using the two-stage payment system, they got a constant stream of working capital from their marketing co-ops.

THEIR RECENT HISTORY AND CURRENT SITUATION

The full history of the European cooperative banks in the twentieth century still has to be written, but we know that they managed to survive a world war and takeover by fascist states that could not tolerate their independence. They then survived a second world war to see the restoration of savings and credit systems in the West and a long period of state control under communism in the East. Surprisingly, the contours of the systems set up by Raiffeisen and Schulze are still discernible. In most countries they survived the trend towards conversion of cooperatives and mutuals into investor-owned companies. The exceptions were Belgium and Sweden where small cooperative banking sectors had developed but did not survive. In Sweden at the end of the 1980s there were nearly 400 cooperative banks organised under 12 regional 'centrals'. It had about 5 per cent of the market in terms of assets, but around 10 per cent of savings and loans. The liberalisation of the market during the 1980s resulted in rapid credit growth and intensified competition, which triggered a debate in the cooperative banks and savings banks about how to meet the challenge. In 1991 a banking crisis led to implementation of plans that had been under discussion for several years. The cooperative banks were in need of a large injection of capital, and so they merged into one national bank that in 1994 converted to investor-ownership and was floated on the stock market (Brunner et al., 2004).

However, in most countries there was resistance to the idea of demutualisation. In Italy in the 1990s the *banche popolari* (set up under Schulze's system) were given the right to convert to investor-ownership but few took the opportunity. During the 1990s, the German cooperative banks considered, but decisively rejected, it as most banks were not willing to give up their cooperative status.

Table 2.2 provides basic statistics on the sector. Each central bank is listed by order of its market share of deposits, which is one of the most important indicators of success. This is a business model that does not involve large-scale borrowing from other banks in the wholesale market, but relies on generating its own capital for lending on to individuals and small businesses. Unless the banks succeed in borrowing the capital their borrowers need, the model does not work. The fact that in the Netherlands Rabobank has captured 40 per cent of the market shows that the model works. Ten more centrals have more than 10 per cent of deposits, seven more have more than 5 per cent, and another seven have less than 5 per cent. We can expect the market share of loans to be less than that of deposits, because the banks need a margin of safety, but where the share of loans

Table 2.2   Basic statistics on European cooperative banks, ordered by market share of deposits[a]

Country	Central bank	Market share – deposits	Market share – loans	No. of local/ regional	No. of customers/ members
Netherlands	Rabobank	40	29	141	10m/1.8m
Finland	OP-Pohjola	32.5	33	213	4.1m/1.3m
Austria	Raiffeisenbank	29.3	25.5	551	3.6m/1.7m
Italy	Bche Popolare	26.9	24.7	100	9.6m/1.2m
France	Credit Agricole	23.9	21.4	39	20m[b]/6.5m
Germany	BVR/DZ Bk	19.4	16.9	1138	30m/16.7m
Cyprus	Coop Central	19.3	20.4	111	746.7k/634k
Switzerland	Raiffeisenbank	18.6	12.1	390	3m/1.4m
France	Credit Mutuel	14.2	17	18	29.2m/7.2m
Luxemburg	Bk Raiffeisen	11	11	13	124.5k/7.5k
Poland	KZBS	8.9	5.7	576	7.5m/2.5m
Hungary	NFS Co-ops	8.6	2.8	112	1.1m/121k
Italy	Federcasse	7.3	7.2	415	5.7m/1m
Austria	GSVerband	7.2	7.3	60	1.5m/701k
France	BPCE	6.7	7.6	20	7.8m/3.3m
Spain	UNCC	6.6	5.3	80	10.8m/2.2m
UK	Coop Bank	5	1.5	n/a	5.1m/2m
Portugal	Credit Agricola	4.5	3.1	86	1.2m/392k
Bulgaria	Central C Bk	4.1	2.3	30	1.2m/7k
Slovenia	DBS	2.7	1.6	n/a	86k/302k
Greece	Assoc Coop Bk	1	1	16	431k/212k
Denmark	SDA	0.6	0.5	16	125k/63k
Romania	Creditcoop	n/a	n/a	48	1.1m/680k
Sweden	Landshypotek	n/a	n/a	10	69k/58k
EUROPE[c]		21	19	3874	181.1m/50.4m

Notes: a. The Association of Lithuanian Credit Unions has been missed out here because it is already counted in the World Council of Credit Unions (WOCCU) figures (it has dual membership); b. The figure for 2010 is 54 million, which includes customers in several countries, notably Italy and Greece, as well as France. The figure of 20m is an estimate based on the proportion of customers to members reported in 2008; c. Note that the Swiss Raiffeisen federation and WGZ Bank in Germany are missing from these totals as they are not members of the European Association of Co-operative Banks (EACB). The Swiss federation is listed separately using 2008 figures.

Source: From EACB (2012), reordered and simplified.

Table 2.3   Cooperative banks in each country by market share of deposits

Country	Percentage
France	44.8
Netherlands	40.0
Austria	36.5
Italy	34.2
Finland	32.5
Germany	19.4 (+ WGZ bank missing from stats)
Switzerland[a]	19.0
Cyprus	19.3
Luxemburg	11.0
Poland	8.9
Hungary	8.6
Spain	6.6
UK	5.0
Portugal	4.5
Bulgaria	4.1
Slovenia	2.7
Greece	1.0
Denmark	0.6
Romania	No info
Sweden	No info

Note: a. Figures from 2008 – the most recent available.

is higher than that of deposits it reflects annual fluctuations rather than a risky business model.

The number of local banks in each country varies widely, but to get a true picture we have to see the numbers as a ratio of the number of customers. Rabobank in the Netherlands has 71 000 customers per bank while DZ in Germany has around 23 000. Another potentially important issue that we will be exploring in Chapter 8 is the ratio of customers to members. The ratio is more than five to one in Rabobank, but less than two to one in DZ. Credit unions differ from cooperative banks in this respect; usually they make all their customers into members. The banks have to decide which type of customer may be offered membership and then whether or not to encourage customers to become members.

Table 2.3 adds together results for each country. Sometimes these are the same as for the central, if there is only one central in a particular country. Sometimes there are two centrals, reflecting their origins on the Raiffeisen and Schulze business models, and in these cases to get a country picture

Table 2.4　　Financial statistics on European cooperative banks with over 1bn euros in assets, ordered by size of assets

Country	Central bank	Savings (billion)	Loans (billion)	Total capital ratio	Assets in euros (billion)
France	Credit Agricole	812	882	11.7	1731
Germany	BVR/DZ Bk	620	583	13.7	1020
Netherlands	Rabobank	299	436	5.2	653
France	Credit Mutuel	228	323	4.7	591
Italy	Bche Popolare	425	378	11.2	481
France	BPCE	168	123	11.1	349
Austria	Raiffeisenbank	150	163	11.4	255
Italy	Federcasse	151	135	15.2	180
Spain	UNCC	98	96	n/a	119
Finland	OP-Pohjola	39	57	12.8	84
Austria	GSVerband	30	45	17	65
UK	Coop Bank	39	40	4.6	52
Cyprus	Coop Central	14	13	5	20
Poland	KZBS	13	10	13.6	18
Portugal	Credit Agricola	19	9	13.4	13
Luxemburg	Bk Raiffeisen	4.7	3.7	9.7	6
Hungary	NFS Co-ops	4.2	2	20.8	5
Denmark	SDA	1.3	1.3	12.1	2
Bulgaria	Central C Bk	1	0.6	13.5	1.1
EUROPE		3107	3305	n/a	5647

Source:　From EACB (2012), reordered and simplified.

we have to add them together. The top country is France with a market share of nearly 45 per cent of deposits, followed by the Netherlands. When we plot these on a map we find that the countries where the banks have over 10 per cent of the market are the ones where people responded most strongly to the Schulze and Raiffeisen models coming out of Germany 150 years ago. Those with less than 10 per cent are in two geographical groups: countries that form an outer ring around Western Europe – the UK, Spain, Portugal, Greece, Cyprus, Sweden, Denmark – and recently reconstituted cooperative sectors in Eastern Europe – Poland, Hungary, Romania, Bulgaria and Slovenia.

Table 2.4 provides financial statistics that show just how large the sector is, measured by billions of euros. In 2010 the three French centrals between them had €1208 billion in deposits, and €1328 billion in loans. The German DZ group had €620 billion and €583 billion, respectively, followed by Italy with €576 billion and €513 billion and the Netherlands with €299 billion and €436 billion. This is big business. Capital ratios vary between over 20 per cent in Hungary and just 4.6 per cent in the UK. A simplistic reading would indicate that some banks are more risky than others but, to determine this, a more sophisticated measure of Tier 1 capital is needed; we will be discussing this in Chapter 6. The low capital ratio in the UK reflects the fact that the UK Co-operative Bank is a secondary cooperative, owned by a consumer cooperative group; we will be describing this bank in Chapter 4. Now we will examine the main features of cooperative banking in each country.

COOPERATIVE BANKING BY COUNTRY

In *Germany*, cooperatives have had to compete with savings banks and private banks in the retail market (though less so with the regional public banks that lend more to larger businesses), and they are third in size, doing about as much business as the savings banks. In 1972, the Raiffeisen and Volksbank groups were merged into one, with a three-tier structure of 7000 local banks, regional banks, two centrals (DZ[2] and WGZ), and a national association called BVR. At that time, an important legal change allowed them to trade with non-members. This enabled the sector to grow while also obscuring its nature as a cooperative. Since then, the regionals have disappeared, and the number of local banks has shrunk through mergers to just 1138, and so they are much bigger than they used to be. Attempts to merge the two centrals have so far failed.[3] DZ Bank is organised as a joint stock corporation, with most of its shares held by the local cooperatives. It has 30 million customers of whom 16.7 million are members (EACB, 2012). It is the fifth largest bank in Germany, with a 19.4 per cent share of the market in deposits and a 16.9 per cent share in loans, and it provides 28 per cent of all loans to small and medium enterprises (SMEs). It is ranked the 46th largest bank in the world (Global Finance, 2012). WGZ is much smaller, being the central bank for 230 local banks in Rhineland and Westphalia.

In Germany, the banking market is highly competitive because of a low level of concentration. However, as Ayadi et al. (2010) point out, each cooperative bank and savings bank is treated as separate in the statistics, and so the level of concentration by group is underestimated. In the local retail market competition is intense, because the cooperatives and savings banks are tied to localities and cannot move out. Prices for banking services are comparatively low, and profits also low, and this means that customers are getting a good deal that is directly attributable to the presence of cooperatives.

In *Austria* there are still two movements corresponding to the Raiffeisen and Schulze traditions. Here, cooperative banks have had to compete mainly with savings banks, and together they have 50 per cent of banking assets and most of the retail banking business. The cooperative market share is larger than that of the investor-owned banks and, in contrast to Germany, is twice as large as that of the savings banks. The Raiffeisen banks are organised in a three-tiered system of 541 local banks, eight regional banks and one national. Together they have 3.6 million clients and 1.7 million members. The regional banks carry out clearing functions for the local banks. Their national bank, RZB, is the third largest bank in Austria; as well as providing services to the local banks it is a large commercial bank in its own right. The group has a 29.3 per cent market share of savings, 25.5 per cent of loans, and a 39 per cent market share of loans to SMEs. There is also a parallel structure of cooperative associations that provide consultancy and auditing services to the local banks. One controversial aspect of the work of RZB is its expansion into Central and Eastern Europe, through Raiffeisen International, a company listed on the stock market but majority owned by RZB. This means that many customers in other countries are banking with a cooperative bank that is not giving them the membership rights customers have in Austria.

There is also an Austrian Co-operative Union that explicitly claims the legacy of Schulze and the 'people's banks'. It has 60 primary banks and a central bank called OVAG, 1.5 million customers and 700 000 members. Its market share is 7.2 per cent of savings and 7.3 per cent of loans, and it has a 7.4 per cent share of loans to SMEs. Like other central banks it is more than just a provider of services to the local banks; in 1991 it was allowed to become a commercial bank and it now has private clients and its own network of branches in Vienna. Also, like RZB, it has a whole set of subsidiaries in banking and insurance, and has made serious inroads into Central and Eastern Europe where its Volksbanken International has 600 banking outlets in nine countries (Ayadi et al., 2010). It is even listed on the stock exchange, though the proportion of equity not owned by the cooperative sector is very small.

In sum, in Austria both the Raiffeisen and Volksbank systems are more centralised than in other countries, and the central banks and their subsidiaries are not pure cooperatives but a hybrid of member- and investor-ownership. There is now also the option for local cooperatives to split into two parts, one a cooperative holding company and one a corporation owned by the cooperative that does the business. Only one cooperative has used this option so far, but savings banks have used it extensively. At the regional level, four of the eight Raiffeisen co-ops have converted to joint stock status, though the local banks still own most of the shares. These examples show that hybridisation can occur at any level. The governance of such systems must be particularly difficult, and this is a point we will return to in Chapter 9.

Like the German banking sector, Austrian banking is very competitive because the level of concentration is not high and there are several banks chasing the same business. The return on equity is comparatively low, and Austria is 'overbanked'. This helps to explain why both cooperative bank groups have expanded so much into the neighbouring countries of Central and Eastern Europe (Ayadi et al., 2010, p. 53). It also helps to explain why there has been so much within-group consolidation in the cooperatives and savings banks, since larger banks tend to have lower costs. However, the need to cut costs has not led to a large-scale closure of local branches.

In *Italy*, until the 1990s both movements had a stable market share; the *banche popolare* (BP) had 10–15 per cent and the *banche di credito coooperativo* (BCC) had 5 per cent of total bank assets (Ayadi et al., 2010, p. 58). Then a period of deregulation and privatisation began, and the *casse di risparmio* (savings banks) were demutualised into joint stock companies. In contrast, cooperatives successfully resisted political pressures to convert, and from the mid 1990s began a period of consolidation and consistent expansion of their market share. Federcasse is the central association for 415 local BCCs that follow the Raiffeisen model. It has 5.7 million customers, a million members and a modest market share of 7.3 per cent of deposits and 7.2 per cent of loans. Regional federations provide technical assistance and auditing services, while the central association does strategic planning and provides risk management through deposit guarantee and reserve funds. With the banking crisis of 2008 it introduced a stronger support system of mutual guarantees, but the whole system remains much more decentralised than in Germany and Austria, with the apex organisation being more an association than a bank.

The national federation of the BPs that follow the Volksbank model is much larger; it has 100 banks in its group, with 9.6 million customers and 1.2 million members. It has a 26.9 per cent market share of deposits, 24.7 per cent share of loans and a 27.4 per cent market share of loans to SMEs. Their largest bank, UBI, is the fourth largest in Italy, whereas the largest rural bank, BCC di Roma, ranks 65th; the average BP has ten times the assets of the average BCC. This indicates not that one is more successful than the other but that they continue to do the different jobs they were set up to do. The BCCs still serve the rural communities: 32 per cent of their branches are in areas with fewer than 5000 inhabitants, compared to 17 per cent of the BP branches, and the average size of the BCC group's business loans is much smaller (Ayadi et al., 2010, p. 60). Again, the network is decentralised; the apex organisation provides research, analysis and advice, while a separate institute manages the payments system.

Why is the Italian system so much more decentralised than the German or Austrian? One important factor is the 1993 law on banking that keeps the BCCs locally based and rural. It prevents them from issuing tradable shares and insists they put at least 70 per cent of their profits into the reserves. Members can invest a maximum of €50,000, and loans should be granted primarily to members. Expansion into a nearby area is only possible if a certain number of members live there. In return for these restrictions, the BCCs get important tax reliefs on retained earnings put into reserves and on patronage refunds to members. The same law allows the BPs to be more commercial, to expand the scope and coverage of their business, and even to issue tradable shares (though these are restricted to 0.5 per cent of share capital). They only need to retain 10 per cent of profits as reserves, but on the other hand they get no special tax reliefs.

Both types of cooperative are allowed to convert to joint stock ownership, but only with the approval of the members. Again the BCCs are treated differently, because if they demutualise the reserves have to be given to a fund that supports cooperatives. This recognises the intergenerational nature of their capital; the current members cannot just appropriate it. The law has been used in two directions; weak BCCs have converted in order to be taken over by a BP, and some BPs have merged with other BPs and with joint stock banks in order to form groups. However, even though they may be listed as joint stock companies, BPs are still recognised as essentially cooperatives.

In *France*, bank development was held back by indirect state control of the whole banking sector until a law of 1984 gave banks back their autonomy. From then on the cooperative banks grew rapidly until they now have a pre-eminent position; the market share of the three cooperative groups is an astonishing 55.7 per cent of deposits and 52.7 per cent of loans (figures for 2008 from Ayadi et al., 2010, p. 69). There are three cooperative banking groups. The largest is Credit Agricole (CA). It was founded in the nineteenth century by government to meet the needs of farmers, but in 1988 it was converted to a mutual, and then recently at the national level it was converted again into a joint stock company. It has a mixed ownership: 56 per cent of its shares are owned by 39 regional banks, which are themselves owned by 2531 local banks, which are owned by 6.5 million members. It has 54 million customers, many of whom are in Italy and Greece. In France, it has 24 per cent of deposits, 22 per cent of loans and 25 per cent of the SME loans market.[4] Having expanded into wholesale banking, asset management and insurance, and having bought Credit

Lyonnais in 2003, it has become a major player, being ranked the seventh largest bank in the world by assets (Global Finance, 2012).

Second in size is Credit Mutuel (CM) that represents the Raiffeisen legacy. Like CA it has grown partly through acquisition and partly through diversification into insurance. It has 2065 local banks organised into 18 regional federations. It has 29 million customers and 7.2 million members, and its market share of deposits is 14.2 per cent, and of loans is 17 per cent. In a recent ranking it is rated the 48th biggest bank in the world. Third in size is the Banques Populaires group (BP), part of the legacy of Schultze and the Volksbanks. It consists of 18 regional BPs plus two specialist banks for the education and non-profit sectors. Together they have 7.8 million customers and 3.3 million members. The group has a 6.7 per cent market share of deposits and 7.7 per cent of loans. It has also grown through acquisitions of other banks. In 2006, together with the savings bank group, Caisses d'Epargne (CE), it created an investment bank, Natixis. The savings banks also have an interesting history. Their group consists of 17 regional CEs that were converted to mutual status in 1999. In 2009 BP and CE merged, and the new group, predictably called BPCE, is now France's second-largest banking group with 22 per cent of deposits and 23 per cent of real estate loans. When the two banks are fully merged it is likely that BPCE will also enter the list of the top 50 largest banks in the world.

With all the acquisitions, mergers and diversifications, it is worth asking whether the cooperative banks still serve the people they were set up to serve. One indicator of this is the number and distribution of branches. CA has the largest network after the French post office savings bank, and it still has a third of its branches in sparsely populated areas (less than 75 people per square kilometre). BP has a quarter of its branches in these areas, and CM is mainly based in areas with less than 150 people per square kilometre. In contrast, the commercial banks are based mainly in the cities. Another indicator is the kind of loans they grant. The cooperatives lend mainly to individuals (51 per cent), individual entrepreneurs (12 per cent), and non-financial corporations (27 per cent); the lending by commercial banks to these categories of borrower is respectively 34 per cent, 4 per cent and 41 per cent (Ayadi et al., 2010, 2008 figures). They still operate according to the cooperative principles, whereby each member has one vote and is entitled to an annual patronage refund.

Is this system driven from the top down or the bottom up? It varies. Two of the three groups, CA and CM, have a three-tier system with local, regional and national bodies, while BP has two tiers of regionals and a national bank. CA's central and regionals are listed on the stock exchange, but the regional banks keep majority ownership of the central while providing financing for the local banks. BP's regionals also own the central bank. CM has a more bottom-up approach, with the local banks taking in deposits and granting loans, the regionals providing training and business development and overseeing the governance system. Several national-level organisations then provide specialised services such as managing liquidity and providing mutual support.

In the *Netherlands*, in 1972 the Raiffeisen and Boerenbond federations merged and their central banks became Rabobank Nederland. It serves 147 local banks with 1.7 million members. It has a market share of 43 per cent of deposits, 30 per cent of loans and 39 per cent of loans to SMEs in the Netherlands. It also has a huge international presence in the food and agriculture industries, and is rated 29th in the world by assets. This impressive achievement has not been without cost. Over the period from 1997 to 2010, the number of local banks has declined through merger by more than two-thirds from 481 to 141, and the number of bank branches has halved from 1823 to 911. However, there are limits to how far a cooperative bank can go in the desire for growth. In the late 1990s Rabobank planned to diversify into investment banking, but this decision was reversed as the bank's culture was not able to stretch that far from its roots in retail banking (Vogelaar, 2009). However, a move into wholesale banking was successful; because the demand for loans outstripped supply of funds from customer deposits, the bank began to borrow from the wholesale market. It also expanded internationally, until its subsidiary, Rabobank International, was generating about a quarter of its income.

Of course, both of these moves – into wholesale and international banking – may add to the risk, and we will see in Chapter 6 how Rabobank fared during the recent banking crisis. There is no doubt that this is still a *cooperative* bank; in the late 1990s the option of conversion to a joint stock company was considered but was rejected (Ayadi et al., 2010). The local banks still wholly own it, though most of its subsidiaries are listed as private companies either wholly or majority owned by the bank. The whole system is underpinned by a mutual guarantee scheme. Rabobank acts as a central bank for the local banks, developing products, managing risk, providing liquidity, investing their surpluses and so on. It also acts as a bank in its own right in areas where the local banks cannot go, such as banking for 'high net worth' individual (rich people) and international banking. It also acts as a supervisory body to the local banks, and its subsidiaries provide them with a wide range of services.

It is not surprising that in the late 1990s it began to experience a lack of equity capital, because the traditional method of turning retained profits into reserves was no longer adequate. It turned to two new methods of capital-raising. The first is capital securities: similar to bonds, but with no fixed term, and with interest only payable if the bank makes a profit. The second is member certificates, which enable members to invest their capital and receive a return (again provided the bank is in profit). Neither of these instruments infringes cooperative principles because they do not carry voting rights, but their growth has meant that now people acting as investors rather than as members provide over a third of the bank's capital. At the end of the twentieth century only 6 per cent of the local Rabobanks' customers were members. However, a drive to recruit members has led to a fourfold increase to nearly 24 per cent in 2010. The governance structure of the group is complex, as it has to balance centralising versus decentralising tendencies, and member oversight against effective control by elected boards.

Finland experienced a serious banking crisis in the early 1990s because of an overheated housing market, high levels of public debt and the economic effects of the collapse of the Soviet Union. In the resulting reorganisation of the banking sector, the cooperative sector took over the savings banks, reorganised into a new federation and emerged stronger. Now the banking sector is highly concentrated, with the three top banks having more than three-quarters of the business. In 1997 OP Bank Group was created as the group's only central, then, in 2005, the OP Group became a majority shareholder of a leading non-life insurer, Pohjola. In 2007, the two groups formed the OP-Pohjola Group, which means the bank is listed as a joint stock company, owned jointly by the group's central and local banks (Ayadi et al., 2010). There are 213 local banks, grouped in 16 regional federations, with 1.3 million members, and together they have a 32.5 per cent market share of deposits and 33 per cent share of loans.

In 2001 the central bank was given the duty of supervising the local banks, and a strong mutual guarantee scheme was set up. Then, when it acquired Pohjola it gained investment, insurance and fund management subsidiaries. It now has 25 per cent of the non-life insurance and 30 per cent of the life insurance markets, and is a leading lender to SMEs, farmers and homeowners. As in other countries, the number of branches has been decreasing – from 745 in 1997 to 554 in 2010 – but the group is still by far the biggest branch network.

In *Spain*, a Raiffeisen-inspired movement was destroyed during the civil war of the 1930s, but it began again in the 1960s with the formation of employee credit unions. In 1970 they set up a national association to represent their interests; the Union Nacional de Cooperativas de Credito. Then in 1989 they formed a trade group, Asociation Espanola de Cajas Rurales that operates through a central bank (Banco Cooperativo Espanol). To the outsider, the existence of two national associations would imply two different movements, but the credit cooperatives are members of both.

There are 80 primary co-ops with 10.8 million customers, of whom 2.2 million are members. They have a small but useful market share of 6.6 per cent of deposits and 5.3 per cent of loans, and also a 6.5 per cent share of the mortgage market. As in other countries, the cooperatives are more active in the more isolated rural areas. Though they have been growing slowly, their main competitors, the savings banks, have been growing much faster, and have now overtaken the private banking sector, with a market share in deposits of 56 per cent and loans of 48 per cent (Ayadi et al., 2010). Growth has come at an eventual cost; we will see in Chapter 8 that these savings banks are in trouble and have to be bailed out by the government.

Credit cooperation came to *Portugal* in 1911, though it built on a long tradition of community warehouses that provided credit to local farmers (Stafanetti, 2010). The cooperative banks are grouped into Credito Agricola, which has nearly 1.2 million customers of whom 392000 are members. It has only a 4.5 per cent share of deposits and 3.1 per cent of loans, but as in other countries plays an important role in bringing banking to rural areas. There are 86 local banks (EACB, 2012), but this is a much-reduced number because of many recent mergers. There are seven regional unions and a national federation, Fenacam. The cooperative group is reported to have a higher profitability than other types of bank, and has the highest level of capital adequacy (Stefanetti, 2010, p. 22).

In *Cyprus* the first cooperative credit bank was established in 1909, explicitly to combat the problem of usury. In 1914 a regulatory framework was created, and in 1937 a Co-operative Central Bank was founded (Cotugno, 2010). It now has 111 local banks in membership, serving 747000 customers of whom 634000 are members. It has a market share of deposits of 19.3 per cent and of loans of 20.4 per cent. Raiffeisen *Switzerland* has 350 local banks in membership with 1.65 million members and three million customers. It is third in the Swiss banking market in terms of assets, with 21 per cent of deposits and 15 per cent of the mortgage market (Raiffeisen Federation, 2012). *Luxembourg* has Banque Raiffeisen, with 13 local banks in membership. It has nearly 125000 customers and 7500 members, and even though it is so much smaller than the banks we have been describing so far, it is after all working in a very small country. It has an 11 per cent share of both deposits and loans. *Denmark* still has a small group of 20 Raiffeisen banks. *Sweden* has one credit union called Landshypotek serving 69000 customers, of whom 58000 are members. It specialises in lending to farmers. The Association of Co-operative Banks of *Greece* has 16 local banks in membership, with 431000 customers, of whom 212000 are members. It only has a 1 per cent market share of savings and loans, but again it is not the volume that matters but the quality.

As Henry Wolff noted on his travels in the 1890s, Raiffeisen sectors were being set up in Central and Eastern Europe, but these later lost their independence under communist states. With the fall of communism some of these have been reconstituted and there are growing sectors in Poland, Romania and Hungary. The cooperative credit system began in *Poland* in 1861 in the city of Poznan. By the start of World War II there were 1600 cooperative banks; those under German occupation were kept going, but those under Russian occupation were dissolved. After the war they were compelled to join a state cooperative bank, BGZ, that was, of course, a contradiction in terms. In 1989 the Polish parliament began the reconstruction of the banking system, in a passage to a market economy that resulted in many bank failures. In 1991 the cooperatives set up a National Union of Co-operative Banks. BGZ was turned into an investor-owned company, and the cooperative banks established three regional banks to meet their needs. There were great differences in the level of efficiency and effectiveness of the banks, and this hindered the setting up of a mutual guarantee system. However, in 2001 the whole system was reformed. Smaller local banks were confined to their province and were required to affiliate with one of the regionals and a national credit guarantee fund was set up (Cotugno, 2010). As in other countries there has been a gradual concentration of the sector through mergers, and there are now 526 local banks with 7.5 million customers, of whom 2.5 million are members. The sector has an 8.9 per cent market share of deposits and a 5.7 per cent share of loans (EACB, 2011). There is also a new credit union movement that we will be describing in the next chapter.

In *Hungary*, the cooperative movement began very early, with a visit from Raiffeisen in 1885 to a conference in Budapest. However, in 1947 the communist government dissolved all the cooperatives and centralised everything into one national bank. After the introduction of a market economy the banking sector went into crisis and in 1991 the most important commercial banks had to receive a government bailout. In 1992 a law on cooperatives was passed that gave the cooperative banks a modern legal framework, allowing them to set up a National Federation of Savings Co-operatives (OTZ) and a mutual guarantee scheme. They signed an integration agreement, and in 1997 became part owners of a central bank: the Bank of the Hungarian Savings Co-operatives. The main shareholder was the German cooperatives' central, DZ Bank, that took a 71 per cent capital share. Then, in 2004 the cooperative sector became sufficiently mature to be able to become the majority shareholder of the bank with a 64 per cent share (Cotugno, 2010). There are 112 banks with 1.1 million customers and 120000 members (EACB, 2011). Their market share of savings is 8.6 per cent and of loans is just 2.8 per cent.

In *Romania*, the first 'people's bank' was founded in 1851, at the time when Raiffeisen was first beginning his work. The first real credit cooperative was founded in 1867 in Rasinari, and then in 1870 a savings and loan society was founded on the Schulze model in Bucharest. Cooperative banks then grew rapidly, only to lose their autonomy during the communist period. It was only in 1990 that they gained a legal framework based on cooperative principles, and their work was restricted to members only. In 1996 they gained the right to trade with non-members, and were organised on the three-level structure familiar in so many other countries. However, during 1997–98 new 'people's banks' were set up that failed to respect cooperative principles and operated with dangerously low capital levels. The government stepped in and forbade the establishment of new credit cooperatives, organised proper supervision and insisted that each cooperative should have a minimum capital. This resulted in a wave of mergers so that there are now 48 local banks, with just over a million customers, 680 000 of whom are members (market share figures are not available). A central Creditcoop was set up in 2002 and this provides a mutual guarantee scheme, and the kind of services the member societies need in order to meet the government's regulatory demands; those credit cooperatives that cannot meet the requirements have been liquidated (Bussoli, 2010).

CONCLUSION

The history of the cooperative banks shows that they were well designed by their founders, but that they have evolved to suit the circumstances in many different times and places. Mainly it has been a process of good design and vigorous promotion by dedicated individuals in each country. Government has been asked to provide a safe environment, but otherwise the banks stand on their own merits. There are some unanswered questions about the role of membership, the quality of governance and the control of subsidiaries. Some commentators think there has been a shift of power towards the centre (Ory and Lemzeri, 2012). We will be considering these questions in Chapter 9. For now, let us just pause to consider what an achievement the European cooperative banking system is. It has survived everything that has been thrown at it: world wars, fascist and communist governments, economic crises, attempts at demutualisation, and a revolution in banking technology. Despite the complexity, and the differences between the systems in each country, at its core it still transmits the 'DNA' of Schulze and Raiffeisen.

NOTES

1. This section follows closely the analysis provided in Birchall (2010, Ch. 7).
2. At that time called DG.
3. Though they have recently merged their private banking business based in Luxembourg.
4. Figures from 2009. These were not updated in the EACB statistics for 2010.

3. The evolution of credit unions

There is a particularly acute collective action problem in relation to cooperative banks. They are costly to set up, requiring much dedicated time and effort, the learning of new skills and the building up of trust among large numbers of people. It also helps to have rich supporters who can invest the start-up capital. As in Europe, so in America, it took specialist promotion by individuals who were strongly motivated and well connected, such as Alphonse Desjardins in French-speaking Canada and Edward Filene in the USA.

THE MOVEMENT SPREADS TO CANADA AND THE USA

Desjardins was working as a translator in the Canadian House of Commons in 1887 when he observed a debate over usury that impressed him with the extent of the problem (MacPherson, 1999). He read Wolff and Luzzatti, and in 1900 with a lot of help from his wife, Dorimene, opened the first *caisse populaire* in his hometown of Levis. It was based on a combination of the ideas of Raiffeisen and Luzzatti, and emphasised the importance of thrift through regular savings as well as of the need for credit. In the first seven years the caisse made 2900 loans totalling $350,000 without a single loss, forcing three moneylenders to give up business. The idea spread slowly through parishes throughout Quebec and other French-speaking provinces, and by the time of his death in 1920 he had organised 175 caisses. The Great Depression of the 1930s forced the caisses populaires to become disciplined, with an integrated structure of four regional unions and a provincial federation and a rigorous auditing system. By 1940 there were 562 caisses with $25 million in assets. The pattern was set for a distinctive movement that enabled caisses to remain small and parish based, while benefitting from strong centrals and specialised subsidiaries providing other products such as life insurance.

In the USA, the movement began with Quebecois immigrants who had moved to New England in search of work. In 1908 a Catholic priest, Monsignor Hevey, invited Desjardins to Manchester New Hampshire to explain the system and a society was set up. The New Hampshire legislature then passed a law to provide statutory authority for it. Banking was a major issue at the time, with a widespread sense that the commercial banking system was not meeting the needs of working people and small businesses, and with the federal government searching for ways to provide credit to farmers. Edward Filene was a member of a merchant family with a large department store in Boston. He travelled round Europe looking at cooperative banks, read Wolff's books and visited Desjardins. Together with Pierre Jay, the state commissioner for banks, in 1909 he achieved a Massachusetts Credit Union Act. He used the term *credit union* so as not to confuse it with the mutual building and loans societies that at the time were referred to as cooperative banks. The rules were mainly from Raiffeisen but with distribution of surpluses allowed as long as 20 per cent of surpluses went to a reserve fund.

For the next ten years there was slow progress, but in 1920 Filene and Roy Bergengren set up a Credit Union National Extension Bureau that Bergengren then managed and Filene spent much of his personal fortune to finance. During the 1920s, with the growth of mass production, rising wages and improved transportation, people began to become consumers, buying new items such as cars, refrigerators and radios. Retailers set up instalment plans but they charged high interest rates, and employees saw the benefits of being in a credit union. Expansion had to await enabling legislation; in 1921 there were only four state laws, but by 1934 there were 32, and a federal law of 1932 provided universal coverage. The movement continued to grow during the Great Depression and hardly lost any money; a Princeton University study found in 1937 that banks had lost 34.5 per cent of their deposits, and buildings and loans societies 32 per cent, but the credit unions had only lost 6.7 per cent (MacPherson, 1999, p. 22).

Employment based credit unions became the norm, with their low administrative costs, easy deductions from salaries and low-risk loans. The idea was widely promoted by professional groups such as teachers, enlightened employers, trade unions, the Roman Catholic Church, ethnic groups (who were aware of the European legacy), and the established consumer and agricultural cooperative movements. Using these networks, the resources provided by Filene and strong state leagues, by the mid 1930s they had created over 3000 credit unions. In 1934 the extension bureau became the Credit Union National Association, and it formed two important subsidiaries: CUNA Mutual, providing insurance, and CUNA Supply, providing joint purchasing. By 1941 there were nearly 11 000 credit unions, and in a postwar explosion of consumer demand the sector grew even more: by 1954 there were 15 000 with more than seven million members.

In English-speaking Canada it was 1930 before Roy Bergengren got round to organising the first credit union (at Welland, Ontario among a group of employees). What really got the movement going here was a combination of adult education and local economic development. The Extension Department of the St Francis Xavier University in Antigonish, Nova Scotia developed a method for study clubs under the direction of two priests, Jimmy Tompkins and Moses Coady. The method was simple; an organiser from the Extension Department would come to a community and set up a meeting. Local people would look at their needs and consider the possibilities and then, in study clubs that met weekly for a year or more, would establish a cooperative (MacPherson, 1999). The movement that grew out of this was different from the American movement in being community based and linked to other types of cooperative.

During the 1940s there was remarkable expansion; in 1941 there were nearly 1500 credit unions, and by 1954 there were 3800 with 1.5 million members. The movement expanded in the west, where farmers in the prairie region of Saskatchewan and Alberta took to the idea. It reached Ontario and British Columbia, but here it was largely urban and employee based. Why did it grow so fast? One underlying reason was that there was not much competition; there were no other community based banks, the larger banks did not meet people's needs, and unlike in the USA there were no savings and loans societies (which meant credit unions could offer mortgage loans).

In the late 1940s the idea reached Australia, where credit unions began to be formed along American lines, mainly as 'closed bond' employee unions; by 1962 there were 126 in New South Wales and 36 in Victoria. In Ireland there had been a false start when the promoter A.E. Russell had set up cooperative banks early in the twentieth century, but in the turmoil of independence and the Irish civil war they had all collapsed. A new beginning was made in 1958 and by 1970 there were 366 unions with over 220 000 members.

COLONIAL PATRONAGE AND GOVERNMENT CONTROL

During the early twentieth century colonial governments began to see the value in financial cooperatives as a way of countering usury and enabling indigenous people to make the transition to a modern world of business and markets. It began in India, where colonial officials identified indebtedness as the main problem holding back rural development. The problem was that farmers had to pay their taxes in cash and so they had to go to moneylenders to provide it. Once in the clutches of the 'usurers' they became more and more indebted so that the crops they had not yet grown were mortgaged, and sometimes their children had to be 'sold' as indentured labour. In 1884, one colonial administrator put it very dramatically:

> The power that stands in the way of India's economic development is the power of evil finance . . . the land lies blighted by the shadow of the usurer (Sri Daniel Hamilton, quoted by Huss, 1924, p. 83).

In the early 1890s Sir Frederick Nicholson was seconded to study the Raiffeisen system in Europe, and he concluded that this was just what India needed; his message was 'Find Raiffeisen!' His report was published in 1894, only five years after the first credit cooperatives legislation was passed in Germany. This was not as strange as it seemed. Farmers in India and Germany were both suffering from indebtedness and a lack of credit with which to improve their businesses, and they both suffered from periodic famines. Reformers in India had also tried the same remedy as in Germany – the distribution of food aid – and it had achieved very little.

In 1904, a Co-operative Credit Societies Act was passed supporting agricultural credit cooperatives. It was very much a top-down approach based, as Munkner describes it, 'on an imported theoretical concept without practical experience with this form of organisation under socio-economic conditions prevailing in India' (1989, p. 101). Because there was no indigenous support for the idea, it had to be promoted at first by a specialist government agency, headed by a registrar whose powers went far beyond those of the Registrar of Friendly Societies in Britain. This was the beginning of what has been called the 'classic British-Indian pattern' that influenced cooperative development throughout the British Empire (Develtere, 1994, p. 41). In 1912 a second act expanded the law to cover all types of co-op, introduced limited liability and allowed the formation of secondary and tertiary societies. By 1915 there were 15 000 rural credit societies with 700 000 members, but they were seen by their members more as state agencies for granting loans, and with only small amounts saved on deposit (Fay, 1938). In 1919 a new law decentralised the administration of the credit co-ops to the provincial governments.

An optimistic reading of their early history is that they had a great start. They expanded more rapidly than in any other country including Germany (Seibel, 2009b). A contemporary observer noted that their regulation and supervision were good, and they were firmly in the hands of their members, with 50 per cent of the capital in member shares, 10 per cent in deposits and only 40 per cent in commercial borrowings (Strickland, 1922). By the mid 1920s there were 50 000 societies. However, in several provinces there was serious over-financing, and in the depression of the 1930s a quarter of the by now 80000 societies had to be liquidated. The colonial authorities had studiously set up a three-tier system with, in each province, a provincial bank, district centrals and local primary cooperative credit societies. It was a cumbersome system to regulate. In 1934 the Reserve Bank of India (RBI) was set up, and it began to provide central oversight and refinancing. From 1942 onwards it started extending credit facilities to the provincial banks for seasonal agricultural operations and crop marketing.

This may have seemed like a good idea at the time, but it was a serious mistake. It gave the farmers the impression that government was handing out credit they did not need to pay back, and it led to a rapid increase in overdue loans. As Seibel puts it, this

> opened the floodgates of a generous government supply of financial and human resources. This led to a long drawn-out process of restructuring and reform in reverse, which eventually turned a self-help movement into a vast network of public institutions (Seibel, 2009b, p. 1).

In 1945 the central government set up a Co-operative Planning Committee to look into the state of agricultural finance. A large number of co-ops were found to have frozen assets due to heavy 'overdues' on debt repayment. The committee recommended that the frozen assets be liquidated, and the debts be adjusted to the members' capacity to repay. A recent task force comments that this 'marked the beginning of State interference in the management of co-operatives and the consequent erosion in the credit discipline of the members' (Vaidyanathan and Task Force, 2004, p. 16). A Banking Regulation Act of 1949 gave the RBI the responsibility for supervising the larger cooperatives at the apex of the system. However, this did not really help matters, as it led to a dual system that was confusing and inefficient.

After India gained its independence, the cooperative sector was seen as an important agent of development policy. A rural credit survey recommended a state partnership in governance and management of the cooperatives, paving the way for direct intrusion of government in the running of the co-ops. They began to be seen as merely institutions for the delivery of state credit. State governments were given full authority to appoint chief executives, suspend elected boards, merge societies, amend by-laws, veto decisions, and generally tell the cooperatives what to do. They also participated in ownership by taking up shares, all in direct contravention of cooperative principles.

During the 1960s an urban cooperative banking sector also began to be promoted, and in 1966 it was included under the same confusing dual supervision system that applied to the rural banks. In 1969 the major commercial banks were nationalised, and government interference in cooperatives increased. The recent Vaidyanathan report describes a system in which the state and the workforce began to act like 'patrons' over the members of the cooperatives. In 1989 a loan waiver scheme was introduced whereby government wrote off farmers' debts. Not surprisingly, loan recovery rates fell. This greatly aggravated the already weak credit discipline in the cooperative system. It spawned a series of schemes by state governments to waive interest, and partially write off debts. The Vaidyanathan report puts it like this:

> The competitive populism adopted by the political class . . . severely impaired the credibility and health of the co-operative credit structure (Vaidyanathan and Task Force, 2004, p. 19).

The state used cooperatives to channel rural development schemes, and in particular subsidy based programmes for the poor. The primary credit cooperatives became a conduit for distributing political patronage and it was not surprising that politicians dominated their management boards.

In the 1990s there was a change of attitude. There was 'an increasing realisation of the disruptive effects of intrusive state patronage and politicisation of the co-operatives' (Rangarajan, 2008, p. 69). In 1995 some states began to pass new laws that provided for cooperatives to be democratic and independent. However, the old laws were not repealed, and no effort was made to encourage co-ops to re-register under the new acts. Most continued to adhere to the old law. A new generation of autonomous financial co-ops did begin, slowly and unevenly, to emerge but mainly in commodity sectors rather than in savings and credit.

A similar pattern of colonial promotion of a credit cooperative sector began in what are now Pakistan and Bangladesh in 1904, Sri Lanka in 1911, Malaysia in 1922, and Singapore in 1925. The results were similarly disappointing. In Sri Lanka, in 1911 the colonial government enacted the first credit cooperative law and took an interest in promoting the idea, but the dominant form was the consumer cooperative, set up during World War II to distribute rationed goods; by 1945 there were over 4000 societies and more than half the population were 'being clothed and fed through Co-op stores' (Jayaweera, 1987). After independence, in Sri Lanka 75 different types of cooperative had grown up, all single purpose, and reflecting the needs of the members. However, they were small, often not viable, with one village having seven or eight different types (Rajaguru, 1996). The government began to promote multi-purpose cooperative societies (MPCSs), one per village, which combined provision of consumer goods with agricultural supply, and savings and credit cooperation. By 1968 there were over 5000 societies, with a total membership of 1.1 million people. But they had lost their autonomy: they became, essentially, agencies of government for delivering rationed goods to the rural population, and gathering in savings to be invested in government bonds. In 1970 they were amalgamated into 371 societies covering 10–20 villages each. As one historian comments: 'Co-operatives were born from the pen of the Registrar and not from voluntary association' (Rajaguru, 1996, p. 17). Nominations to boards ensured a pro-government majority at all times.

Government control of the MPCSs continued during the 1990s, despite the process of structural adjustment and partial privatisation of the economy. Other types of cooperative declined under the impact of growing competition from private traders, the exception being the credit cooperative movement that, under the name Sanasa, in the late 1970s began a strong revival. Sanasa was never under government control, and as a genuine social movement was too small to attract much interest from politicians, but it remained neglected until in the 1970s a social reformer, P.A. Kiriwandeniya, saw its potential and began to revive it. By 1994 there were over 7000 primary societies, with 27 district unions and a national association (Birchall and Simmons, 2013, forthcoming).

Credit unions came to China as early as 1919, when they were promoted by an international famine relief commission and then by missionaries. By the mid 1930s an American observer counted 9000 societies with almost five million members (Warbasse, 1936). After the communist takeover in 1949, the new government supported them, and they were still allowed to be genuine grass-roots cooperatives organised by their members. However, with collectivisation in 1959 they became subordinate arms of the communes, and control was transferred to local brigades dominated by the Communist Party. In 1979 the commune system collapsed. Four big state-owned banks were created, and the rural credit co-ops became branches of one of these, the Agricultural Bank. Loans were given to state-owned enterprises, and the rural credit cooperatives (RCCs) just became cashiers and involuntary suppliers of funds to the bank (Ong, 2006). During the 1980s, county level credit cooperative unions were set up, bringing some coordination and support for the local societies, but they were more like departments of local government, characterised by poor management and government interference (Swoboda and Ruibin, 2007).

The modernisation of the economy in the 1990s led to the failure of many older manufacturing businesses that were owned by local authorities and financed by the RCCs. New businesses set up by local officials to create employment also failed. By the end of the 1990s, 26 per cent of their loans were non-performing, though unofficial estimates put this as high as

50 per cent. In 1996 their oversight was transferred to the People's Bank, but they were still not allowed to be autonomous (Empel and Smit, 2004).

The French colonialists introduced credit unions into Vietnam under the influence of the Raiffeisen model; by 1960 there were around 5500 of them. The system was badly disrupted by wars, and after independence was achieved in 1975 they became part of a command economy under the leadership of the Communist Party. They were used to collect small savings and provide credit to production cooperatives, state-owned enterprises and farm households, and by the mid 1980s there were nearly 7200 of them covering almost all the communes. At the end of the 1980s, the whole system collapsed and nearly all were closed; Seibel estimates that out of total assets of around $550 million close to $500 million were lost (Seibel, 2009a). They had not been regulated or supervised properly, capital requirements had been minimal, and they had been left as isolated units, with no network or apex bodies to help them out. Their loss was not mourned, as the ordinary people had not identified with them. Happily, the story does not end there; as we shall see below, a new network was successfully created.

THE IDEA SPREADS FURTHER

In some ex-colonial countries small, genuinely member-controlled credit unions began to emerge, wherever they were too small for governments and politicians to take an interest. In Africa, there was an existing traditional form of informal, pre-cooperative saving and lending. Tontines were popular, which, like the box clubs of eighteenth-century Britain, consisted of a group of people who saved regularly and took it in turns to take loans. The credit unions (or savings and credit co-ops as they are usually known) developed naturally, in the same way as in other regions. They were promoted by charismatic leaders, often linked to churches and supported as soon as possible by national leagues. For instance, in Zimbabwe in 1962 local priests introduced the idea of credit unions using the Antigonish method of promotion. By 1968 there were 11 registered unions, over 30 savings clubs and a national council, and by 1983 these had grown to 5000 unions with a membership of 125 000. In Togo, a missionary introduced the idea in 1967 and by 1984 there were 103 unions with a membership of 11 000 and a national union. A similar story can be told of Cameroon from 1963, Burkina Faso from 1970, Rwanda from 1975, and so on (Birchall, 1997).

From 1941 onwards, Catholic priests began to promote credit unions in Jamaica using the Antigonish method. Other churches and trade unions supported the idea, and the movement grew rapidly and gained affiliation to the American Credit Union National Association (CUNA). It soon became the 'most vibrant section' of the wider cooperative sector, and set up its own Caribbean Confederation of Credit Unions. The idea travelled all round the Caribbean until by 1962 there were 406 unions in the region, with 62000 members. Without government support it was free of the 'clientalism' that bedevilled the official cooperative sector, and became the strongest of the cooperative sectors with over 70 per cent of co-op members. For instance, in Jamaica in 1984 it had 292000 out of a total of 413000 cooperative members, and in Trinidad 138000 out of 188000 (Develtere, 1994). By 1995 the Caribbean movement taken together had 401 unions, with 931000 members, and 23 per cent of the savings and loans market.

Jamaican immigrants then introduced them into Britain. This was a fascinating historical twist of fate, since the great advocate of cooperative banks, Henry Wolff, had failed to interest the British public 50 years previously. In 1955 another priest introduced them into Latin America via Peru; by 1970 the region had 3000 credit unions organised in 15 leagues, with nearly a million members (MacPherson, 1999). Critics say they had an explicit social welfare focus, lacked professional management and were weak at loan recovery and at earning enough profits to fund expansion. Organised by Catholic priests and Peace Corps volunteers, they grew rapidly, relying on 'substantial grants and soft loans available from external donors', and when these sources dried up in the 1980s many of the movements foundered. Where they were successful, it was because they paid attention to crucial business factors such as loan repayment rates, attraction of savings and earned profits (Westley and Shaffer, 1999, p. 1305).

Several attempts were made to reform these credit union sectors. In Guatemala, in 1987 the United States Agency for International Development (USAID) funded a seven-year Co-operative Strengthening Project that helped test and refine a 'new model credit union' methodology (Richardson, 2000). The national federation and 20 primary unions were modernised using the World Council of Credit Unions' 'Pearls' ranking system that provides a systematic way of measuring the health of a union. Similarly, USAID funded a strengthening programme in Honduras. Here, adverse economic conditions combined with a faulty development strategy of subsidised lending by donors that undermined the unions. The result was that by 1987, 34 unions had ceased operations, another 30 were in financial trouble and only 12–15 were functioning normally. However, the project was so successful that a line of credit from USAID was never needed; the unions reformed themselves (Arbuckle and Adams, 2000).

From the 1950s onwards, Catholic activists also began to promote credit unions in several Asian countries. They began to be promoted actively in Africa through aid programmes. They were organised mainly along traditional Raiffeisen lines: small, volunteer-led, and based on a specific community or place of employment. The problem soon became how to stabilise a huge movement that was growing very quickly and lacked stability. The World Council of Credit Unions (WOCCU) took on this process of stabilisation through a programme of international lending and technical assistance, overseeing a worldwide expansion in the sector that is still continuing.

In contrast, during the 1960s, growth in new credit unions was slowing in the USA and Canada and in some areas had stopped. Unions were starting to diversify and amalgamate in search of economies of scale, and a minority were expanding because they really wanted to grow. The larger ones became more professionalised and evolved into a more 'managerial' type, with salaried staff, a wider range of financial 'products', growing technological sophistication and a more indirect form of member governance. With greater use of advertising and the introduction of teller lines in their branches, they were beginning to look more like the commercial banks. During the 1970s, the American movement continued to grow until in 1978 it had nearly half the total number of credit unions worldwide, but 72 per cent of the total membership and 73 per cent of the total assets (MacPherson, 1999, p. 106).

In 1977 new legislation allowed them to provide mortgages, then in the 1980s they experienced a heady mixture of deregulation, inflation, increased competition and the introduction of electronic banking. They weathered the storm very well, resisting the temptation to demutualise and keeping their distinctive set of values while at the same time competing successfully with the private banking sector. By 1995 there were 12 300 unions serving 70 million members, and with more than $300 billion in assets. They held 13 per cent of the consumer credit market and 8 per cent of consumer savings (Birchall, 1997). However, all this success led to a reaction among people concerned to keep the idea focused on low-income people. They set up a National Federation of Community Development Credit Unions that promoted new community based unions in a self-conscious attempt to return to the movement's roots.

SOME CLASSIFICATION SYSTEMS

Before we begin to describe the current credit union sector in each region, we need to make a few important distinctions. First, unions may be classified according to a common bond. This may be defined by where people live, what association or church they belong to or where they work. The bond may be narrowly or broadly defined. It tends to be defined narrowly and then to be broadened as the union grows. For instance, in many countries it begins with members of a church and then grows to include members of the wider community. Employment based unions do not have to extend the bond because they include all employees of a particular employer, and this may make them very large to begin with. Here, size is not really an issue, and employment based unions can grow very large. In fact, the largest in the USA is the Navy Federal Credit Union with three million members whose bond is that they are members of the armed forces and their families. Community based unions cannot, by definition, grow larger than the number of people who live in their area. Advocates of the community based union see the growth of unions as diluting the common bond. Advocates of large size see unions more as potential cooperative banks that bring a much broader range of services to their members, who are seen more as customers than as community members.

Second, unions can be classified by their level of development. Sibbald and colleagues suggest a three-fold typology of nascent, transitional and mature stages in the growth of a credit union sector (Sibbald et al., 2002). In the *nascent stage*, unions have a small asset size, a restricted range of savings and loan products, and are run mainly by volunteers. Often they rely on financial help from aid agencies, local government or a wider credit union movement to get them going. They are 'missionary in nature, with a tendency for zealous leadership', and have a commitment to the ideal of self-help (Sibbald et al., 2002, p. 402). They are highly regulated, and legislation severely constrains their growth within the common bond. In the *transition stage*, the asset size has grown much larger, they begin to rely on paid employees and products become diversified. The regulatory framework is relaxed to allow a wider membership outside the original bond. There is a shift of values towards growth and professionalism. In a *mature* industry, there is large asset size, a loose common bond (with an emphasis on members as customers), well-developed central services, highly diversified products and rigorous financial management. The shift of values is towards long-term sustainability and the ability to compete with investor-owned banks. This typology implies that there is a natural growth pattern, but unions may stay nascent or transitional and never advance to the mature stage.

Richardson provides a similar typology, classifying unions in developing countries in three phases. Phase 1 is characterised by dependence on outside bodies for help and a poor image. The institution is financially weak, has inadequate controls and non-standard operations, provides credit only and has entrenched leadership, untrained employees and a stagnant membership base. This type is really a conduit for lending by donors. Phase 2 is characterised by independence and a good image, with a financially strong institution that has adequate controls and standardised operations. Its services have expanded to include savings, credit and insurance, and it has products that are competitive. Its leadership is balanced, the employees are properly trained and the membership base is expanding. Phase 3 is characterised by interdependence in a network of unions and an excellent image. It has consolidated financial strength, interlinked controls and good supervision. It provides a full range of financial products, under professional leadership and management, and has a diverse membership base (Richardson, 2000). Some credit union activists disagree with this kind of typology, as they want to stop at Phase 2 in order to concentrate on serving people on low incomes and contribute towards local communities (Power et al., 2012). They do not want their union to become a bank.

The reliance on apex bodies at national level to provide services to the primary societies complicates matters. Primary-level unions do not always have to grow bigger; the mature stage can be reached with a combination of small, local unions and an effective national apex body. Here, another typology is relevant; Desrochers and Fischer (2005) identify three types of cooperative banking system: atomised, consensual and strategic. *Atomised* systems consist of primary societies that are not federated together and so stand on their own. *Consensual* systems have a national federation that provides them with a range of services and some influence over their environment, but has no authority over them. A *strategic* system is one in which a central bank provides essential services such as liquidity management and deposit insurance, often in conjunction with a national federation that looks after the political interests of the sector. Here, the primary societies cede real powers to the centre. There is a clear division of authority between national and local levels, with the locals electing representatives to the central, and the central supervising the locals. Again there is a normative edge to the typology; nobody wants to be in an 'atomised' state. However, the advantages of consensual versus strategic systems do need to be discussed because, as we shall see in Chapter 6 when discussing the banking crisis, there are sometimes real problems of governance in strategic systems, when members lose control over subsidiaries. For the moment we will pass over these issues and use the typologies just to describe the current situation.

Table 3.1   Credit union basic statistics 2011

World region	Number of countries	Market penetration[a]	Number of credit unions	Number of members
World	100	7.8%	51013	196.5m
Africa	24	7.2%	18221	18m
Asia	22	2.7%	19798	39.7m
Caribbean	19	17.5%	433	2.9m
Europe	12	3.5%	2321	8.1m
Latin America	15	5.7%	1750	18.1m
North America	2	45%	8164	104.5m
Oceania	5	23.6%	326	5.1m

Note: a. Penetration rate is calculated by dividing the total number of reported credit union members by the economically active population aged 15–64 years.

Source: Edited from WOCCU (2012a).

THE CURRENT SITUATION OF CREDIT UNIONS WORLDWIDE

Credit unions are well established in around 100 countries, and most are members of WOCCU. Western Europe is missing from the picture because it is the home of the older cooperative banking sector that, by historical accident, has retained its own distinct identity and its own organisation, the European Co-operative Banking Association. Looking at the WOCCU statistics we can gain a snapshot view of the important characteristics of the sector (see Table 3.1). There are around 51 000 credit unions, served by over 100 'centrals'.[1] Their spread around the world is impressive; at the end of 2011 they had assets of $1,564 billion and reserves of $141.3 billion, they had just over $1,000 billion out on loan to members, and held $1,222.6 billion of their savings. This makes them – collectively – very big business.

The number of credit unions is not a good indicator of the importance of the sector because the size of each union can vary so much. However, by dividing the number of members by the number of unions we can get an insight into the average size of unions in each region. They fall into three types. Africa and Asia have the smallest unions (averaging 985 members in Africa, 2006 in Asia). Then come the middling regions, the Caribbean and Latin America (with 6804 and 10335). Then there are the most developed regions, Oceania and North America (with 15706 and 12804 members per union). Europe is a bit of an anomaly with only 3502 members per

union, because as a more economically developed region we might expect
it to have large unions. This may be because much of the development in
Eastern and Central Europe is recent. We shall see when we look at the
regions in more detail.

Unlike the European cooperative banks that have been allowed to
provide services to customers who are not members, the credit unions are
fully mutual.[2] This means that in order to save with, or borrow from, a
union, one has to be a member. In the credit union system, 196 million
people are *members*, which means – if one or two persons per household
are members – that a lot more people depend on them for savings and
loans. Which of the seven world regions has the most members? North
America leads with 104.5 million, followed by Asia, with 39.7 million, and
then Africa with 18.2 million, Latin America with 18.1 million, Europe
with 8.1 million, Oceania with 5.1 million, and the Caribbean with 2.9
million members (see Table 3.1). However, it is all relative to the size of
population in each region, and this is measured (roughly) by WOCCU in
what it calls 'market penetration'.

Market penetration is the number of recorded members as a percentage
of the economically active population (defined as people aged 15–64).
A more accurate way to estimate the financial importance of the sector
is through *market share*. This has been done for the cooperative banks
and building societies, but only for some of the credit unions and in some
countries. What WOCCU does is to calculate market penetration instead,
and at least this gives a consistent indicator. Worldwide, the market
penetration is 7.8 per cent. It is highest in North America at 45 per cent.
Oceania is second with 23.6 per cent, and the Caribbean next with 17.5
per cent. Africa has 7.2 per cent, Latin America 5.7 per cent, and Europe
only 3.5 per cent. It is lowest in Asia, where it is only 2.7 per cent, which
indicates that there is much more to be done in this region to reach people
who are still 'unbanked'.

We should expect unions in wealthier countries to be themselves
wealthier on average. To test this simple proposition we can calculate
the average amount of savings each member has deposited (see Table 3.2
for total savings). The regions fall into three types. First come the richer
countries: Oceania comes first with $13,369 and North America with
$9,260 per member. Then come a middle group of Asia with $3,067, Latin
America with $1,850 and the Caribbean with $1,444. Africa lags behind
with only $240 per member. Again Europe is not easily classifiable as, for
a comparatively rich region, it has only $2,742 per member and we will
have to find out why.

Table 3.2   Credit union financial statistics 2011

Year/region	Savings	Loans	Reserves	Assets
World	1222.6	1016.2	141.3	1563.5
Africa	4.3	4.2	0.3	4.9
Asia	121.8	88.1	8.6	140.2
Caribbean	4.3	3.5	0.54	5.2
Europe	22.3	111.9	3.1	24.6
Latin America	33.5	30.5	7.3	50.3
North America	968	808.8	114.8	1253
Oceania	68.4	69.1	6.6	85.2

Note: Figures are in billions of US dollars, rounded to nearest tenth of a billion.

Source: Edited from WOCCU (2012a).

Credit Unions in Africa

Africa has 24 countries with credit unions, but only eight have a membership of over a million. Still, this is an increase from six countries in 2010. Kenya comes first with over four million members, followed by Senegal with just over two million. Yet in terms of market penetration, it is the smaller countries – Benin, Senegal, Mali and Togo – that have over 20 per cent. Senegal claims nearly 33 per cent market penetration with 235 quite large unions averaging nearly 9500 members each. Contrast Ethiopia, which has only 0.6 per cent market penetration, yet has over 4300 unions, giving an average of only 62 members each. A lot depends on the policies of each government. Sometimes an ambitious government sets up cooperatives and credit unions in every village, but most of them remain on paper. When governments leave unions alone but regulate them effectively, a more balanced picture emerges. In Tanzania, for instance, market penetration is 4 per cent, and there are just under a million members and over 5000 unions, making an average of 177 members per union. We know from our own research that this is a real social movement (Birchall and Simmons, 2010).

Credit union membership is growing quickly throughout Africa. There is a lot of institutional strengthening going on, with help from mature unions in other countries. In Malawi, the Canadian Co-operative Association (CCA) is providing support for the Malawi Union of Savings and Credit Co-ops and its member savings and credit cooperatives (SACCOs), aiming to increase membership and improve risk management. In Uganda, CCA and Uganda Co-operative Alliance are linking agricultural cooperatives and SACCOs, while WOCCU and CCA are helping the Uganda Credit and Savings Co-operative Union to establish a supervision unit, and to prepare for government supervision. It is found that better supervision leads to increases in membership, and in savings. In Ghana, the CCA is working with the Credit Union Association of Ghana, and in 25 years the sector has gone from near collapse to 400 thriving SACCOs. Here the emphasis is on building the board of directors, increasing staff capacity and improving the role of women in leadership.

In Tanzania, WOCCU has been invited by the Bank of Tanzania to develop and implement a regulatory framework for SACCOs, and to train the regulators from the Co-operative Development Department. The sector has grown almost too fast; in 2009 there were more than 5500 unions serving 800 000 people, an increase of more than 50 per cent in just three years. There is a need for central oversight to ensure discipline. The aims are to provide risk-based supervision, an early warning system for failing SACCOs, policies for intervention and guidance to help them improve their operations. Similar kinds of strengthening are happening in Ethiopia and Kenya. In Sierra Leone, after a terrible civil war, CCA and the Irish League are strengthening the few unions that still survive.

Credit Unions in Asia

In the WOCCU statistics, the Asia region has 20 per cent of the members (39.7 million) but less than 10 per cent of the assets, which indicates that they are (not surprisingly) much less rich than the Americans! They have 39 per cent of the world's total number of unions, indicating that they are generally small in size and are not under such pressure to merge into larger units. In general, unions in *Asia* have a very low market penetration of only 2.7 per cent. From the statistics there are three distinct groupings. First there are established, well-integrated sectors in five countries: South Korea (16.5 per cent penetration), Thailand (7.4 per cent), Philippines (6.7 per cent), Singapore (6.4 per cent) and Sri Lanka (6.3 per cent). In Korea there are 954 unions with 5.8 million members and a market penetration rate of 16.5 per cent. In terms of membership, they are third in size after the USA and Canada. They operate at a high level of integration, with a strong national federation that provides central liquidity, a single central-ised IT system and a common brand.

The Sanasa movement in *Sri Lanka* is also notable. There are 8424 societies in membership, with 805 000 members (Sanasa Development Bank, 2012). This means that if families are added in it covers 3.1 million people. This is a genuinely democratic movement. At the village level, it competes with two similar membership based credit societies:

the government-sponsored Samurdhi banks and the non-governmental organisation (NGO)-sponsored Sarvodaya Movement. Politicians have recently suggested that these be merged into Sanasa, which has the better track record for sustainability, and has a vertical structure of federation and a national bank that the others cannot match (Birchall and Simmons, 2013, forthcoming). Also in Sri Lanka there is a large Women's Development Services Co-operative Society (known as Women's Co-op) that has 57 000 members. It does not feed into local societies but works through a network of 120 branches. WOCCU has been working with the cooperative to help strengthen it through developing group lending products, and improving farm incomes through improving value chains. It has introduced computerised accounting, increased liquidity from savings products, and a better brand image. As a result, loan delinquency is down from 20 per cent to 1.8 per cent (WOCCU, 2012b).

The second set of credit union sectors consists of seven countries with between 1 per cent and 4 per cent market penetration: Nepal (3.6 per cent), India (2.6 per cent), Vietnam (2.5 per cent), Hong Kong (1.4 per cent), Mongolia (1.2 per cent), Taiwan (1.2 per cent) and Indonesia (1.1 per cent). In India there are two national federations of urban and rural cooperative banks, both of which are under the same three-tier system, with primary societies, district and state cooperative banks. The National Federation of Urban Co-operative Banks and Credit Societies (NAFCUB) is included in the WOCCU statistics. It has 1645 societies, with 20 members in membership, but it has a small market share of 3.5 per cent of deposits and 2.9 per cent of loans (Malegam and Expert Committee, 2011). In some respects it is outgrowing the three-tier system; there are 42 multi-state urban cooperative banks (UCBs), and some are very big. The sector has some serious problems. An expert committee convened in 2011 has identified these as stemming from a liberal licensing policy followed by the RBI between 1993 and 1999; many UCBs licensed during the period have become financially weak. In 2004 licensing was discontinued, and the RBI entered into a memorandum of agreement with state governments to coordinate regulation. Since then, there has been an improvement in the performance of UCBs, but the expert committee found that only 57.6 per cent were sound. Those with a larger deposit base were sounder, but 88 have a negative net worth.

There is uneven geographical spread, weakness in structure, and capital is below the required norms. Almost a third of those with a deposit base of less than 10 crore (100 million rupees, about $1.8 million) have inadequate safety for depositors. The increase in their size of operations means member ownership has been lost, but nevertheless they are important players in the drive for financial inclusion; more than 90 per cent of their loans are below 5 lakh (500 000 rupees, about $9000). Despite the problems with existing UCBs, the committee concludes that there is a need for new ones in unbanked districts. The main problem is the duality of control between the state-based Registrar of Co-operative Societies and the RBI. This explains the less than satisfactory performance. The committee concludes that there should be a clearly defined control system in place, with the cooperative character of the UCBs controlled by the registrars and the banking aspect controlled by the RBI. They need professionally competent managers, freedom from vested interests and competent supervision. Interestingly, the report suggests they move to the continental European system of a two-tier board.

Vietnam is distinctive in having a new system of people's credit funds to replace the old government-controlled system that collapsed. This is quite an achievement. It began in 1990 with a new legal framework, and a set of pilot projects aimed at establishing a new network fully in line with international best practice; the development arm of the Desjardins unions in Quebec (Developpement International Desjardins, DID) gave technical assistance. The result is a substantial three-tier network of people's credit funds (PCFs), a central bank (Central People's Credit Fund) and a national federation (Vietnam Association of PCFs). At first, local government had a lot of influence over the primary societies, but direct influence has gradually given way to genuine self-management as directors and managers have gained more confidence in running their own affairs. Government interference only occurs at the top level, with the State Bank of Vietnam setting maximum interest rates. After a period of consolidation in which 100 societies were closed down and regional apex bodies were collapsed into the central, the movement has achieved a stable state. It has strong capital adequacy, a healthy ratio between savings and loans, and loan default rates of less than 1 per cent (Seibel, 2009a). Now there are 1095 primary societies, with 1.6 million members, and total assets of $1.6 billion (WOCCU, 2012a).

The third set of credit unions consists of very small sectors in nine countries, with less than 1 per cent market penetration: Afghanistan (0.5 per cent), Azerbaijan (0.3 per cent), Bangladesh (0.3 per cent), Cambodia (0.4 per cent), Iran (0.03 per cent), Kyrgyzstan (0.7 per cent), Laos (0.4 per cent), Myanmar (0.2 per cent), Malaysia (0.9 per cent) and Kazakhstan (figures not available). There are various reasons for this neglect. Bangladesh has the famous Grameen system that is not counted as a credit union sector. Afghanistan and Cambodia have suffered terrible conflicts. Credit unions in Azerbaijan, Kyrgyzstan and Kazakhstan are only just beginning after the long Soviet rule. In these countries, the emphasis is on establishing new credit union movements with help from unions in developed countries. For instance, in Cambodia, the Canadian Co-operative Association is helping to establish a brand new credit union system. In Afghanistan, a Rural Finance and Cooperative Development programme is developing credit unions to increase financial access primarily in southern and eastern Afghanistan. WOCCU is working in partnership with Afghan leaders to set up new unions, strengthen their apex association as a supervisory body, and develop long-term loan products. What is distinctive about this initiative is that savings and loan products are being invented that are Shariah-compliant, enabling Islamic cooperatives to be developed. The mutual ownership and shared risk of cooperative members was found to be in line with Islamic values and helped the unions to attract new members and the support of local religious leaders (WOCCU, 2012b).

There are also large credit cooperative sectors that do not figure in the WOCCU statistics, and it will be interesting to find out why. These include the Shinkin banks in Japan, the Indian rural credit societies and the rural credit cooperatives in China. In Japan, the Shinkin banks were founded in 1951, and they have 292 local banks and a central. They are a variant on the credit union, but with the express purpose of lending to SMEs; they can accept deposits from non-members and can make loans to larger companies of over 300 employees that are prohibited from membership. In 2001 they had their own banking crisis when 20 of them failed and had to be merged with other Shinkin banks. There were three causes of the failure: loan delinquency by SMEs that were struggling under a prolonged recession, losses in securities owing to a downturn in the stock market, and a reassessment by the regulator of their bad debts that led to a shortage of equity capital (Kurimoto, 2012).

In India, the rural credit societies (RCSs) have their own National Federation of State Co-operative Banks (NAFSCOB). It is just as well that this sector is not included in the statistics. Although it is a vast banking empire, it is in a poor state and is not really cooperative. On paper it is very impressive. There are 93 000 primary societies with a membership of 121 million and 290 000 staff (NAFSCOB, 2012). However, this is down from the 112 000 societies with 132 million members quoted in the report of a task force in 2004 (Vaidyanathan and Task Force, 2004). There are 371 district banks and 31 state cooperative banks that support the primary societies as well as doing business on their own behalf. There is one society for every six villages, and the borrowers are mainly small farmers and members of scheduled tribes and castes who are among the poorest people. Like the Sri Lankan multi-purpose societies, a large proportion of them are also outlets for farm inputs and public distribution of food and essential items. Needless to say, the commercial banks do not reach this far and so the RCSs are vital for any strategy of financial deepening (see World Bank, 2008).

Their performance is poor and deteriorating rapidly. In the early 1990s they accounted for over 60 per cent of lending for agriculture, but by 2003 it had fallen to around 34 per cent. In 2004, the task force estimated that 63 per cent of the primary co-ops were viable, 30 per cent potentially viable, 8 per cent dormant or under liquidation. In contrast, the share of the commercial banks was up from 33 per cent to 57 per cent. In 2009, Seibel commented that the situation was even worse than the task force had admitted. In his view:

> Large numbers of co-operative banks, and more than half the primary credit co-operatives, are loss-making. Many are technically bankrupt but are kept open thanks to lenient supervision and political pressure (Seibel, 2009b, p. 1).

Many more would be in trouble if international accounting standards were applied. Three-quarters of cooperative credit is for crop loans, which shows that, after all the effort put into supporting agriculture, farmers have not yet become self-sufficient. The primary societies are really just channelling agents, with a large part of the funds provided by the National Bank for Agriculture and Rural Development (NABARD), guaranteed by state governments, and rolled over perpetually. If NABARD finance were recalled the cooperatives would collapse.

Does it matter if the rural credit societies go down? After all, they are not true cooperatives. It does matter, because there is no alternative. The commercial banks do not have the reach that the cooperatives have, and they have cut back their branches so that they are even more remote from the poorer farmers. The reach of the cooperatives extends to nearly half the population, and is supposed to underpin the broader cooperative movement. It affects the inputs and marketing linkages of the entire farm sector, and so its decline is a major impediment to rural development (Seibel, 2009b). Also the banks' depositors are at risk of losing $4.3 billion.

What has gone wrong? The task force found that borrowers, not depositors, drive the business, and that conversion to a more balanced savings and credit cooperative model is needed. Governance is deeply impaired, with the lower tiers managed by the higher tiers and with little involvement by members. Elections and auditing are dependent on the state governments and they have an interest in keeping control. Elections have not been held for a long time (more than ten years in three states!), boards are frequently replaced, audits are delayed, government officials are put into top positions, and there is interference in operational decision-making. Supervision is not as stringent as for commercial banks (Vaidyanathan and Task Force, 2004). A reform process has begun that is estimated to cost $3 billion. The aim is to restructure the cooperative banks, wipe out their losses, restore the members' capital, achieve a minimum 7 per cent capital to risk weighted assets ratio, and initiate major regulatory and governance reforms. There is a strong focus on restoring the cooperatives to their members and encouraging them to monitor the banks themselves.

In China, a reform process began in 2000. It was always going to be a huge task; at that time there were 35000 primary societies, 2439 county, 67 district, and 6 provincial banks. How important is it to reform them? Like the Indian credit cooperatives, they may be in financial trouble and are not genuine member-owned banks, but they are still needed; they hold 12 per cent of China's bank deposits and 11 per cent of loans, but account for more than 90 per cent of legitimate lending in rural areas (Swoboda and Ruibin, 2007). The big four banks have withdrawn from rural areas to serve the urban areas. The government recognises the importance of the RCCs in developing a diversified rural economy, creating employment and preventing the drift of population to the cities. Up to 75 per cent of people in China still did not have access to financial services in 2005 (Planet Finance, 2005). The contribution of NGOs is insignificant. The Agricultural Bank does micro-finance, but it has a poor record with 25 per cent of its loans non-performing, and it is withdrawing from the agricultural sector. So the RCCs are still the key vehicle for loans to farmers, SMEs and individuals.

By 2002 the situation was desperate. Thirty-seven per cent of the sector's outstanding loans were non-performing, amounting to a staggering $62 billion (Empel and Smit, 2004). Nearly 20000 RCCs – 55 per cent of them – were technically bankrupt (Ong, 2006). They faced competition for savings from postal banks that were able to pay higher interest, yet had their interest rates fixed by the Central Bank. They had been forced to take over a weak loan portfolio from a network of rural credit foundations that were closed down. They still had no national network, so that depositors could not get access to their money except in their local RCC.

Reform began. In 2001 rural credit cooperative unions (RCCUs) were set up to provide centralised data processing, investment and liquidity services, and back office support; under their strong managerial control, the RCCs began to function more like branches. The Central Bank pumped $9 billion into the system. In 2003, supervision was transferred from the People's Bank to a new China Banking Regulatory Commission (CBRC). This accelerated a process of merging RCCs into each other and then into the RCCUs. The total number of RCCs declined from 40000 to 25000, but their supervision was still a huge task; the CBRC had an average of only one supervisor for more than ten RCCs (Planet Finance, 2005).

The reform process began in eight provinces and then late in 2004 expanded throughout the country. The management control rights of the RCCs were transferred to provincial governments, and then various shareholding models were tested, including full and partial demutualisation. People's Bank bonds were issued to write off bad debts, subsidised loans were given to fund more lending to farmers, tax reliefs were given and RCCs were allowed to charge higher interest rates. Provincial RCCUs were created as centrals. Most of the city based RCCUs converted into investor-owned banks that then began to grow very fast, but some chose instead to become rural cooperative banks.[3] In Guinzhou province, a partnership between WOCCU and the People's Bank of China began to modernise the RCCs. Here, in this very poor region, most of the RCCs remained cooperatives. Two thousand village-level RCCs were merged into 84 country RCCUs and four rural cooperative banks. The system became much more professional and properly audited, and in 2005 showed a small profit. Steps were taken to convert them into real cooperatives. The lower tiers began to elect the board of the provincial central, and some elections began to be contested (Swoboda and Ruibin, 2007).[4]

There is a lot at stake here. If the reforms fail, the only alternative is demutualisation. In 2010 the government announced that it wanted to encourage investors to buy into the RCCs; domestic banks can buy up to 100 per cent and foreign banks up to 20 per cent of their equity. The direction of the reforms will determine whether they become true financial cooperatives or small investor-owned banks.

Credit Unions in Oceania

Oceania includes Australia and New Zealand, Fiji, Papua New Guinea, the Solomon Islands and Tonga. Most of the members (4.5 million people) are in Australia, but there are 413 000 members in Papua New Guinea and 195 000 in New Zealand. Australia and New Zealand are like North America, with a few large unions (106 in Australia, 22 in New Zealand) doing a lot of business. The islands are more like Asia, with much smaller unions working among much poorer populations; the number of unions in Tonga is higher than in Australia and New Zealand put together. The market penetration in Australia is an impressive 30.6 per cent, in Papua New Guinea 11.1 per cent, and New Zealand 6.9 per cent, after which it drops to 3.8 per cent in Tonga and 1.6 per cent in the Solomon Islands (WOCCU, 2012a).

During the 1990s a large part of the Australian building society sector demutualised, but credit unions have resisted the temptation; only two attempts have succeeded, and three have failed because of opposition

from members. Instead they have merged and consolidated: the numbers
are down from 291 in 1995 to 106 in 2011, and the top ten unions have
increased their asset share from 25 per cent to over 50 per cent (Davis,
2007; WOCCU, 2012a). They have 4.5 million members, and a market
penetration of over 30 per cent. As in the UK, the threat of demutualisation and the unpopularity of the big commercial banks have sharpened
members' understanding of the benefits of being a mutual. The unions are
represented in a trade body, ABACUS, which includes the whole mutual
financial sector: building societies, credit unions and friendly societies.
This is the kind of development we can expect to see in other developed
countries; in the UK for instance, though the trade bodies remain separate
the underlying similarities of the 'financial mutuals' are being recognised.

There is a trend towards credit unions becoming cooperative banks. In
New Zealand, the Public Service Investment Society was founded in 1928
to serve the needs of civil servants (NZCB, 2012). In 2011 it registered as
a bank, and gave its 130 000 members one share each, with equal voting
rights. The New Cooperative Bank only has 0.6 per cent of the market,
but with a customer satisfaction rating of 96 per cent its managers expect
it to grow into a fully-fledged retail bank. In Australia, recently the federal
government called for higher levels of competition in a market dominated
by a few large investor-owned banks. Several credit unions responded by
merging together to form Bankmecu. It only has 134 000 customers, but
expects to grow quickly, boldly proclaiming its status as 'Australia's first
customer-owned bank' (Bankmecu, 2012). Here is an extract from its
website that neatly sums up the benefits of customer-ownership:

> At bankmecu we are accountable to our customers because collectively they own
> the bank and its profits. When you become a customer, you also become a part
> owner of the bank. We don't need to pay dividends to investors because we don't
> have any. Our profits are 100% owned by our customers, and go back to them in
> the form of better rates and lower fees. Some profit is also retained and invested
> back into developing the bank for the benefit of all customers. So the more
> banking customers do with us, the more everyone benefits (Bankmecu, 2012).

The bank calculates that in 2010 its customers were collectively $31 million
better off (in pricing benefits) than if they had banked with Australia's big
banks; this works out at $231 per customer. In 2011 it had profits of $27
million, and achieved a 94 per cent satisfaction rating.

Credit Unions in Latin America and the Caribbean

There are credit union sectors in 15 countries in Latin America and no
one country predominates. From a regional total of 18 million members,

Brazil has 4.4 million, Mexico 3.8 million, and Colombia another two million, but Chile, Ecuador and Guatemala each have well over a million, and Bolivia, Costa Rica, Honduras and Paraguay have over 600 000. Only in El Salvador, Nicaragua, Uruguay and Panama do they fall below 200 000. The highest penetration rates can be found in Ecuador (20.3 per cent), followed by Costa Rica (19.3 per cent) and Paraguay (16.5 per cent), but Honduras and Guatemala are close behind (with 13.8 per cent and 12.6 per cent respectively). It is hard to generalise about this region. There are sectors that consist of small, weakly integrated unions serving low-income rural populations, just as in parts of Africa and Asia, and these are being strengthened by collaboration with experts from countries where the unions are well established. For instance, in Colombia, WOCCU is developing micro-credit and savings products for around 200 unions that serve more than two million members. Field officers are now aided by mobile telephones and hand held printers.

Then there are large urban unions that are more like commercial banks. Caja Popular Mexicana is the largest union in Latin America; 62 unions, state federations and a national federation all merged to form it, with technical assistance from WOCCU funded by USAID. The results have been spectacular, with assets increased nearly fourfold, loan delinquency down to 4 per cent and membership growing at 14 000 people per month. The union has 3500 employees, and is hoping to offer online banking and credit cards. In Chile, Coopeuch is the largest union, second largest in Latin America. It has 85 branches that serve 417 000 members nationwide and holds US$1.8 billion in assets. In Brazil, the Sicredi credit union system has 144 primary societies, four central unions and a bank, with two million members in ten states. It has averaged 15 per cent membership growth and 30 per cent asset growth annually for the past five years, and its members have access to all the sophisticated financial products provided by commercial banks. In 2010 Rabobank's development arm took a minority stake of 24.9 per cent, in a move that signals growing solidarity between credit unions worldwide.

In the *Caribbean*, 19 countries have credit union movements. Most have small memberships numbered in the tens of thousands, but the largest, Jamaica, has 920 000 members and a penetration rate of 51.5 per cent. Some of the populations are quite small, and so even with small numbers of members by international standards, several countries have high penetration rates; St Vincent has 81 per cent, Barbados 76.9 per cent, St Lucia 74.3 per cent, Belize 63.7 per cent, Grenada 61.6 per cent, Trinidad and Tobago 56.4 per cent, and so on. Clearly the credit union movement is well established in this region and has an important economic role. Only five countries have a share of less than 10 per cent. Haiti is one of them, and here WOCCU is working with USAID funding to strengthen value chains and provide financial products, again using 'mobile money' techniques (WOCCU, 2012b).

Credit Unions in Europe

Europe offers a mixed picture that requires several different stories to be told. The credit unions are all around the edge of the core of cooperative banking countries, in the UK, Ireland, Russia, the Baltic, and Central and Eastern Europe. In terms of membership, Ireland leads with over three million, followed by Poland with 2.3 million, Ukraine with 1.1 million and then Britain with 983 000. In all of these countries the unions are small, only in Ireland reaching over 6000 members per union, with the next largest being Ukraine with 2400 per union and Britain with an average of 2000. Ireland stands out from the crowd; here the penetration rate is an astonishing 72.2 per cent, the next in line being Poland at 8.4 per cent. However, in the ex-communist countries the sector is growing fast from a standing start when the Soviet Union collapsed; Lithuania has a 5 per cent penetration rate, Ukraine 3.5 per cent and Moldova 4.3 per cent. Everywhere else the rate is negligible.

Credit unions in Ireland are well established. Beginning in 1959, they developed at first 'under the profound influence' of the Catholic Church, with a residence based rather than employment based common bond (McCarthy et al., 2000, p. 45). They formed their own trade body in 1960 and gained legislation in 1966 (updated in 1997), and so we might expect them to be in the 'mature' category of unions that are able to offer a wide range of banking services, as in New Zealand or the USA (Sibbald et al., 2002). However, the movement was set back in the mid 1990s by an information technology project that went wrong and had to be abandoned. The banking crisis did not affect the unions directly, but the subsequent downturn certainly did. Lending has decreased, arrears have increased dramatically, and some unions find themselves seriously under-capitalised. Will this credit union sector develop from the transitional to the mature stage? There is some resistance among supporters to moving from a community based, volunteer-led union to a more 'mature' system dominated by professionals (Power et al., 2012). Yet there may not be a choice. A recent report from a government commission recommends the merger of weaker unions with stronger ones, an improved regulatory framework and a governance standard (McKillop, 2012).

There was a thriving credit union movement in Poland before World War II, but communist rule destroyed it. In 1989, leaders of the Solidarity Party visited the USA to find out more about them and linked up with officials from WOCCU. They set up a foundation, and then in 1992 a National Association of Co-operative Savings and Credit Unions (NACSCU), with help from WOCCU and funding from USAID. This was a bold, 'top-down' approach to development that had no parallel elsewhere; most development begins by founding and then strengthening primary societies, but here the apex body came first and it promoted the primary societies. Another difference was that it focused on workplace unions in heavy industries such as mining, factories and shipbuilding rather than on rural areas. By the end of 1998 there were 220 unions, with 268 000 members and, remarkably, NACSCU had become self-sustaining. Now, after considerable consolidation the sector has 59 unions, with assets of \$4.6 billion. The market has changed, with heavy industry giving way to a wider common bond that is driving rapid growth (WOCCU, 2012b).

The Polish sector is a real social movement that has grown faster and provided a wider range of services than any other movement in recent history. Its success can be explained like this: there were strong macro-economic reforms that eased the tradition to a market economy; there was unwavering political support from the Solidarity trade union and party; and there were strong, dynamic leaders coming out of that movement; they obtained favourable legislation and tax regulations; there was strong social capital, a general distrust of banks and unmet financial needs (Evans and Richardson, 1999). Unfortunately, because of this unusual combination of success factors, the Polish experience is not likely to be replicated, but this has not stopped the movement from helping unions to become established in neighbouring countries.

In Britain, community based credit unions began in 1964, and employment based unions in the early 1980s. They achieved a clear legal basis in a law of 1979, and then began to be supported by local authorities as part of their local economic development strategies; by 1999, 83 per cent of all community credit unions had been formed with local authority support. They began to make 'significant headway' in the late 1990s (Jones, 2012, p.1). The sector remains small, with a large number of unions (405 in 2011) but less than a million members, and an asset base of just under \$1.4 billion that is only 30 per cent the size of the assets held by the Polish movement (WOCCU, 2012a). To put it bluntly, the British credit union sector is 'not regarded as being successful'. It has been aimed at areas of deprivation, but it is the larger unions in more affluent areas that have been successful (Ward and McKillop, 2005, p. 461). It has been held back by a lack of charismatic leadership, competing trade associations and reliance on 'top-down' promotion by local governments.

It is growing, though; in the last ten years membership has increased by 128 per cent, savings by 214 per cent and loans by 177 per cent. There are now several unions with over 20 000 people in membership (Jones, 2012). Mergers have reduced their numbers but there is a more professional and business-like approach. Gradually, restrictive legislation has been modified to allow a wider common bond, larger memberships and higher ceilings on the amounts members can save and borrow. From 2006, a Labour government gave £100 million to expand the availability of credit, and then from 2010 a Coalition government pledged up to £73 million to modernise delivery and customer support systems. They are still in the 'nascent' stage of development, but with help from the Co-operative Bank, 25 of the larger unions have begun to offer a current account and a prepaid Visa card (ABCUL, 2011). The biggest federal, ABCUL, is setting up a company to provide back office functions and so the sector may finally be maturing.

In some other European countries the sector is brand new and needing the same kind of help that sectors in Asia and Africa obtain. In the North Caucasus, for instance, rural credit cooperatives are being strengthened with technical help from ACDI/VOCA, an agency set up originally by American agricultural cooperatives. In Belarus, a national association has been formed with help from WOCCU and the Polish national association.

Credit Unions in North America

North America, consisting of the USA and Canada, is predominant in the world of credit unions, with 80 per cent of the total assets and 53 per cent of the members (104.5 million), which indicates (not surprisingly) that they are also much richer than average. In the USA there are 7351 unions with 93.9 million members and 63 per cent of the total assets of credit unions worldwide (WOCCU, 2012a). Their market penetration is an impressive 44.9 per cent. Their financial statistics are so large they have to be expressed in hundreds of billions. They have $982.1 billion in assets, $586.6 billion in loans, $845.9 billion in savings and shares, and $99.8 billion in reserves (WOCCU, 2012a). The three largest unions each have over $10 billion in assets; Navy Federal is largest with more than $45 billion and 3.8 million members. They have demonstrated what we might call 'scalability' (Rosenthal, 2012).

They have a very large and complex system that defies simple description. First, unions can choose to be either federally chartered or state chartered; currently the ratio is about 60 to 40. The two types come under slightly different legislation and regulation, which makes things complicated. Then they have a three-tier system, with regional and national corporates that provide services to the primary unions. Currently there are 12 federally insured state corporates and 14 federal corporates, but the largest federal corporate, Central Federal, has been closed down because of its losses in the recent banking crisis, and another four centrals have been taken into administration. The majority of unions serve 'solidly middle class' members, but there are 1128 low-income unions that deliberately aim to serve low-income and minority communities. Not surprisingly, the credit unions in the USA have been badly hit by the banking crisis and subsequent 'great recession', and so we will be telling their story in greater detail in Chapter 6.

In Canada there are 813 unions with 10.6 million members and over 17 per cent of the total assets worldwide. Their market penetration is even higher than in the USA, at 45.5 per cent. The Mouvement des Caisses Desjardins, known more prosaically in English as the Desjardins Group, is the jewel in the crown of the worldwide credit union movement. There are three features that make it special; its sheer size in relation to the banking sector in its region, the complexity of its organisational structure and its strong cooperative ethos. Then there is a fourth feature that comes from these, its socio-economic impact. The only movement that rivals it in these ways is the Mondragon cooperative system in the Basque region of Spain, which has a savings bank at its centre but is organised around a different principle, of worker cooperation. The success of both movements has been explained by their situation; an ethnic group who are in the majority in their region but form a minority within a larger nation state where the majority speak a different language. The result is a strong sense of social solidarity that translates into high levels of social capital. However, this is only part of the explanation. They are also very good at banking.

Desjardins is the leading cooperative financial group in Canada, and sixth largest in the world, so that it stands on a level with the credit union sector in the USA and the biggest European cooperative banking sectors. There are 397 caisses Desjardins (377 in Quebec and 20 in Ontario), with 5.8 million members, 42500 employees and 5400 elected officers (Desjardins Group, 2012b). The group has $190.1 billion in assets (up 6.3 per cent on 2010), $125.2 billion out on loan, and $123.4 billion in deposits. It is the market leader in the Quebec region for just about everything to do with finance. Its market share of residential mortgages is 38 per cent, of consumer credit 22.8 per cent, of business credit 27.9 per cent, and of agricultural financing 42.7 per cent. It is the largest credit and debit card issuer, the leading direct insurance provider and the largest life and health insurer in Quebec. In Canada as a whole it is ranked second in the group insurance market, fifth in life and health insurance and seventh for property and casualty insurance. It achieves all of this while having a Tier 1 capital ratio of 17.3 per cent, which is much higher than the regulator requires; it is ranked 18th among the 50 safest banks in the world.

A major factor in this success story is the tightly integrated and efficient group structure. The caisses network is served by just one central, Desjardins Group, that has a unitary board, with a chief executive officer (CEO) who is also president. It has a democratic structure of regional general meetings, councils and an assembly of representatives. It has four business sectors, for personal services, business and institutional services, wealth management and life and health insurance, and property and casualty insurance. It has a corporate executive division that supports the network and its democratic governance, and also carries out financial and risk management. This structure works well, both as a business and as an association of people. The word 'mouvement' is a loaded one, and suggests more than just a group of businesses that collaborate together. It suggests a sense of common purpose, of community and of shared values. In this case we do not just talk of a sector but of a genuine social movement.

The credit union movement in the English-speaking regions of Canada is less highly integrated than Desjardins but is also very impressive. There are currently 363 credit unions with over five million members. They are collectively big business, having $142.5 billion in assets, $126.3 billion in deposits, $117.6 billion in loans and nearly 27 000 employees (CUCC, 2012). They hold 6.2 per cent of the residential mortgage market, 2.4 per cent of personal loans, 18.3 per cent of loans to SMEs, and 11.1 per cent of agricultural loans. Their share is stable apart from a decline in the personal loan business, and they have recovered well from the banking crisis of 2008. They have a three-tier system, with five provincial centrals whose main role is to maintain liquidity in the unions, and an apex body, the Credit Union Central of Canada.

Over the last 20 years, there has been a dramatic decline in the number of unions, and an increase in assets. Unions have declined at an average of 40 per year, from 1203 in 1990 to 409 in 2009, and now 363. There has also been consolidation; the largest ten unions had 24 per cent of the assets in 1990, and now have 43 per cent. As a CUCC report puts it 'Rationalisation has been part of the credit union system for decades' (CUCC, 2010, p. 5). The smaller ones merge in order to reduce overhead costs, afford new technology and offer better products. As a result, over the last 20 years assets have quadrupled, growing at an average of $4.6 billion per year. Access to banking facilities by members has not been sacrificed; the number of branches has decreased much more slowly, from 2026 to 1747, with only nine branch closures in the last nine years. The main challenge for the Canadian unions is stagnating membership. There are over five million members, but the annual growth rate has been under 1 per cent, and the average age of members is 12 per cent higher than for the population. Forty-five per cent are retired or near retirement age and only 1.8 per cent are between 18 and 24. In consequence, many unions now have strategies to attract younger members.

CONCLUSION

This description of credit unions around the world raises several important questions that we will be pursuing in later chapters. One question keeps on cropping up: how large can unions become before they lose their purpose and just become commercial banks? Small, community based unions are attractive to some people because they foster a sense of community and build up social capital. However, they may not be very effective. Many are reliant on government grants and if these are withdrawn they collapse quickly. Many do not serve their community very well, because they have a low membership and do not reach enough people. Nor do they supply their members with what they need; their savings and loan products are too restricted. There is a strong argument that people on low incomes have just as much right to modern banking services as anyone else.

To the historian it is obvious that unions set up as an 'atomised' or 'nascent' sector will not be able to deliver. The successful sectors have always combined small, local unions with national-level federations that provide them with the services they need to make them effective. However, this does not allow us to avoid the question about how large a primary level union should be. Even in a strategic system unions can be too small and have to merge in order to be financially viable. How we value this trend depends on how we define community; people's loyalties may be to a region as well as to a village or town, especially if the region has a different language from that spoken in the rest of the country. There comes a point at which residential common bonds no longer apply. If they have a dedicated membership strategy, can national-level customer-owned banks also inspire loyalty and a sense of ownership?

NOTES

1. The WOCCU statistics do not include the centrals, whereas the European Association of Co-operative Banks statistics begin from the central banks and then mention the number of local banks. This is a significant difference of emphasis.
2. There are exceptions to this rule but they are minor.
3. Despite being urban banks, they still kept the name of rural credit cooperatives.
4. Also, in the West Guangzi region the International Fund for Agricultural Development (IFAD) has been working for a long time in parallel with the RCC reform process, training managers to apply modern micro-finance appraisal technologies so they can improve their loan repayment rates.

4. The evolution of mutual building societies

History is messy. The story of cooperative banks is one of continual expansion and change, and it is only complicated by the name change from cooperative bank to credit union half way through. It would be good if we could integrate the history of building societies into this wider history, but there is very little point of contact between them, hence the need for a separate chapter. On the other hand, both cooperative banks and building societies and – where they are strong, credit unions – have evolved into broader banking activities that include mortgage lending for property, so that now the consumer is faced with a variety of customer-owned banks that all offer the same range of services. In order to understand their history we have to make these distinctions, but looking to the future they will be less and less relevant.

Before we begin to discuss the provision of mortgage lending it is worth pausing to reflect on why it is needed. In the past (and also the present in low-income countries), people built their own homes using materials that were to hand: stone, thatch, slate, wood and mud. With the development of urbanisation that accompanied the industrial revolution it began to be impossible for people to house themselves without help. In Britain, during the nineteenth century, factory workers, lured to the city by higher wages than they could get in the countryside, had to rent a home from a new class of landlords who began to build on a large scale for the new working classes. In countries where common land is available, shanty towns have grown up in which the residents gradually build for themselves, beginning with the most rudimentary of dwellings and improving them with more durable materials, adding a second storey and so on. However, in developed countries land is under private ownership and is simply not available for people to build for themselves even if they have the skills and can afford the materials.

The problem is that housing is an unusual kind of commodity. People need shelter as much as they need food, but it costs a lot more to produce and lasts for more than a lifetime. Two solutions have been found to this problem: renting and mortgaged ownership. In the recent past, most people living in cities rented from a landlord who had money to invest and who made a return on that investment by turning a long-term capital asset into a commodity rented by the week. Building societies were invented in order to enable people who could not afford to buy such an expensive commodity outright to find other people who were prepared to lend them the capital to buy it gradually. It was not easy to find a method by which this could be done. Borrowers needed to borrow long term while depositors needed to lend short term; their interests were at odds. Commercial banks would not touch such a difficult contract because of the risks involved.

The solution came in two stages. First, the terminating building society was invented that was based purely on mutual self-help among people who could afford to save money regularly. The members could use the funds they accumulated to enable them to build their own homes one at a time until everyone was housed and the society was wound up. The problem was to find a way of allocating the funds fairly, and two methods were used: a lottery and an auction of the right to be next in the queue. The only problem was that members had to be in from the start; anyone joining later would have to put in a lump sum to enable them to catch up with the contributions made by the rest. Membership was restricted to people who could afford the weekly payments and could wait for the opportunity to build for themselves, and so it was the skilled workers in regular employment who joined. The second stage was the invention of the permanent building society, in which a large group of depositors were attracted by the offer of interest-bearing savings accounts, while a smaller group of borrowers were able to borrow out of the resulting pool of capital.

What about the problem for the building society of borrowing short and lending long? This was solved by the development of a business model that concentrated on the efficient cycling of money from the depositor to the borrower, and back to the society in the form of mortgage interest. Because this was the society's only business it could avoid the more risky types of investment that commercial banks made. Because it was lending on property it could secure the loan on the value of the property. This meant that, unless there was a drastic downturn in property values, if a borrower defaulted it would get its money back. Also, because it was locally based, and had a rule that borrowers be savers first, it could rely on good knowledge of the reputation of the borrower. Lastly, because it was owned and controlled by the depositors and borrowers as members, it had no incentive to make profits beyond those needed to cover management costs, and was inherently risk-averse. That, at least, is the theory. As we will see from the history of the building societies, they also required government protection against fraud and mismanagement.

The history of the building societies (which are known in the USA as savings and loans) is much more patchy than that of the cooperative banks and credit unions. The idea spread from Britain to many countries, but only in Britain and the USA is the sector large enough for a story to be told. For this reason we will be focusing on the history of this type in these two countries.

THE INVENTION OF THE BRITISH BUILDING SOCIETIES

In Britain, the European cooperative banking movement never caught on, despite some vigorous promotion towards the end of the nineteenth century by advocates such as Henry Wolff (1893, 1907). This was partly because commercial banking was better established than in continental Europe, and reached down further into the small business sector. It was also because, after the invention of the permanent building society in the 1840s, a uniquely British way of organising working-class savings had already developed that provided a safe haven for people's money.

The first recorded building society began in 1775 at the Golden Cross Inn in Birmingham. They quickly became established in areas such as Birmingham, Leeds and South Wales. They were 'terminating societies', whose members deposited their 'club money' in a box in a public house until there was enough to start building. Some had houses built for the members, while others allocated money so the members could build their own homes. Then houses were allocated by ballot or by auction as they became available, and loans were sometimes taken by the society to speed up the process. The officers were unpaid, and a system of fines encouraged members to keep up their payments and take part in governance. Money was deducted for drink at the regular meetings; for the first 50 years, as one historian coyly puts it, 'history reveals no society unattached to licensed premises' (Boddy, 1980, p. 6). All of these features were the same as in the friendly societies that insured people against sickness and provided basic medical care, and also the 'box clubs' that enabled people to save to meet more humble needs, such as for boots or clothes.

By 1825 there were well over 250 of these societies, terminating eventually when all members were housed. They were popular but had a more limited appeal than other mutuals, such as the friendly societies that provided health insurance. The reason is obvious; the rates of subscription were too high for most workingmen. Like other mutuals, at first they had no legal status and so no redress against fraud. A Reform Act of 1832 extended the parliamentary vote to smaller property owners, and this greatly increased their business because working-class people could gain the vote provided they qualified as property owners. Freehold land societies began with the express purpose of dividing up land to offer as freeholds, and a number of them registered as building societies. Then a Building Societies Act of 1836 recognised them, gave them the same kind of protection as friendly societies had obtained in 1793 and made them exempt from stamp duty on shares, a vital concession if they were able to prosper. From then onwards there was tremendous growth. During the 1840s, 767 terminating and 81 permanent societies were established (Cleary, 1965, pp. 286–9).

THE INVENTION OF THE AMERICAN SAVINGS AND LOAN ASSOCIATIONS

In the USA, building societies were called 'building and loans', later 'savings and loans' (S&Ls for short), but most people referred to them as 'thrifts'. Like the British building societies, which they copied, they began as terminating then developed into permanent societies. During the eighteenth century there was no need for institutional home finance; land and raw materials were available in abundance, and people built their own homes and helped each other through informal mutual aid traditions that are familiar to pre-industrial societies the world over. The first industrial revolution began in the 1790s, and it resulted in cities such as New York and Philadelphia experiencing phenomenal growth, similar to that of the English cities such as Manchester and Birmingham. Housing became more expensive and began to require financing and, as in Britain, informal arrangements between friends and family proved inadequate to the task (Mason, 2009). Again, as in Britain commercial banks were not able to meet the need, because bank deposits could be withdrawn on demand and they could only lend for up to five years. Their terms were also onerous; mortgagees usually made interest only payments during the life of the loan and then had to pay the principal at the end of the loan period.

Mutual savings banks also came to America from Britain, in 1819. They were not mutuals at all, but trustee-based institutions like the British savings banks, and their purpose was not lending but attracting savings. They invested mainly in low-risk government bonds, but they did also provide home loans. Unfortunately, they required large down payments and their coverage was inadequate since they were confined to cities in the north-east of America. Insurance companies were another potential source of funds. They invested their policyholders' money in bonds and also in long-term commercial and residential mortgages. Again, they required a large down payment that made these unavailable to working-class people.

The first savings and loan association was the Oxford Provident Building Society in Frankfort Pennsylvania, founded in 1831. The organisers came from the English midlands and they copied the familiar building society model. Members subscribed for shares paid for in monthly instalments. They received loan advances on these shares through an auction in which they had to submit bids indicating the loan fee and interest rate they were prepared to pay (Mason, 2009). This meant profits could be made on repayments by borrowers, and these were distributed to members as dividends. When everyone had paid in full, the association would terminate. Like the building societies, this first S&L also emphasised the importance of instilling a habit of saving, and there were fines for late payments and an emphasis on good character among the members. Dividends were credited to the account of each member rather than paid in cash, and this both preserved the funds available for lending and enabled them to build up substantial savings. However, the associations suffered from the same disadvantages as in Britain. It was difficult for people to join after an association had started, and new members had to make back payments. Later in the life of the association, when the loans were nearing maturity, they had more funds than they needed, and so members were required to take a loan or to cash in their shares. Of course the main problem was that they terminated, and this made it difficult for them to become institutionalised as a social movement.

GROWTH OF A MOVEMENT IN BRITAIN

In Britain, the first of the permanent societies, the Metropolitan Equitable, began in 1845. We can understand how this happened. When they terminated some societies ended up with a surplus that they would lend to other societies. They began to take in deposits from investors looking for interest rather than a loan, so as to increase the funds available for members to borrow. The interest was paid out of subscriptions from borrowers. Also, the practice began of forming terminating societies in series, so as to accommodate new groups of applicants in succession (Gosden, 1973). In 1847 the idea was set out in detail by a reformer, Arthur Scratchley, that they should separate the borrower from the investor and run the society like a bank with depositors and mortgage loan holders. This meant the length of term of the loan could be increased, and as long as the income from borrowers covered the interest to saving members (plus management expenses) they would be sound. Generally, both savers and borrowers could become members; it was realised that if borrowers were excluded the societies would become more like investment clubs for the wealthy. In effect, they became savings banks, accepting money on deposit and paying depositors at lower rates than shareholders. In this they were very secure. There is an old joke in building society circles that sums up the simplicity of the form: 'You borrow at one percent, you lend at two percent and you are on the golf course by three.'

The permanent societies grew rapidly. By 1873 there were 540 of them, compared with 959 terminating societies (Cleary, 1965), but of course they were much bigger. They became increasingly attractive to investors. A Royal Commission report set up to investigate the societies and recommend further legislation commented:

> A building society, with its money secured on freehold land and leasehold property, and a constant incoming of repayments by monthly instalments may fairly be preferred . . . to a bank (Cleary, 1965, p. 197).

However, the new type of society was quite different in spirit from the old. The 1872 commission noted that they were 'mainly agencies for the investment of capital rather than for enabling the industrious to provide dwellings for themselves' (quoted in Cleary, 1965, p. 205). They had changed the character of the building society movement. While the smaller societies were still under the management of the working classes, the larger permanent societies were 'under the direction of the middle class'. They required skilled management rather than voluntary work by officers elected by the members, and the new members were not so motivated to get involved. The societies became disassociated from the local pub and met in schoolrooms or temperance halls, while the larger ones such as the Halifax acquired office premises just like any other business.

The Royal Commission commented that the term 'building society' was a misnomer, since they did not build but made advances on building. They were better understood as investment associations mainly confined to 'real securities'. They were lending not just to individuals but also to house builders and landlords, and some even made loans to industrialists and landowners (Boddy, 1980). The commission decided that the more commercial societies were becoming just like banks, but with the difference that they mainly lent on property. However, they were still a distinct corporate form because they were founded on membership rather than on capital.

With such a big shift in character, the sector was in need of new legislation, which, on the recommendation of the Royal Commission, was provided in 1874. Members gained limited liability, while the society itself rather than its trustees could now hold mortgage deeds and stand security for loans. Societies were allowed to offer small paid up shares as well as the subscription shares that involved long-term saving, and they could borrow from depositors up to two-thirds of the sum secured by mortgages. They were not allowed to invest surplus funds anywhere but in mortgages or securities underpinned by a government guarantee. The government gave itself regulatory powers, and the Act gave the sector a sound basis on which it relied right up to the 1986 Act that allowed demutualisation. However, the law did not stop some societies getting into immediate difficulties. First, in the 20 years after the Act there was an era of economic depression that meant societies experienced falling property values and lack of demand for loans. At the same time, they attracted an increasing volume of savings that they found it difficult to invest. The result was that societies with surplus funds moved into more risky areas and many got into difficulties. They began to advance money against poorer security, financed commercial enterprises and began to do more purely banking business (Boddy, 1980).

Two societies went bankrupt: the Liberator in 1892 and the Birkbeck in 1911. The reasons are uncannily similar to those that have tested societies in the recent banking crisis. The Liberator grew quickly, financing property and industrial companies that then defaulted on their loans. The reason for the Birkbeck's failure was different. It had in effect become a bank, with most of its assets in government securities; when the market value of these declined it got into trouble. These failures were compounded by the invention in the 1860s of a new form, the Starr-Bowkett society. These societies, named after their inventors, proved popular; there were more than 1000 of them by 1892. They invited people to invest small sums and then enter a lottery, the winner of which got an interest-free loan for housing. However, this was more like gambling, and the high salaries of the officers and their rules that prevented office-holders from being dismissed made them notorious. In 1892 two of these societies collapsed through fraud.

By 1894 the assets of the movement as a whole had fallen by £10 million to £42 million, and it was realised that the law had to be strengthened. That year a new Act was passed that made the lottery illegal in newly formed societies and toughened the law against dishonesty. Powers of inspection were given to the Chief Registrar, societies were required to make an annual return, and members were given the power to dissolve a society. Societies now had to declare mortgage arrears and properties taken into possession, just as banks now have to make realistic write downs of their assets after a property bubble has burst. However, during this period much good had been done; it was estimated that between 1836 and 1896, because of the work of the societies, at least 250000 people had become homeowners. By 1910 there were 1723 societies with 626000 members and assets of over £76 million (BSA, 2010).

GROWTH OF A MOVEMENT IN THE USA

In the USA, growth was slow until the 1870s when, as in Britain, it was helped by the invention of the new type of permanent society. S&Ls began to issue shares periodically on a 'serial plan', so that new members could join without having to make back payments. This meant that some members who did not need a loan could use the association just as a savings bank. However, as Mason (2009) points out, this also caused problems because it necessitated the association keeping detailed records of each period. Then from the 1870s onwards a new form of permanent S&L began, in which, as in Britain, the associations could issue shares whenever they wanted. This meant that if they made losses on loan defaults they could no longer charge individuals equally for the loss, but had to set aside part of the profits as reserves. Some thrifts began to accept deposits from non-members and to allow them to make payments at any time. The officers began to fix interest rates on loans without the need for an auction, and developed amortising mortgages that charged interest only on the remaining balance. In all these ways, as the Royal Commission of 1872 noted in Britain, they were becoming more like banks.

At this time, the thrifts were small and locally based, holding an average of $90,000 in assets, and with nearly 60 per cent having fewer than 200 members (Mason, 2009). Like the European cooperative banks, they were low-risk institutions, relying on local knowledge of people's creditworthiness, tying borrowers in as members and giving them voting rights. Their leaders described the business as a movement, and allied it with social reform campaigns and popular movements. Growth was slow, until in 1869 one of the leaders, Edmund Wrigley, wrote a book promoting the idea, and then followed it up with a guide for people wanting to set up their own S&L (he was the American equivalent of Arthur Scratchley). Also, from then on a second industrial revolution began, which had the effect of boosting urban growth and increasing demand for housing. From the 1870s onwards, the numbers of 'building and loans' (as they were known at the time) increased rapidly. By 1890 they had spread to all the states. Philadelphia had 900 thrifts, and Chicago, Baltimore and Cincinnati had similar concentrations.

They were succeeding in reaching down to people on low incomes. A survey carried out in 1893 found that 26.9 per cent of members were labourers and factory workers, 17.7 per cent housewives and housekeepers, 14.5 per cent artisans and mechanics, 12.3 per cent merchants and dealers, and only 2.9 per cent described themselves as 'capitalists' (Mason, 2009). By now, more than 85 per cent were organised under either the serial or the permanent plan; as in Britain, the terminating society was becoming less important. The movement reported a foreclosure rate of only 2.4 per cent, which indicated that it was very safe. It was also quite egalitarian by the standards of the day; about a quarter of the members were women.

We have seen how in Britain there was a growing need for government regulation and supervision to stop the idea from being exploited by people who were simply out to enrich themselves. In the USA, national building and loans began to be formed that were, as the name suggests, nationally based and with local branches. These were investor-owned 'for-profits', that were often formed by bankers or industrialists, and they had prominent politicians on their boards. These organisers invested the $5 million that were needed to start them off, and had voting rights based not on the one member, one vote principle but tied to the size of their shareholding. They intended to make a return on their investment.

They paid very high interest on savings and charged higher rates on loans, and employed promoters to sell shares through local branches. The effect was to spread the S&L sector into rural areas where they had not been before, but the organisers, managers and promoters all earned large salaries, and most spent between 6 per cent and 11 per cent of revenues on operating expenses (the rate for the local, mutual S&Ls was 1–2 per cent). Also, they had twice as many paid staff as the locals. In this they were very like the Starr-Bowkett societies in Britain, and eventually they gave the movement a bad name. At first they expanded very quickly; in 1893 there were 290 of them, and three years later there were 361 (Mason, 2009). The high interest rates on savings were offset by high fees and fines for premature withdrawals, and so the deal was not as good as it seemed. The nationals were also much more risky. They gave mortgages on inflated estimates of the value of property, and asked for inadequate security. Because the branch agents were paid on the number of members signed up, they had an incentive to make more risky loans.

By 1895 the locals had begun to hit back by publicising these disadvantages. They drafted state laws that limited the scope of the nationals and promoted better business standards, and by 1900 nearly every state had its own thrift law. The Depression of 1893 confirmed the locals' argument. Real estate prices fell, and the nationals soon began to make losses. Between 1893 and 1897 more than half of them went out of business, taking the savings of thousands of working-class people with them. By

1910 all had gone. There are obvious parallels with the S&L crisis of the 1980s, and with the recent banking crisis of 2007 onwards. The damage done to the movement was serious. In areas where the nationals had collapsed, there was a general loss of confidence in S&Ls, and it became difficult to set up any new associations. The locals resented the damage done to their reputation by the nationals, and they realised the benefits of government regulation and of maintaining decent reserves against potential losses. They set up state-level leagues, and in 1892 formed the United States League of Local Building and Loan Associations. These helped to promote the movement, create uniform business practices and sponsor favourable legislation.

EXPANSION IN BRITAIN DURING THE TWENTIETH CENTURY

In Britain, World War I did not stop the expansion of the sector. By 1920 there were 1271 societies, with 748000 members and £87 million in assets. They were poised for massive growth during the interwar period. During the 1930s there was a building boom that mainly produced houses for owner-occupation. The effects can still be seen in every town in Britain, with large, sprawling suburbs of semi-detached houses, mainly built in red brick and with three bedrooms, an upstairs bathroom (which was a rarity in older houses), and front and back gardens. It was a style that was easy for intellectuals to despise but it gave a whole generation of middle-income people a chance to own their own home away from the slums of the inner city. The building societies survived the economic crisis of the early 1930s almost untouched, with the slump checking their growth for only a few years. The high rate of return on their shares and the security they offered made them highly attractive to savers. The building boom was fuelled by the rising wages of those in work, and by static house prices, but the availability of large amounts of money on loan from the building societies was crucial. The sector was instrumental in maintaining consumer demand and helping the country get out of the recession.

However, there was a down side. Societies were competing with each other to lend, and they increased the loan term from 20 to 25 years, and began to accept additional forms of security that allowed them to lend more than 75 per cent of the value of the home. Insurance companies provided guarantees in return for a single payment by the borrower, while housing developers deposited cash with the societies that they could draw on if borrowers defaulted. The attempt to extend ownership to lower income groups meant the quality of housing declined, and in 1939 a new

Table 4.1   British building society growth during the twentieth century, before the 1986 deregulation

Year	No. of societies	No. of depositors (thousand)	No. of borrowers[a] (thousand)	Deposits from shares £m	Mortgage assets £m	Total assets £m
1910	1723	626	Inc	?	60	76
1920	1271	748	Inc	64	69	87
1930	1026	428	720	303	316	371
1940	952	771	1503	552	678	756
1950	819	654	1508	926	1060	1256
1960	726	571	2349	2721	2647	3166
1970	481	618	3655	9788	8752	10819
1980	273	915	5383	48915	42437	53793

Note: a. The figures show many more borrower than depositor members, but the statistics excluded millions of small shareholders.

Source: Extracted from BSA (2012).

Act reined the societies in by defining what were accepted forms of collateral. By 1940 the number of societies had fallen to 952, but this reflected more the wind up of terminating societies (that still accounted for 16 per cent of societies in 1932) than a process of consolidation; that would come later. The number of members had grown dramatically to over two million and the assets to £756 million (see Table 4.1).

The building societies emerged from World War II with a massive surplus of funds. While the Labour government restricted the development of new homes other than public sector housing for rent, the societies were able to take advantage of a decline in private renting. With rent controls still in place, landlords wanted to sell off property for owner occupation. With the return of a Conservative government in 1951, the political pendulum swung back towards private housing. Between 1959 and 1962 the government lent the societies £100 million to encourage the private market, and in 1962 owner-occupiers were exempted from paying income tax on the imputed rental value of their homes. A new Labour government elected in 1964 switched from an ideology of 'council' housing for general needs to one of support for owner occupation, and in 1967 introduced an option mortgage scheme that gave people on low incomes a reduced mortgage rate (by returning to them the tax relief they would have paid if their incomes had been higher). A Conservative government then came back in, and during the financial crisis of 1973, which was caused by the oil price shock, gave the societies a bridging grant to enable them to keep their mortgage rate down. An incoming Labour government did the same in 1974; it seems that whatever political ideology was in power the building societies were favoured.

The result was that by 1980 the sector had become huge: it had nearly £54 billion in assets, more than 25 million households were saving through deposit or share accounts, and more than five million were borrowing on a mortgage. This meant that nearly half the adult population were involved in one way or another. The sector was second only to the insurance companies in size, having outgrown pension funds, high street banks, savings banks and national savings. They dominated the mortgage market, providing over 85 per cent of the funds for house purchase (Boddy, 1980). Their effects on the British way of life had been profound; the percentage of people owning their own home had increased from less than 10 per cent before World War I to 54 per cent in 1979. The number of societies had fallen to 273, achieved mainly through the transfer of engagements of smaller societies to larger ones. However, this resulted in a very unbalanced profile; the 36 largest accounted for over 90 per cent of the total assets, while the top 20 had 84 per cent (Boddy, 1980). The registrar approved this general trend because it meant that societies that were in financial difficulties did not fail but were rescued by another society. Even when, in 1978, the Grays failed because of a fraud that cost it £8 million, the result was not bankruptcy; in this case the Woolwich took over its assets and the members of the Building Societies Association contributed to a compensation fund. In contrast to the European cooperative banking sector, the UK building society sector was never integrated but loosely federated in a trade association, but societies effectively covered each other's losses.

EXPANSION IN THE USA DURING THE TWENTIETH CENTURY

In the USA in 1900 there were 6600 S&Ls, rising by 1920 to 8633 and by 1930 to 11 777, with 22 per cent of all mortgages and 10 per cent of the population in membership. During the 1920s just 2.3 per cent of all thrifts failed, compared to 21.3 per cent of banks. During the Great Depression they also tended to survive better than banks; for instance, in 1931 only 2 per cent of thrifts failed, while 20 per cent of banks went out of business. Their numbers did fall to just over 9000 in 1937, but this was mainly through mergers rather than failures. In some states their assets grew because investors began to see them as a safer place to put their money. Then, as the depression got worse deposits began to fall away and unemployment began to affect members' ability to pay their mortgages. Commercial banks that had been used by the S&Ls to provide them with services folded, and in these cases, like other creditors, the S&Ls lost their money. Despite their longstanding reservations over asking for government help, the movement's leaders began to realise they needed support.

Compared to the European cooperative banks, the thrifts had not yet benefitted from having a central bank and unified regulation. In 1932 their trade association worked with Congress to create a Federal Home Loan Bank Board (FHLBB) to regulate the sector, and 12 regional Federal Home Loan Banks (FHLBs) to raise money in the wholesale markets to lend on to S&Ls. These were federally sponsored but owned by the S&Ls through stock holdings. The S&Ls elected two-thirds of the directors of each FHLB (while the Bank Board appointed a third), and they received dividends on its profits (White, 1991). In 1933 a federal charter was established that allowed thrifts to choose between being state or federally regulated. Then in 1934 a Federal Savings and Loans Insurance Corporation was founded to provide a deposit insurance system, and this was put under the authority of the Bank Board. The league helped thrifts to see themselves as part of a movement, and got them to agree to the common term 'savings and loans' rather than the variety of names they had used before. It lobbied successfully for exemption from federal taxes on the grounds that the S&Ls were not for profit. A close association began between the movement and its regulators that was to last for the next 40 years. From the government's point of view, S&Ls were an essential partner in meeting public policy goals; they helped to stabilise the banking system, and continue the trend towards home ownership.

During the 1930s the S&Ls improved their quality of management, moved towards common accounting standards and improved their public image by adopting modern advertising techniques and moving to better quality office accommodation. Their competitors were insurance companies that either lent mortgages short term and required a large payment at the end, or lent on an interest-only basis, with the principal being paid at the end; they could not match the products the S&Ls were able to offer. On the savings side, banks offered only short-term deposits with penalties for early withdrawals, while the S&Ls offered longer-term savings to members, who earned compound interest as profits were distributed to share balances. They also had a distinct social movement approach to their work, an attitude of 'social uplift' that gave them a moral edge.

During World War II, thrifts experienced a surge in deposits and a lack of demand for home loans, and so the movement specialised in buying and selling government war bonds. By the end of the war, nearly 28 per cent of their assets were in government securities, so they were well placed to capitalise – literally – on the postwar building boom; in 1945 they had 7 per cent of consumer savings and 23 per cent of home loans, but by 1965 they had increased their share of the market to 26 per cent and 46 per cent respectively. They increased in size rather than in numbers of societies, which remained stable at just over 6000. This was the most successful period in their history, as they rode the wave of suburban housing development, much as the British building societies had done in the 1930s.

During the 1950s some S&Ls began to convert from mutual to investor ownership. The regulatory Bank Board was critical, believing that this was done just to enrich their managers, and in 1955 it put a moratorium on conversion of federal S&Ls. However, in 1961 it lifted the ban. The number of conversions soared, but as Mason (2009) points out in his history, so did the abuses, especially by insiders who opened large accounts just before the thrift was to issue stock. A prohibition was reintroduced in 1963 that would stay in place for the next ten years. However, this did not apply to state-chartered S&Ls and by 1967, 23 states had allowed their S&Ls to convert. At this time most were still mutual; only 12 per cent were investor-owned 'stock associations', but these were very large and controlled more than 20 per cent of the industry resources (Mason, 2009). They also began to set up holding companies that could control several thrifts under one umbrella, and that could then set up subsidiaries for other products such as insurance.

This move away from pure mutuality was controversial. Supporters argued that by issuing stock they could better meet the demand for home loans, and that because the managers were usually also the owners they had a vested interest in ensuring financial soundness. Opponents argued that they raised serious conflicts of interest and undermined the idea that thrifts were local institutions owned by their customer-members. Regulators were worried that the investor-owned thrifts would pursue more risky business so as to maximise profits for their new owners, and that this would prove costly for the Federal S&L Insurance Corporation. In 1960 an Act was passed in Congress limiting holding companies to owning one thrift each, but they caused increasing problems for the regulators in the years to come.

The thrifts had a major competitive advantage over the banks in being able to set their own interest rates on deposits, while the banks had to adhere to rate ceilings under a rule called 'Regulation Q'. Because of complaints from bankers, the Federal Reserve began to raise the ceiling until banks could compete more effectively, and competition to pay the highest rates became fierce. In 1966 the S&Ls, who through their national league had become very effective lobbyists, succeeded in getting Congress to agree that they would always be able to pay slightly higher rates than the banks. Their argument was that a rate differential was needed to ensure that they could continue to provide loans to meet the aspirations of American citizens for home ownership. This might seem a fairly unimportant event, but it proved to have dire consequences for the S&Ls. The league was determined to keep this permanent advantage over the banks, and so resisted all attempts at deregulation until the end of the 1970s. As we shall see below, this postponement of necessary deregulation caused enormous damage.

During the 1970s, the S&L sector had to contend with a very unstable economic environment, with oil price shocks, recession, rising inflation and high interest rates. Greater competition and new technology also came into the mix. The national league was determined to resist deregulation if it meant losing their built-in interest rate advantage over the banks, and so the S&Ls were not prepared for the recession that began in 1979 (Mason, 2009, Ch. 7). The idea of the mutual S&L was beginning to be seen as old-fashioned, and in 1974 the league tried to modernise its image with a change of name to the 'United States League of Savings Associations'. Savers began to be much more footloose in their choice of where to put their money, and switched it constantly to get the best interest rates. New financial products were developed that made it difficult to tell the difference between the types of bank. There was a wave of acquisitions of smaller thrifts by large ones that were seeking to expand, and the gap between the small, community based thrifts and the large, commercially minded ones, got larger.

Profitability declined, and so did capital adequacy, and the large thrifts wanted to raise more capital by issuing securities but the Bank Board would not let them. Another way to raise capital was to end the ban on conversions to stock companies, but the regulators were worried about managers taking large benefits for themselves and then moving the business into riskier lending strategies so as to boost earnings and share prices. In 1975 the ban on conversions was lifted, and over the next four years the number of stock S&Ls rose by 25 per cent to 805. Sure enough, a report from the General Accounting Office confirmed the regulators' concerns, finding insider abuse and a move to riskier loans. By 1979, the aggregate reserve ratio for these investor-owned S&Ls had declined to 4.8 per cent. The S&L crisis of the 1980s was an accident waiting to happen.

DEMUTUALISATION AND FINANCIAL CRISIS IN THE US SAVINGS AND LOAN SECTOR

Problems began in the late 1970s in the USA, when the economy went into recession. To combat 'stagflation', the deadly combination of high inflation and economic stagnation, the government dramatically raised interest rates. In the British model, mortgages were set at a variable rate that moved up and down at a fixed percentage above the Bank of England base rate. This meant that when the UK government raised interest rates there was increasing pain for mortgage holders and an increase in loan defaults, but the societies remained basically sound. In the USA, the S&Ls were not allowed to offer variable rate mortgages. They lent long term on fixed interest rates, which meant that when the return to savers overtook the return from loans the societies quickly ran into trouble. The league put its faith in Regulation Q, the rule that said S&Ls would have a built-in half a percentage point advantage over the banks for savings. However, during the 1970s the increasingly sophisticated financial products that were being offered by banks (especially money market mutual funds) had got round this. By early 1980 a third of the sector was reporting losses, and there was a consensus that something had to be done, and quickly. Congress passed two laws to deregulate the federally regulated sector, allowing thrifts to offer adjustable rate mortgages, and removing restrictions on what else they could provide. They were allowed to issue credit cards and checking accounts (in the UK called current accounts), to offer consumer loans, and to invest directly up to 3 per cent of their assets in joint ventures. The Regulation Q interest rate ceiling was phased out, and deposit insurance increased. Some of the states, not to be outdone, deregulated their S&L sector even more. In this way it was hoped that thrifts would become profitable again.

An interpreter of this period, Lawrence White, says that 'the major deregulation actions ... were fundamentally sound and sensible' (1991, p. 74), but that they needed to be accompanied by an *increase* in other types of regulation. To understand this crucial point, we need to appreciate that there are three types of regulation. There is *economic regulation* that limits prices and restricts who can enter a market, and who can provide particular products. Then there is *safety regulation* that ensures consumers are protected. This focuses on the soundness of the business, in particular on making sure it has enough retained capital and ways of managing the risk derived from making loans. A third form of regulation is *consumer information and protection*, which prevents discrimination against consumers and discloses all the information they need to make a considered judgement on what to buy (White, 1991, Ch. 3). White's argument is that economic deregulation should have been balanced by *tougher* safety-and-soundness regulation. Thrifts now had the opportunity to take risks, they had the capability and they had the incentive. Between the first half of 1981 and the end of 1982 the sector suffered a steep decline in its net worth. Four hundred and fifteen thrifts became insolvent, accounting for a third of the sector's assets, and the solvent thrifts had lost half their net worth. In fact, the situation was even worse because they had not yet begun to write down the value of their loans to reflect the decline in property values.

At this time, 80 per cent of the S&Ls were still member-owned; the rest were investor-owned 'stock associations' that had very restrictive rules to make sure they were owned by large numbers of local people, no one of whom could gain a controlling interest. They had to have 400 stockholders, each with no more than 10 per cent of the stock, no controlling group could own more than 25 per cent, and 75 per cent of owners had to reside or do business in the market area. For these stock associations the rules were swept aside and it became possible for anyone to buy their own S&L. The results were dramatic. In the previous 45 years only 143 S&Ls had failed, but in the early 1980s, 118 societies failed, with many more merging in order to survive (FDIC, 1999).

Why did so many fail? First, to meet the competition they had to be deregulated to offer higher interest rates, but because they lacked the authority to make variable rate mortgages they were unable to generate higher incomes. Second, there was a decline in regulatory oversight and so unscrupulous managers were able to avoid scrutiny and use the S&Ls for their own gain, and insider mismanagement and fraud resulted. Managers pursued a 'go for broke' lending strategy, making high-risk loans as a way to recover, knowing that if the loans were defaulted on federal insurance would cover the losses. Also, many managers lacked the experience to calculate risks in deregulated areas; bad loans were made from well-intentioned decisions. Third, regulation of the sector was faulty. The regulator, the Federal Home Loans Bank Board, was small and used to overseeing a public service industry with low risk; it was not designed to function in the new environment of the 1980s. Also, the sector was regulated by one body and insured by another, which meant that poor inspection reports were not followed up. Fourth, the stock associations became targets for speculators, and new owners came in who just wanted to make money; they were prepared to make high-risk loans and pay high interest on deposits.

A drop in interest rates in 1982 helped the sector to return to solvency. Between 1982 and 1985 there was very rapid growth, with 492 new S&Ls being founded and the sector's total assets increasing by 56 per cent. Yet conversion from mutual to investor-owned status meant there was an

Table 4.2   Conversions of FSLIC-insured mutual thrifts to stock thrifts, 1980–86

Year	Number of conversions
1980	16
1981	32
1982	31
1983	83
1984	96
1985	78
1986	86

Source: FHLBB data, cited in White (1991, p. 107).

opportunity for new people to gain control and milk a society for high salaries and dividends. Healthy S&Ls became contaminated by having to keep up with the rest, illustrating the old saying that 'bad money drives out good'. White argues that the years 1983–85 were the real 'debacle', because this is when the losses made on the real estate market had to be recognised and written down. In 1989 the federal government finally created a programme to resolve the crisis by *reregulating* the sector through a new Office of Thrift Supervision. A report from the Federal Deposit Insurance Corporation estimates that during the 1980s, 747 S&Ls had failed at a cost of $160 billion, of which $132 billion had to be paid by federal taxpayers. Coupled with the larger failure of 1530 commercial banks taking with them more than $230 billion in assets, it had been the most expensive financial collapse in American history (FDIC, 1999).

The conversion of member-owned S&Ls to investor-owned status was a major part of the disaster. Table 4.2 shows how the number of conversions grew during 1983–86, as existing mutual managers and new entrepreneurs realised the opportunity to take over. At the start of the crisis, 20 per cent of the thrifts were investor-owned, controlling 27 per cent of the industry assets, and it is mainly in this group that the failures occurred; of the 'soon-to-fail' thrifts identified by the Bank Board in 1985, 86 per cent were investor-owned.[1] We should not overemphasise the difference between mutual and investor-owned thrifts, since there was very little involvement of members in the governance of the mutuals. They tended to be controlled by a self-perpetuating management group, with no incentive to members to participate, particularly since their deposits were covered by federal insurance. However, with demutualisation managers were free to become owners and maximise their own interests, which usually meant pursuing higher risk strategies. A similar process has been blamed as one of the causes of the boom and bust real estate cycle in New England during the mid to late 1980s that led to the failure of mutual savings banks (FDIC, 1999).

The legislation of 1989 prevented the crisis from occurring again. Between 1980 and 1989, 890 S&Ls, with $348 billion in assets, had failed. They amounted to 35 per cent of the sector. Amazingly, others grew and weathered the storm, so that during the same decade total sectoral assets had nearly doubled. The majority of those that remained were mutuals that had continued to focus on what they were good at: providing a safe place for people's savings and using them to provide residential mortgages (Mason, 2009, Ch. 8). With hindsight we can see that the original problem was not deregulation but over-regulation; in the 1970s this prevented them from adapting to market conditions. Deposit insurance made things worse by ensuring that investors' money flowed to the riskiest financial institutions that gave the highest returns. It was a mishandled industry restructuring problem that, if it had been handled better, would not have led to demutualisation (FDIC, 1999).

DEMUTUALISATION IN THE UK

In the *UK*, demutualisation occurred in a completely different context. Building societies were basically sound, but had been chafing at the restrictions put on them by the regulator (the Building Societies Commission) and wanted powers to compete with the commercial banks. The 1986 Act gave them these wider powers to engage in personal banking, but it also gave them the option to convert to investor-ownership providing 75 per cent of their members voted in favour. In 1989 Abbey National resolved to convert. Then in 1995 Cheltenham and Gloucester converted and was taken over by Lloyds Bank Group. An Act of 1997 then provided the societies with the more flexible operating regime they had been looking for, though in return they had to take measures to increase the accountability of boards to members. This satisfied some society boards, who began to take steps to resist calls for demutualisation, but ten of the biggest societies converted, taking with them around 70 per cent of the sector's assets. Among the biggest, only the Nationwide resisted the siren call (see Table 4.3).

The official reason for conversion was to seek a more liberalised trading regime and to be able to raise more capital. However, from 1997 onwards the building societies felt they had a liberal enough regime, and did not need to raise capital on the stock markets. After all, their main business proposition had always been that they recycled small savings into mortgages for house purchase. At the time, critics argued that the real reasons for demutualisation were greed on the part of management, who benefitted through enhanced salaries and bonuses and stock options. Evidence has emerged to back up these claims. In the year following demutualisation, the salaries and bonuses of Halifax directors increased by 38.5 per cent, of Northern Rock by 32.4 per cent, of Bradford and Bingley by 40.2 per cent, and Alliance and Leicester by 26.8 per cent (All-Party Parliamentary Group for Building Societies and Financial Mutuals, 2006, p. 30). In the years to follow, the average yearly growth in remuneration was 8 per cent, well in excess of the rate of inflation. None of this includes the share options granted, which should also be taken into account. A study focusing on the years from 1993 to 2000 by Shiwakoti found that the total remuneration of chief executives of demutualised firms increased by 293 per cent, compared to an increase of 65 per cent in mutuals. These rises were not due to improved performance, because the rate of return on assets and other measures did not change significantly after demutualisation (cited in All-Party, 2006, p. 32).

There was also a bonanza for consultants advising on the demutualisation process. The Building Societies Association calculated that the total cost of legal, accounting and public relations fees was £550 million. The Halifax conversion alone cost £171 million. The payout for members began with just £130 at Abbey National, but increased dramatically to over £2000 per member at Halifax, Northern Rock and Woolwich. Certainly members were being bribed to vote in favour of demutualisation. Also, boards were able to spend their society's money on persuading members to accept. The information given was very one-sided, and it was not made clear that the members were taking the capital that was supposed to be available to later generations of savers and borrowers. The whole process was made notorious by a process of 'carpet bagging' whereby people would open new accounts in building societies in the hope of getting a windfall profit on conversion.

The eight big demutualisations that took place in the decade between 1989 and 1999 were achieved with the wholehearted backing of their boards of directors, and though there was resistance by small groups of members, generally the members heard a one-sided argument. By 2000, the board of Bradford and Bingley were arguing forcefully that their members would be better off if it remained a mutual, and it was only when a vote went decisively against them that they changed to backing demutualisation (Drake and Llewellyn, 2001). In 2001 the Nationwide fought off a demutualisation attempt and its board affirmed its commitment to mutuality. The building societies changed their rules so that new members had to agree to any 'windfalls' from conversion being given to charity and

Table 4.3   Effects of demutualisation on the UK building society sector

Year	What happened	No. of depositors (thousand)	No. of borrowers (thousand)	Deposits from shares £m	Mortgage assets £m	Total assets £m
1986	Act allows demutualisation	2850	7023	115538	115669	140603
1989	Abbey National floated	4490	6699	143359	151492	187012
1995	Cheltenham and Gloucester taken over by Lloyds	6307	7178	200826	233358	299921
1997	Alliance and Leicester, Halifax, Woolwich, Northern Rock floated, Bristol and West taken over by Bank of Ireland	964	2872	90093	105803	137864
1999	Birmingham Midshires taken over by Halifax	722	3044	109138	120410	157141
2000	Bradford and Bingley floated	740	3107	119299	134100	177747

this took the incentive out of carpet bagging. This action, combined with the Nationwide fight back, effectively ended the whole demutualisation trend.

In 2005, the Britannia Building Society bought the deposit base and branch network of the former building society Bristol and West from the Bank of Ireland. The deal brought with it 700000 customers, which took membership of Britannia to just under three million. This was significant as it was the first remutualisation of a former building society. It began to raise hopes that Northern Rock could be remutualised. The 'Rock' had been a building society, had demutualised and had got into deep trouble during the banking crisis. It had needed to be bailed out by the UK government to such an extent that it became state-owned. Good arguments were put forward for its remutualisation (Michie and Llewellyn, 2009), but the government decided to accept a bid from Virgin Money that netted £750 billion for the taxpayer. Remutualisation would have meant a much longer payback term.

During the banking crisis, some building societies also experienced losses; we will be looking into this further in the next chapter. The worst affected was the Dunfermline Building Society that had gone into lending on commercial property and become insolvent. The viable part of its business was taken over by the Nationwide and its losses held in a separate fund by government. Societies had always had the option of merging with other societies, but now it was felt that in the face of serious losses or lack of capital more flexibility was required. In 2007, a new building societies act allowed societies to merge with companies. The Britannia took advantage of this by merging, in 2009, into the UK Co-operative Bank. As the bank is a secondary cooperative, being wholly owned by the Co-operative Group (whose roots are in consumer cooperation), the merger was from one mutual to another.

One of the consequences of the massive bailout of banks in the UK has been that building societies have found it difficult to raise capital for expansion. In 2008, the wholesale money market froze and then slowly began to lend again, but the massive injection of government funds into the big banks gave them an unfair advantage. At this time, Kent Reliance was the fastest growing building society. It had achieved this mainly through a subsidiary that had bought the Jersey mortgage business of a bank. It had also kept its costs down by hiving off much of its administration to two subsidiaries in India. By 2010, it was in sound condition but could not find the capital to enable it to continue to expand. In 2011 the society demutualised into a new investor-owned bank called OneSavings Bank. There are only two owners: the private investment firm JC Flowers, who have a 41 per cent ownership stake, and a new Kent Reliance Provident Society, that owns 59 per cent. This means that, through the provident society, the members of the original society still have a substantial ownership share, but at one remove from the business.

In *Australia*, a similar deregulation of the finance industry in the 1980s led to a spate of demutualisations, with at least 18 building societies converting (Delisted, 2010). The smaller societies were taken over while some of the largest became banks. However, eight societies still remain mutual. In *New Zealand*, the finance company crash of 2006–08 and the follow on from the credit crisis have led to merger and demutualisation, leaving just two building societies. In *Ireland* there used to be around 40 societies but through a process of merger and demutualisation they have all disappeared. In *Germany and Austria*, there are specialist mortgage lenders that could be roughly translated as building societies, owned either by the savings bank or cooperative bank sectors, and they have not been affected at all by the demutualisation trend.

THE CURRENT SITUATION

In the UK there are now 47 building societies, with £330 billion of assets, of which £212 billion are mortgage assets, and with £215 billion in savings balances. It is a sector that is no longer based on local economies but has become highly consolidated. In 1995 the largest five societies already had 67 per cent of the total assets, but by 2010 they had over 86 per cent. If we take the same statistic for the largest ten societies, they had 85.7 per cent and now have 94.4 per cent (BSA, 2012). If we then take the largest 20 societies the statistic is not much different, because the societies from 11 to 20, by size, only add another 3.3 per cent to the total assets. Dominating the whole sector is the Nationwide Building Society that, as its name suggests, has a national presence and has over 60 per cent of the sector's entire assets. It has 12 million investing members who make up 60 per cent of the total for the sector, and 1.4 million borrowing members, 54 per cent of the total. It has 800 branches out of a total of 1652 and so it dominates the building society share of the 'high street'. Next is Yorkshire BS, with around 10 per cent of the assets and of investing and borrowing members. Coventry BS has around 7 per cent of the assets, Skipton BS has around 4.5 per cent, and Leeds has 3 per cent. Between them these big five societies have most of the assets, and they are getting bigger. The ninth largest society, Norwich and Peterborough, has recently merged with Yorkshire, which gives the 'big five' a combined asset share of 88 per cent.

In the USA, since the crisis of the 1980s, the remaining S&Ls have made a complete recovery and consumers have regained confidence in them. Their leaders have rebranded them as community banks, alongside other small banks that have different ownership structures, and so it is impossible to find statistics that identify the mutual associations. In 1991, the league merged with the National Council of Savings Institutions to become 'America's Community Bankers'.[2] They have a variety of ownership types in membership, but the focus is still on locally based relationship banking of the kind that the mutual S&Ls have always practised.

In Australia the remaining mutuals have joined together with the credit unions in a new national association called Abacus. They still hold 8.4 per cent of the new home loan market and 11.4 per cent of household deposits, and they are growing strongly by an average of 4.9 per cent per year (Abacus, 2012). With 4.5 million members they have a market penetration of 20 per cent. Unsurprisingly, they are safer than the investor-owned banks: their Tier 1 capital ratio is 15 per cent compared to the banks' 10 per cent, and they are very confident about their mutual identity.

NOTES

1. The figure given by White (1991, p. 116) is 71.5 per cent, but even of 669 soon-to-fails, 100 had been converted from state-chartered investor-ownership to federal mutual status in order for regulators to manage their failure. If we recalculate taking this into account the figure is 86 per cent.
2. The regulator, the Bank Board, became an Office of Thrift Supervision and then in 2011 was taken into the Office of the Comptroller of the Currency. All the comptroller can confirm is that as at June 2012 there were 586 federal savings associations, down from 642 in 2011.

5. The evolution of banks owned by other types of cooperative

Sometimes cooperative banks have been set up as an extension of the work of other types of cooperative. Networks of consumer, worker and producer co-ops have all, at various times and places, developed their own banks. Governments have also seen the benefits of providing credit to cooperative sectors as part of their wider economic policies. Sometimes they have set up state banks to do this, but more often than not they have set up a bank and then given it to a cooperative sector to run. Banks owned by cooperatives tend to be less independent than the cooperative banks and credit unions, and their democratic structures are indirect, but they are still member-owned rather than investor-owned. Like the other customer-owned banks, they have tended to become much more general in purpose, providing a wide range of financial products not just to cooperative businesses but to individuals as well.

Seen from below, by customers looking at a bank branch on the high street, they are all quite similar. Seen from above, by someone interested in who owns and controls them, they are quite different. But then there is a further complication, some banks have been demutualising in order to raise more capital and be able to expand the business. In the case of banks owned by a cooperative, the change to investor-ownership creates a hybrid in which the cooperative still owns a substantial part of the business. Another complication is that cooperative insurance companies have been evolving into 'bancassurance', a cross between an insurance company and a bank, but we will leave the exploration of this type until Chapter 10, when discussing the evolution of cooperative insurance.

The most common type is the *agricultural cooperative bank*. In the USA, the federal government set up the provision of credit for farmers in a scheme reminiscent of the French system of *credit agricole*. In 1916, Congress established a system of farm credit banks and associations designed to guarantee that farmers obtained the capital they needed. There were 12 district banks covering the whole of the USA, funding local associations of farmers and ranchers. It was supplemented in 1933 by CoBank, set up to lend to large agribusinesses, cooperatives and rural utilities. Although the farm credit system was government sponsored and initially government owned, by 1968 all the farm credit banks had repaid their federal capital debt and the farmer-borrowers had become the complete owners of their banks. During the 1980s, a new Farm Credit System Insurance Corporation was set up to administer their insurance fund and a Funding Corporation to sell system-wide securities. Federal Land Banks were allowed to merge with the credit associations to become full-service agricultural credit associations.

Now the system is slimmer but just as comprehensive. The Insurance Corporation and Funding Corporation serve just four regional farm credit banks (FCBs): they are AgFirst FCB; Agribank FCB; Farm Credit Bank of Texas; and CoBank (recently merged with US AgBank FCB). They provide more than $177 billion to more than half a million borrowers, including farmers, ranchers, rural homeowners, agricultural cooperatives, rural utility systems and agribusinesses. One interesting feature of the system is that it has never relied on taking deposits from farmers in order to finance loans, but instead has sold system-wide bonds in the capital markets. They make up more than a third of all lending in the rural US (AgFirst, 2012). The rural utility cooperatives sector in the USA also has its own bank, CFC. It was set up in 1969 to raise funds from the capital markets to supplement loan programmes offered by the government's Rural Utilities Service. In 2011 it had over $20 billion outstanding in loans.

In Asia, the agricultural cooperative systems of several countries incorporate a bank. In Korea the agricultural cooperative federation, Nongyup, has a very successful banking arm. In 2012, under pressure from bank regulators, this has been separated from the agricultural supply and marketing division and has to stand alone; the federation now has two separate holding companies. This will cause problems, as the federation is used to subsidising its loss-making marketing operation with the profits from the bank. In Japan, the Norinchukin Bank is part of the agricultural federation, Zen-Noh. During the 2008 banking crisis it suffered huge losses from derivatives, and this issue will be discussed in the next chapter.

Another type is the *consumer cooperative bank.* Consumer cooperatives are customer-owned businesses whose members get together to provide themselves with goods and services. Because they return surpluses to the members in proportion to the business they do with the co-op, they are effectively a way of eliminating the 'middleman', and ensuring that they pay cost price for the goods. But in order to do this without the business being subverted, they have a simple one person, one vote system that ensures governance by consumers. The history of this business model follows a similar trajectory to that of the building societies in the UK and cooperative banks in Germany, beginning with a successful society that is then copied; the consumer co-op story begins with the Rochdale

Pioneers in 1844, and travels all over Europe, wherever there were strong working-class cultures where people could see the benefit (Birchall, 1994). Traditionally, in countries where they are strong (such as the UK, Italy, Sweden, Japan, Singapore) they have focused on food retailing, but in response to demand from their members they have gone into many other market sectors such as funerals, travel, insurance and – sometimes – banking.

In some respects, the customer-owned banks introduced in the last three chapters could also be seen as a type of consumer cooperative. We will be exploring these links further in Chapter 10. There are only a few consumer cooperative-owned banks, and if it were not for the importance of the UK Co-operative Bank and the Finnish S-Bank, they might not be worth mentioning. Why are there so few? In some countries the law disallows this model (for instance Japan), and in others it never developed beyond the banking department in a cooperative wholesale society. Let us look briefly at the UK Co-operative Bank, a wholly owned subsidiary of the Co-operative Group. In 2009 it merged with the Britannia Building Society, which was at that time the second largest society in the UK. At the time of writing it has agreed to take control of 632 branches of the Lloyds Banking Group, moving its market share from 2 per cent to 7 per cent of UK current accounts. The bank is about to become a serious challenger to the 'big four' investor-owned banks that dominate UK banking but have become so discredited.

The bank was set up as a banking department of the Co-operative Wholesale Society (CWS) in 1872, to provide the retail societies with a safe place for their members' savings, to finance their expansion plans, and to act as a reserve fund in case societies got into trouble. The first reason was the most important. The private banking system of the time was very unreliable. One reason for the initial success of the Rochdale society was that in 1849 a local savings bank had collapsed, and people had rushed to invest in the cooperative. There were crises in 1857 and again in 1866 in which many banks collapsed (before the Bank of England took charge of the system). A historian tells of how one society treasurer had to hide money under the floorboards of his own bedroom, and how some societies paid their bill to the CWS with half a banknote, followed later by the other half (Redfern, 1913).

As CWS grew, so did the Banking Department. By 1876 turnover had passed £10 million, and by 1912 it had reached £158 million. The bank consistently out-performed private banks in rates of interest on both borrowing and saving, but business was mostly confined to the retail co-ops. From 1910 onwards, deposit accounts were offered to individuals who had already invested to the limit in their retail societies, and then trade unions, local authorities and many other cooperative, mutual and voluntary organisations began to bank with the Co-op. From 1919 onwards it began to expand through using retail society stores. By 1939, CWS was one of the world's biggest wholesaling and manufacturing businesses, with 155 factories, 12 overseas depots and extensive tea plantations in India and Ceylon (Birchall, 1994). During World War II, restrictions on spending led societies and individuals to put their surpluses in the bank, and so after the war it was able to finance rapid expansion by CWS into new areas of production. From the 1970s onwards, the bank began to become a highly successful business in its own right (Birchall, 2005).

In 1971 an Act of Parliament allowed it to become a separate company, and in 1974 it became a clearing bank. It did something no bank had ever done before – it offered free banking to those who remained in credit on their current accounts. The bank also consistently charged lower interest rates on personal loans, and surveys revealed that it received the highest customer satisfaction rates of all the banks. The CWS shareholders received dividends on the bank's profits, but they did not insist on a high return, and this policy was justified as the return of a kind of dividend to customers. The Co-op was the first bank to publish its commission charges and to adopt a 'truth in lending' policy. However, in a decade of high inflation and economic instability, such rapid expansion did have its dangers. Overheads were high, the rate of return on capital was half that of the big four high street banks, and regular injections of capital were needed from CWS. From the mid 1980s onwards, the bank's expansion began to be rewarded with reasonable profits, yet the CWS was content to leave these to fund expansion and increase liquidity through reserves; its shareholders were able to take a long-term view that encouraged expansion.

From 1992 onwards the bank was committed to an ethical policy that declared it would not invest in oppressive regimes, would not finance the sale of weapons to them, would encourage business customers to take a proactive stance on the environmental impact of their business, would try to ensure its financial services were not used for money laundering, and so on. The policy proved highly popular and won many awards, and the bank began to make significant profits every year. Yet critics pointed out that it was not itself a cooperative; customers could only join the parent cooperative through their local store and then have a very indirect say in how the bank was run. Recently the group changed its rules to allow customers to become members through any of its businesses, and so through a system of area committees bank customers can now make their voice heard.

Another interesting variant on the consumer cooperative bank is the Sri Lankan rural savings and credit banks that are part of a multi-purpose cooperative system. There are just over 300 societies, one in each district, but they are not really multi-purpose; in each location they provide basic consumer goods and a savings bank. Like the Korean agricultural cooperative bank, the multi-purpose co-operative society (MPCS) bank has been under pressure from international regulators to separate from the retail arm but the MPCS directors have resisted. There are advantages in having a bank that generates surpluses that can be used by loss-making parts of the business, but this poses risks for savers. Also, the system has been criticised for taking savings from rural areas and investing them in safe government bonds rather than reinvesting in the local economy (Birchall and Simmons, 2010).

Yet another type is the *worker cooperative bank*. This is not really customer-owned but producer-owned, but it is worth mentioning here just for completeness. The most famous example is the Caja Laboral Popular, founded in 1959 by the Mondragon cooperative group. Operating as a savings bank that then channelled these savings into investment in new cooperatives and expansion of existing ones, the bank had to make sure its investments were sound and so its staff gained expertise in cooperative promotion and monitored the progress of their co-ops through a contract of association. In return for capital, each co-op had to agree to provide equity to a common pool, to allow financial monitoring by the bank, to deposit all surpluses with it, and to allow the bank decision-making powers over relations within the group as a whole (Birchall, 1997, p. 101). In many countries, worker cooperatives have not been as successful as their promoters had hoped. In Mondragon the bank has been a key ingredient in the overcoming of some persistent problems by the worker co-ops. It has provided capital, but also the kind of financial and managerial discipline needed to enable the cooperatives to survive.

There is a type of *multi-sectoral cooperative bank* that is set up to serve the needs of different cooperative sectors. Because they have different interests, consumer and producer-owned cooperative sectors do not usually set these up themselves but rely on governments to do it for them. A good example is the National Co-operative Bank in the USA. It was set up by an act of Congress in 1978, to provide financial services to 'co-operatively structured, democratically owned and controlled enterprises throughout the United States' (National Council of Farmers Co-operatives, 1996, p. 186). From 1981 onwards it was owned and controlled by more than a thousand member co-ops, and began to lend to a wide variety of cooperatives in retail, housing, childcare, education, healthcare, energy and manufacturing. It also finances employee share ownership schemes and securitises cooperative housing mortgages in the wholesale markets. It is described as 'a boutique bank with a special commitment to community' (NCB, 2012). The St Paul Bank for

Co-operatives is a similar organisation, set up mainly to serve co-ops in the Mid-West.

There are a few *investor-owned banks with a substantial cooperative ownership stake.* Kenya Co-operative Bank was established in 1965, with capital raised from the agricultural cooperative sector. In 2008 it was floated on the stock market, with the ownership share of 3800 cooperatives ring-fenced in a holding company with a 65 per cent stake. Taiwan Co-operative Bank is investor-owned, but with a substantial share owned by farmers and fishers. It was established in 1946 with equity capital divided into 250 000 shares, of which the government took 150 000 and the other groups 10 000 each. It specialises in providing finance for cooperatives, the farm and fishing industries more generally, and SMEs.

CONCLUSION

That completes our survey of the history and current situation of the different types of customer-owned bank. The next chapter reports on how they fared during the banking crisis of 2008, and then Chapter 7 brings theory and evidence together for a more systematic analysis of the advantages and disadvantages of this business model.

6. The performance of customer-owned banks during the crisis

How did the banking crisis affect the customer-owned banking sector? There is no magic about the business model. Under the right conditions it can succeed superbly well, but it can also fail. For example, in the Swedish banking crisis of the early 1990s, the cooperative banking sector converted to investor-ownership in order to recapitalise itself (Brunner et al., 2004). In the Spanish banking crisis of the 1980s, the sector suffered the demise of its central bank (Fonteyne, 2007). On the other hand, the Swiss Raiffeisen banks withstood a real estate crisis in the early 1990s better than other banks, the French mutuals suffered less in banking stress during 1980s and 1990s, and before the recent banking crisis the Italian banche popolari and cooperative credit banks had lower loan losses than their competitors (Fonteyne, 2007, p. 26).

Immediately after the banking crisis of 2007–08, Lou Hammond-Ketilson and I wrote a report for the International Labour Organisation that found cooperative banks and credit unions had come through remarkably well. During the crisis, cooperative banks in Europe and credit unions in the USA and Canada increased their assets and the size of their deposits. They increased their lending to make up for the virtual freeze on lending by the investor-owned banks, drawing on their reserves rather than on the wholesale money markets that had ceased to trade. There was a 'flight to quality' among savers, and the number of members continued to grow. Their interest rates were consistently better than those of their competitors, and they were recognised everywhere as being a more stable alternative. We quoted the statement by WOCCU that no credit union anywhere in the world had needed bailout funds. However, this was only true of primary unions, and we reported on the difficulties faced by the US and Canadian centrals, the German DZ Bank and the Japanese Norinchukin Bank. We concluded that, despite these losses, the customer-owned model had particular advantages over the investor-owned model that made it more resilient to crisis (Birchall and Hammond Ketilson, 2009).

However, that report was only the starting point for a proper assessment. This chapter begins by asking whether customer-owned banks were more stable than their competitors before the crisis, and whether, if they *were* more stable, this came at the expense of efficiency and profitability. Then it estimates the impact of the crisis on the sector, looking in particular at the losses made by some of the centrals. Then the chapter looks at the situation after the banking crisis, when a more general recession began to threaten all banks with losses caused by unemployment, default on loans, and loss of savings. Throughout the chapter there are references to the demonstrated advantages of the customer-owned business model, and this leads into Chapter 7, which provides a more thorough discussion of its inherent advantages and disadvantages compared to other types of bank.

PERFORMANCE OF COOPERATIVE BANKS BEFORE THE CRISIS

How well was the sector performing before the crisis? There are two kinds of approach to this question: one is to compare the cost-efficiency and profitability of different banks and the other is to use measures of their relative stability. On cost-efficiency and profitability, a study of German banks found that during the 1990s cooperative banks and savings banks had slight cost and profit advantages over investor-owned banks, explaining this as deriving from their ability to obtain funds at lower cost from small savers (Altunbas et al., 2001). A study of banks in 15 European countries found that cooperatives were more cost-efficient than other banks, even though they were less profitable than investor-owned banks. It suggested that one reason might be the better quality of their loans as a consequence of low-risk lending policies (Iannotta et al., 2007). Another study of the EU-15 over 1998–2003 compared investor-owned, savings and cooperative banks (Girardone et al., 2009). It also found that investor-owned banks were, on average, less cost-efficient than cooperative banks.

These kinds of studies took for granted that it was possible to compare the different types on the same measures, but this obscures the inherent differences between their business models. In a study for the International Monetary Fund (IMF), Fonteyne recognised this (2007). He argued that most literature was flawed as it judged performance of cooperatives with investor-owned banks on just two basic measures – profits compared to inputs. But the business model influences the aims of the bank. Comparing relative efficiency is difficult, since cooperatives pursue a different objective: not to maximise profit but to maximise members' consumer surplus. He found that they were resource-intensive, with a high and inflexible cost base, but achieving a high return on assets. They were profitable even at low leverage ratios, because their business was quite self-sufficient. They were mainly concerned with recycling savings into loans, and much less dependent than their competitors on money markets. The lower cost of their capital allowed them to pursue other objectives than profit maximisation, and they could provide goods and services at below market prices; value was incorporated into the product. Fonteyne also found that their egalitarian culture was a strong counterweight to excessive management remuneration. There was no evidence they were less efficient. He found they had better efficiency ratios, because they made intensive use of a relatively low level of assets to achieve high rates of return. There was no systematic efficiency deficit. In general, they spent more money on branch offices, and had higher net interest margins on assets. But costs per employee were lower than those of their competitors (Fonteyne, 2007).

At the same time as Fonteyne was writing (just before the crisis), two researchers wrote another report for the IMF that focused on the stability of banks in Europe. It showed that cooperative banks were more stable than investor-owned banks (Hesse and Cihak, 2007). They used a huge database of 16 577 banks (including 3072 cooperative banks) from 29 countries that were members of the Organisation for Economic Co-operation and Development (OECD), tracking their progress over a ten-year period to 2004. They took as their dependent variable a Z-score, a 'popular measure of bank soundness' that is 'directly related to the probability of a bank's insolvency' (Hesse and Cihak, 2007, p. 7). The scores for cooperatives were considerably higher than those for investor-owned banks.[1] What made the difference was not profitability or capitalisation, which in the cooperatives were weaker, but the *low volatility of returns* over time. They argued that, because they did not have to make profits for shareholders, when the trading conditions worsened they could use their customer surplus as a first line of defence; 'Co-operative banks in normal times pass on most of their returns to customers, but are able to recoup that surplus in weaker periods' (Hesse and Cihak, 2007, p. 18).

Of course, if their lower returns were the result of inefficiency this would not be possible, but previous studies had shown that this was not the case; cooperative banks chose to have lower returns while being no less efficient than other banks. Hesse and Cihak found that they were less likely to become insolvent than the other bank types, but that they were more stable if they diversified their business and did not just rely on their core customer base. In contrast, the investor-owned banks were already much more diversified and so if they moved further away from the retail business they would become even more risky. In the light of the subsequent banking crisis this is a prescient finding, since it was the most diversified of the investor-owned banks that proved to be the least stable. However, also in the light of the subsequent crisis we know that cooperative banks suffered losses from their international operations operated by subsidiaries, and so this assertion that they will be *more* stable if they diversify may have to be revised.

Just before the crisis, Ayadi and her colleagues from the Centre for European Policy Studies carried out a comparative study of investor-owned, cooperative and savings banks in seven Western European countries, using data from between 2000 and 2008 (Ayadi et al., 2010). They found mixed results regarding *profitability*. In Germany, Italy and Spain, cooperatives had comparable or slightly higher earnings than investor-owned banks. In Finland, they had larger profit margins, although the gap was closing. Cooperative and savings banks were similar, except in France where the latter were significantly less profitable. The results for *return on equity* were similar. German cooperatives out-performed investor-owned and savings banks, French mutuals were similar to investor-owned but better than savings banks, and Finnish cooperatives were similar to other banks. Only in Spain were the other types more profitable. However, we now know that the savings banks were achieving this level of profit through funding a property bubble that has now burst!

What about *cost-efficiency*? Here the results were divided. The cost to income ratios of investor-owned and savings banks were slightly more efficient than those of cooperatives in Austria, Germany and the Netherlands, while the opposite was true for France, Italy, Finland and Spain. Co-ops had less market power in Austria, Germany and the Netherlands but more in France, Italy, Finland and Spain.

Now we come to probably the most important point when viewed from the other side of the banking crisis. In terms of *earnings stability*, in all countries other than Germany and Spain, cooperatives were significantly *more stable* than other banks. Ayadi et al. (2010) report that in some cases the differences were astounding; in France and the Netherlands they were over 50 per cent more stable (as measured by a Z-score). In Germany, they scored better than the investor-owned but not the savings banks. Ayadi et al. sum up their findings in this way; despite slightly lower profitability, the co-ops were not consistently different from other banks in terms of efficiency and market power. They had a stable cushion of earnings that reduced their likelihood of insolvency and contributed to their stability.

In summary then, before the crisis cooperative banks were competing successfully with other types of bank. They were as efficient, or in some cases a bit more or less efficient, than their competitors. They were at least as profitable, and in several countries more profitable, but they were everywhere more stable than the investor-owned banks. It is not surprising that they suffered less from the immediate impact of the 2008 crisis. Table 6.1 compares some key financial statistics for European

Table 6.1   *European cooperative banks before the crisis: top 12 countries*
              by 2010 market share plus EU totals[a]

Country	Years	Assets (billion euros)	Market share of deposits (%)	Market share of loans (%)	No. of customers
France	2005	1857	47	53	42m
	2007	2443	53	45	67m[b]
Netherlands	2005	506	39	23	9m
	2007	571	41	28	9m
Austria	2005	210	33	29	4.3m
	2007	331	36	31	5.1m
Italy	2005	492	29	27	9.5m
	2007	560	34	30	14.3m
Finland	2005	53	32	31	3.1m
	2007	66	32	31	4.1m
Germany	2005	909	18	12	30m
	2007	995	18	16	30m
Cyprus	2005	8.4	23	20	600k
	2007	9.7	20	22	600k
Luxemburg	2005	3.4	10	10	118k
	2007	4.1	10	10	100k
Poland	2005	8.8	11	9	10.5m
	2007	13.3	9	7	10.5m
Hungary	2005	4.2	12	4	1m
	2007	5	9	3	1.1m
Spain	2005	81	5	5	9.7m
	2007	108	5	5	10.3m
UK	2005	16.4	1	0.7	n/a[c]
	2007	17.3	1	3	2.6m
EU totals	2005	4174.1	19[d]	15	123.5m
	2007	5150.2	21	18	135.8m[e]

Notes: a. The Association of Lithuanian Credit Unions has been missed out here because it is already counted in the WOCCU figures (it has dual membership). Totals for 2005 include members in Belgium and Ireland that were not members in 2007, and totals for 2007 include members in Bulgaria, Romania and Slovenia that were not members in 2005. These are small banks so they do not affect the EU totals much. b. This massive increase may be because Credit Agricole began to report its customer numbers worldwide rather than in France. c. At this time the UK Co-operative Bank did not have individual members, as customers joined the group through the retail outlets. A rule change meant bank customers could join the group. d. The EACB explains that these market share figures are estimates. e. The figure provided by the EACB is suspect as Credit Agricole increased its customer figure from 21m in 2005 to 44m in 2007 (moving from counting customers in France to counting customers in several countries). The figure provided in the table uses Credit Agricole's 2005 figure instead.

Source: EACB (2012) reordered and simplified.

cooperative banks for the years 2005 and 2007. We can see that in every country assets increased during these two years. For the European Union (EU) as a whole they increased by over 23 per cent. Market share went down in some countries (Poland, Hungary), stayed the same in others (Finland, Luxemburg, Spain) and in most countries increased. In the EU as a whole, the estimate is that market share of deposits increased by 2 per cent and of loans by 3 per cent. The number of customers increased in most countries, stayed the same in four countries and only decreased in Luxemburg. For the EU as a whole, numbers increased by around 10 per cent. Clearly, the general trend just before the banking crisis of 2007 was upwards.

PERFORMANCE OF CREDIT UNIONS BEFORE THE CRISIS

Like the cooperative banks, the credit unions have faced up to banking crises in the past. They survived the Ecuador crisis of 1999 and the Jamaica crisis of the late 1990s (Crear, 2009). The first few years of the new century were good ones for the credit union movement worldwide. In 2000 there were over 36 000 unions with membership of WOCCU from 92 countries, with over 108 million members. By 2007 there were 49 000 unions from 96 countries, and the membership had increased by 64 per cent to over 177 million (WOCCU, 2012a). Table 6.2 compares the statistics for 2005 and 2007. Over the two years, the amount of savings increased everywhere by an average of 29 per cent, while loans increased everywhere by an average of 39 per cent. Reserves increased by 26 per cent and assets by 32 per cent. The number of members increased by 20 million, which is a 13 per cent rise on average. These figures do not take into account inflation but they are still very impressive. Market penetration also increased everywhere (except Oceania where it dropped slightly) from 6.65 per cent to 7.5 per cent.

PERFORMANCE OF BUILDING SOCIETIES/ MUTUAL SAVINGS AND LOANS BEFORE THE CRISIS

In the USA, scholars have often been attracted to studying the S&Ls because they are a kind of natural experiment in which there are two distinct sub-sectors, mutual and investor-owned. Out of four studies of S&Ls carried out in the 1990s, one found that the mutuals were as efficient as

Finance in an age of austerity

Table 6.2   Credit unions before the crisis

Year/region	Savings (billion dollars)	Loans (billion dollars)	Reserves (billion dollars)	Assets (billion dollars)	Members	Market penetration (%)
World						
2005	763.8	612.2	91.6	894.5	157.1m	6.65
2007	987.9	847.9	115.4	1181.5	177.4m	7.5
Africa						
2005	2.1	2.1	0.1	2.1	9.6m	5.7
2007	3.5	3.5	0.2	3.4	15.1m	8.4
Asia						
2005	47.6	32.8	4	55	31.2m	2.4
2007	78.0	60.1	4.6	96.9[a]	33.1m	2.6
Caribbean						
2005	2.2	1.7	0.34	2.6	1.7m	41
2007	2.6	2.1	0.35	3.2	1.9m	41.4[b]
Europe						
2005	17.7	10.3	1.9	19.9	6.7m	2.9
2007	24.8	15.4	2.8	28	8.2m	3.6
Latin America						
2005	11.5	11.6	2.5	17	12.4m	4.2
2007	19.7	19.8	4.0	30.4	15.1m	4.8
N America						
2005	659.2	531.8	80.4	772.1	91.2m	41.3
2007	827.5	716.5	100.2	983.0	99.4m	43.8
Oceania						
2005	23.5	20.7	2.3	25.8	3.8m	19
2007	31.0	28.9	3.3	36.5	3.9m	18.5

Notes: a. Figures for Central Asia were presented separately in 2007, so these have been added to the Asia figures. b. In 2007 Dominica claimed a penetration rate of 118 per cent which seems implausible. In the 2010 statistics Dominica provides no return. This explains part of the large leap in penetration rates, though there has been a rise overall.

Source: WOCCU (2012a), reordered.

the investor-owned (Cebenoyan, 1993), while three others found that the latter were slightly more cost-efficient (Mester, 1993; Esty, 1997; Caudhill et al., 2001). As we have seen in Chapter 4, the mutuals were much more stable during the crisis of the 1980s and did not have to be bailed out, so a little less cost-efficiency may be a small price to pay. Two studies showed that, like the cooperative banks, the S&Ls were more stable than their investor-owned competitors. The first found a decline in credit quality was more pronounced among converted mutuals (Murphy and Salandro, 1997), which is not surprising since so many of them failed! The second found that, not only were 'stock' S&Ls less efficient, they were more likely to fail (Garbaccio et al., 1994). We know this already from the historical account provided in Chapter 4, but it is good to have this verified by statistical research.

In the UK, the building societies have been another setting for comparative research into the relative merits of mutual and investor-ownership. Valnek compared 17 building societies and seven retail banks over the ten years from 1983 to 1993, and found that the societies were more profitable than their competitors. By aligning the interests of savers and borrowers, they avoided the agency costs incurred by privately owned banks (Valnek, 1999). One of his conclusions was that since the societies have outperformed the banks, the latter should consider mutualising! A slightly later study by Heffernan (2005) found that demutualised societies' rates on deposits and mortgages were more favourable to shareholders than to customers, with the remaining mutual building societies offering consistently better rates. Following conversion to bank status, the rates on all the deposit products of the converts were permanently lower, and their mortgage rates permanently higher. Heffernan's conclusion was that:

> Converts are keen to earn higher spreads because they are no longer answerable to their customers. The building societies offer many more bargains because they are more likely to do the best for their customers, who are their shareholders (2005, p. 794).

This finding was confirmed by an All-Party Parliamentary Group enquiry in 2006. The 'best buy' tables were consistently placing mutuals higher than investor-owned banks on savings and mortgage rates, and with-profits policies (All-Party Parliamentary Group, 2006). In its evidence to the enquiry, the Building Societies Association calculated that having to pay dividends to shareholders added 35 per cent on to the costs of the non-mutuals. The mutual pricing benefit had totalled over £3.7 billion over the decade to 2006. Because there was no evidence that banks were more efficient, societies could retain this advantage. In addition, their performance was achieved without extensive cost cutting. One of the main fixed costs of banks that rely on taking in savings is the maintenance of an extensive branch network. As soon as they demutualised, the new banks began to cut; between 1995 and 2000 they closed 24 per cent of their branches, compared to the mutuals' 2 per cent. Then in the four years to 2004 they closed another 7.2 per cent, compared with the societies' 2.7 per cent. Halifax sold off many of its automatic teller machines (ATMs) to charging companies

Table 6.3   UK building societies before the crisis

Year	No. of societies	No. of depositors (thousand)	No. of borrowers (thousand)	Total assets (£billion)	Deposits from shares (£billion)	Deposits and loan balances (£billion)
2005	63	449	2822	265.2	171.9	71.7
2007	59	460	2941	330.3	206.8	98.4

Source: BSA (2012), reordered.

after demutualisation. Nationwide campaigned against this, calculating that the public would soon have to pay £250 million a year to get their own money out (All-Party Parliamentary Group, 2006, p.14).

In the parliamentary group's enquiry, the most convincing counter-evidence came from Northern Rock, whose managers claimed that its much faster growth would not have been possible without demutualisation. However, the bankruptcy of the Rock just a year later makes this rather less convincing! Table 6.3 shows that just before the crisis the building society sector in the UK was stable, with a slight decrease in the number of societies and increases in borrowing and saving members, but a considerable increase in assets.

THE IMPACT OF THE CRISIS ON COOPERATIVE BANKS

In Europe, a report produced at the height of the banking crisis from Rabobank summed up:

> While all the large co-operative banks have suffered substantial losses on risky investments, they do seem to have been hit relatively less hard by the direct effects of the crisis than private and investment banks (2009, p. 9).

Two of Rabobank's researchers went into more detail in a study of 45 European banks (Groeneveld and de Vries, 2009). They compared the performance of cooperative banks in Europe with their investor-owned competitors on a crucial variable called Tier 1 ratio. This is a measure of bank stability that puts equity over risk-weighted assets. They found that, while the market required Tier 1 ratios of 8 per cent, the cooperative banks all had higher ratios than this (except for DZ Bank, but not including its local banks). Their explanation for this was that the cooperative banks focused more on retail and added profits to reserves, while their competitors were more diversified and had to distribute profits to their shareholders. The study of 45 banks showed that the average Tier 1 between 2002 and 2007 was 9.2 per cent for the cooperative banks compared to 8.4 per cent for the investor-owned banks, so that they went into the crisis with a strong capital base which they subsequently strengthened. During 2008, Raiffeisen, Rabobank and Pohjola Banks all had over 12 per cent Tier 1, while others strengthened theirs to over 8 per cent.

By April 2009, the *ratings* for cooperative banks from the three main rating agencies were all still good at A upward, with Rabobank taking the prize as one of the world's strongest banks with an AAA rating. Profitability was lower than for the investor-owned banks because of the cooperative banks having a higher capital core and lower leverage, which makes them less risky. The study showed that from 2002–08 cooperative banks had a return on equity of 9.3 per cent compared to the investor-owned banks that had a return of 13.4 per cent. This is to be expected because, as we have already noted, cooperative banks do not maximise return on equity in their business model (Fonteyne, 2007). Does the absence of a profit maximising objective make them less efficient? Groeneveld and de Vries (2009) found there was little difference. They had a cost to income ratio of 62 per cent, compared to 61 per cent in the investor-owned banks. They were more efficient than their competitors in every country except France, where they were the same.

The financial stability of cooperative banks was substantially higher than that of the investor-owned banks: in 2007 their average Z-score was 54 over 41. They entered the crisis with larger buffers, and then proved to be very stable. What about their losses? They had limited exposure to toxic mortgages and the volatile wholesale banking business. Their write-downs and losses between 2007 and 2008 were bearable; as a percentage of equity they were 6 per cent at Credit Mutuel and Rabobank, 9 per cent at Banque Populaire, 14 per cent at DZ and CA, and 15 per cent at RZB. There is a question mark over Credit Agricole, which is one of the most commercial cooperative banks, and those banks that have substantial business in Central and Eastern Europe have suffered losses in these operations. The lesson from all of this is that those that remained true to their traditional business model came through the crisis much better.

A more recent report from Rabobank (2011) has confirmed this rather optimistic picture. It quotes Bloomberg data revealing that cooperative banks accounted for 7 per cent of all the European Banking Industry write-downs and losses between Q3 2007 and Q1 2011, even though they had 20 per cent of the market. This is because of their limited exposure to sub-prime mortgages, and fewer investment activities (Rabobank, 2011).

It confirms that the strengths of cooperative banks are continuing to be evident, but also that their profitability has improved. Between 2003 and 2010, cooperative banks had an average return of 7.5 per cent, while the investor-owned banks had a return of only 5.7 per cent. Their Z-scores also continued to be higher.

Using statistics provided for European cooperative banks by the European Association of Co-operative Banks, we can bring the picture up to 2010. Table 6.4 summarises the situation of cooperative banks in Europe at two key points – 2007 and 2010 – that together enable us to see how the crisis affected them. Their assets grew by nearly 10 per cent over the three years, decreasing in only one country, Austria. Their market share of deposits and loans remained roughly the same, rising marginally and falling in various countries with no clear pattern. The number of customers increased by 14 per cent. Table 6.5 goes into more detail during the crisis. Assets dropped, presumably because of losses and write-downs during 2009, but then they recovered so that the 2010 total is nearly 10 per cent higher than in 2007.

How did the crisis affect cooperative banks in different countries? Here we rely on the study by Ayadi and her colleagues published in 2010. In *Germany*, the local banks in the group have not suffered much, for two reasons. Their business model is fairly conservative and they have not been left holding toxic assets. Having a relatively high level of capital has helped them. In 2007 they entered the crisis with a Tier 1 ratio of 9.4 per cent compared to the industry average of 7.8 per cent, and they kept this lead in 2008 with 10.5 per cent compared to 9.3 per cent (Ayadi et al., 2010, Table 3.1.2). They also had a protection scheme dating back to 1934, which protects local banks that get into trouble, so that no bank in the group has ever needed government support. At first there was a 'rush to quality' among customers, and the second largest Volksbank in Frankfurt reported that 2008 was the best year in its history. The future depends on whether the wider economy will weather the storm, because their lending to retail customers and SMEs could be affected if the borrowers get into difficulties. There are two exceptions to this optimistic report. The largest bank, Ärzte und Apothetekerbank, Dusseldorf, did have toxic assets and reported heavy losses that were supported through the guarantee scheme. The central, DZ Bank, was caught out because one of its roles is to act as an interface between the local banks and capital markets; it lost around €1 billion in 2008 (though it returned to profit in 2009) and had to reorient its activities more around its core business of supporting cooperatives. Ayadi et al. (2010) conclude that, despite these two cases, the group as a whole has been a winner in relative terms during the crisis. Table 6.4 shows a slight increase in market shares and in assets.

Table 6.4   *European cooperative banks during and after the crisis (top 12 countries by 2010 market share plus EU totals)*[a]

Country	Years	Assets (billion euros)	Market share of deposits (%)	Market share of loans (%)	No. of customers
France	2007	2443	53	45	67m
	2010	2671	45[b]	46	91m[c]
Netherlands	2007	571	41	28	9m
	2010	653	40	29	10m
Austria	2007	331	36	31	5.1m
	2010	**320**	37	33	5.1m
Italy	2007	560	34	30	14.3m
	2010	662	34	32	15.3m
Finland	2007	66	32	31	4.1m
	2010	84	33	33	4.1m
Germany	2007	995	18	16	30m
	2010	1020	19	17	30m
Cyprus	2007	9.7[d]	20	22	600k
	2010	20	19	20	747k
Luxemburg	2007	4.1	10	10	100k
	2010	5.9	11	11	125k
Poland	2007	13.3	9	7	10.5m
	2010	17.6	9	6	7.5m
Hungary	2007	5	9	3	1.1m
	2010	5.1	9	3	1.1m
Spain	2007	108	5	5	10.3m
	2010	119	7	5	10.8m
UK	2007	17.3	1	3	2.6m
	2010	51.8[e]	5	1.5	5.1m
EU totals	2007	5150.2	21	18	158.8m
	2010	5647.3	21	19	181.1m

Notes: a. The Association of Lithuanian Credit Unions has been missed out here, because it is already counted in the WOCCU figures (it has dual membership). b. Market share for Credit Agricole is no longer reported, so the 2008 figure is used. c. This massive increase may be because Credit Agricole began to report its number of customers worldwide rather than in France. d. This figure is domestic only, that is, the local banks' assets. e. This massive increase in assets, market share and customers reflects the bank's takeover of Britannia BS.

Source: EACB (2012), reordered and simplified.

Table 6.5　Effects of the banking crisis on European cooperative banks over four years

Year	Assets (billion euros)	Market share of deposits (%)	Market share of loans (%)	No. of customers
2007	5150.2	21	18	158.8m
2008	5581.5	21	19	176.5m
2009	5523.7	18.8	20.1	176m
2010	5647.3	21	19	181.1m

Source:　EACB (2012).

In *Austria*, again the conservative business model has helped the local cooperative banks; their lack of investment in toxic assets and their cautious lending have served them well. However, the central banks have suffered from exposure to deteriorating conditions in Central and Eastern Europe, where lending tends to be more risky. The wider recession provoked by the banking crisis hit these countries in 2009, and default rates have soared. Many foreign banks operating here have incurred heavy losses. The Volksbank central, OVAG, had to ask for government support with an equity injection of €1 billion and guarantees for its bonds issues. Table 6.4 shows a decline in assets in Austria. The decline has not been in the Raiffeisen Group but in the OVAG Group, where assets have declined from €94 billion in 2007 to €65 billion in 2010, and its deposits have more than halved from €63 to €30 billion. Has the emphasis on seeking profitable banking business in other countries been a mistake? Should the volksbanks have stuck to the conservative business model of just serving their members? Time will tell.

In *Italy*, the crisis has had very little effect on the cooperative banks, for all the usual reasons: lack of exposure to toxic assets, a low-risk business model, and reliance on own capital for lending. Again, the impact of the wider recession is expected to be greater, as borrowers begin to default, but the figures for 2010 show continuing increases in assets, deposits and loans in both cooperative groups. For instance, the total deposits held by the Banche Popolari almost doubled from 2007 to 2010 (up 92 per cent), though its loans only increased by 18 per cent. It is expected that the banks, which are less highly integrated than in Austria or Germany, will begin to introduce more central support systems for the local banks.

In *France*, losses have been incurred, but they are relatively modest compared with the huge losses made in the UK, Germany and Switzerland (Xiao, 2009). In October 2008, at the height of the crisis, all three banking

groups accepted help from the government. Credit Agricole (CA) received
€3 billion, Credit Mutuel (CM) €1.2 billion and Banques Populaires (BP)
€950 million in the form of subordinated debt, calculated in line with the
size of the banks' balance sheets and market shares in customer loans
and deposits (Ayadi et al., 2010). The worst losses were made in CA's
investment banking arm, Calyon; out of €8.5 billion lost by the group
as a whole, €6 billion were in Calyon. CA launched a rights issue of €5.8
billion and restructured its investment arm to more closely integrate it into
the group, rebranding it as CA Corporate and Investment Bank. Natixis,
the investment arm jointly owned by Caisse d'Epargne and BP, lost €2.8
billion, which amounted to more than a third of their total losses during
the crisis. In response, the government agency responsible for the banks,
State Shareholding Corporation (SPPE), has helped the merger of the two
groups into BPCE, with a second tranche of €5 billion. The new group
has issued €1 billion of deeply subordinated debt. It retains control over
Natixis with a stake of over 70 per cent, while the French government is a
minority shareholder with a 20 per cent stake in convertible bonds.

A comparison of the 2007 and 2010 statistics from Table 6.4 shows that
the three groups taken together lost 8 per cent of market share in deposits,
but kept up their share of loans and managed modestly to increase their
assets. By early 2010 CA and CM had repaid their loans, and all three
groups are now growing again. Even in the middle of the crisis, opportunities arose to expand through acquisitions. In 2008, CM bought Citibank's
retail arm in Germany (now known as Targobank), and took a majority
stake in a consumer credit company. BP took over HSBC's regional subsidiaries and branches in France, while CA merged its asset management
operations with those of Society Generale, with CA taking a majority
shareholding in the new company, Amundi. CA also created an online
bank (Ayadi et al., 2010).

In the *Netherlands*, the impact of the crisis has not been so severe,
mainly because of Rabobank's strong capital position; in 2008 its Tier 1
capital ratio was 12.7 per cent compared to the average for all banks of 9.7
per cent. It was the only large bank in the Netherlands that did not need
government support. However, it lost 6 per cent of its equity, and profits
declined by 17 per cent in 2009, mainly because of a drop in demand for
household loans (Birchall and Hammond Ketilson, 2009). It did have
some exposure to toxic instruments such as mortgage-backed securities
and collateralised debt obligations, but the results from the member banks
were enough to deal with the losses. Table 6.4 shows it holding its market
share at the end of 2010 while increasing its assets. Between 2007 and 2010
its Tier 1 ratio increased from 10.7 per cent to 15.7 per cent, which makes
it very strong (EACB, 2012).

In *Spain*, banks have been damaged more by the wider economic crisis that was triggered by the banking crisis. It is not toxic assets that are the problem but falls in the value of property and a slowdown in construction that have impacted on bank loans. However, by the end of 2009 the ratio of non-performing loans to good loans was 3.8 per cent for the cooperative banks and over 5 per cent for investor-owned and savings banks (Ayadi et al., 2010). Going into the crisis they limited their exposure to the real estate and construction sectors, and during the crisis were better at getting loans repaid than the other banks. At the end of 2009 their non-performing loan (NPL) rate for household mortgages was 1.6 per cent compared with 3 per cent for savings banks and 2.4 per cent for investor-owned banks, while in the real estate sector the cooperatives' NPL rate was 7.6 per cent compared with the investor-owned banks' rate of 10 per cent. This may have to do with the kind of relationship the cooperatives have with their borrowers. Their ability to screen potential borrowers and monitor their progress in paying off a loan is a distinct informational advantage that is more apparent in an economic downturn.

However, Ayadi et al. (2010) highlight one disadvantage; they find it more difficult than investor-owned banks to raise capital in the money markets, finding its supply is uncertain and it costs more. In 2007, the cooperative banks set up a mutual protection scheme enabling them to share liquidity, improving access to capital markets and guaranteeing the solvency of each bank. In Spain, then, we can see that they have not been as badly affected as their competitors, at least not yet.

In *Finland*, the impact on the central bank, OP-Pohjola, has been felt through its subsidiaries in investment and life insurance rather than in its banking business. In 2007 its return on equity was 13.7 per cent, but in 2008 this fell to 4.1 per cent, recovering in 2009 at 5.9 per cent and again in 2010 at 6.8 per cent (EACB, 2012). The losses were due mainly to poor investment performance on the insurance side. Now it is expected that, as the economy weakens, non-performing loans will become a problem. However, the group has performed well under the circumstances.

In general, the European cooperative banks have come out of the crisis very well. Seven of them are in the top 50 safest banks in the world, and across Europe they exceed the minimum legal capital ratio requirement of 8 per cent, with an average ratio of about 9 per cent. This is reflected in very good credit ratings, which range between AA and AAA for the largest cooperative banking groups in Western Europe.

THE IMPACT OF THE CRISIS ON CREDIT UNIONS

In a report on the crisis, the then president of WOCCU, Pete Crear, said

> not a single credit union, anywhere in the world, has received government recapitalisation as a result of the financial crisis and they remain well capitalised (Crear, 2009, p. 1).

This is certainly true for primary-level unions, but not, sadly, for some of their centrals. The worldwide picture is one of strong growth during the period 2007–10 (Table 6.6). There has been a slight decline in the number of unions and a slight increase in the number of members, but the real change has been in terms of performance. Savings increased by only 1 per cent in 2008 but then by 15 per cent in 2009, and another 7.3 per cent in 2010. This is an increase of almost a quarter on 2007. Loans decreased very slightly in 2008 then grew by 7.6 per cent and 5.3 per cent over the next two years, making a total increase over the three years of more than 13 per cent. Crucially, reserves increased by over 14 per cent, indicating that the system is in good health and that risks are being kept low. The figures for 2011 show that the post-crisis downturn has affected savings, but that all the other indicators show continued good health.

In Africa, the banking crisis was hardly felt at all by the credit unions. In the period 2007–10 savings grew by 34 per cent and loans by 37 per cent. However, the continued downturn in the world economy has affected them, with a slight decline in the indicators for 2011. It is important to remember that the amount of business done in such a large and needy region is still very small.

In the Asia region, savings dipped by over 8 per cent in 2008, but then increased dramatically in 2009 (by nearly 28 per cent). Over the three years to 2010 they increased by 38 per cent. Lending also fell at first, but surged ahead in 2009. Again, 2010 saw a large increase on 2007 of more than 34 per cent. The figures for 2011 show continued modest growth in all areas.

Taking 2007 as a base line again, the level of savings in the Caribbean grew steadily to 2010 by an astonishing 50 per cent and loans by 57 per cent. Here, as in Africa, the amount of business done is very low by the standards of richer countries, but because the penetration rate is much higher the unions are having a much greater effect on the local economy. In 2009, Crear reported that some unions had been directly affected by the crisis, in tourism, shipping and sugar, with their members affected by layoffs, salary cuts and business closures (Crear, 2009). Those with high dependence on remittances had also been affected. The 2011 statistics show a levelling off in the rate of growth, with indicators showing only small increases.

Table 6.6   Credit unions during and after the crisis

Year/region	Savings (billion dollars)	Loans (billion dollars)	Reserves (billion dollars)	Assets (billion dollars)	Members	Market penetration (%)
World						
2007	987.9	847.9	115.4	1181.5	177.4m	7.5
2010	1229.4	960	131.7	1460.6	188m	7.5
2011	1222.6	1016.2	141.3	1563.5	196m	7.8
Africa						
2007	3.5	3.5	0.2	3.4	15.1m	8.4
2010	4.7	4.8	0.3	5.8	17m	7.6
2011	4.3	4.2	0.3	4.9	18m	7.2
Asia						
2007	78.0	60.1	4.6	96.9[a]	33.1m	2.6
2010	107.7	80.7	7.8	139.4	37.8m	2.6
2011	121.8	88.1	8.6	140.2	39.7m	2.7
Caribbean						
2007	2.6	2.1	0.35	3.2	1.9m	41.4[b]
2010	3.9	3.3	0.42	4.8	2.8m	16.6
2011	4.3	3.5	0.54	5.2	2.9m	17.5
Europe						
2007	24.8	15.4	2.8	28	8.2m	3.6
2010	22.1	13	3.1	25.4	8.3m	3.5
2011	22.3	11.9	3.1	24.6	8.1m	3.5
Latin America						
2007	19.7	19.8	4.0	30.4	15.1m	4.8
2010	29.2	30.6	6.9	48.1	15.7m	5
2011	33.5	30.5	7.3	50.3	18m	5.7
N America						
2007	827.5	716.5	100.2	983.0	99.4m	43.8
2010	1015.7	784.5	108.4	1182.8	102.5m	44.1
2011	968	808.8	114.8	1253	104.5m	45
Oceania						
2007	31.0	28.9	3.3	36.5	3.9m	18.5
2010	46.1	43.2	4.7	54.2	3.8m	17.3
2011	68.4	69.1	6.6	85.2	5.1m	23.6

Notes: a. Figures for Central Asia were presented separately in 2007, so these have been added to the Asia figures. b. This figure is too high because some countries counted multiple memberships and youth memberships. It declines to 23.4 per cent in 2008 and 18.9 per cent in 2009. From 2010 it looks to be more accurate.

Source: WOCCU (2012a), reordered.

In Europe, during the four years to 2010, savings and loans both declined slowly year by year, and savings are now 11 per cent lower and loans 16 per cent lower than in 2007. The explanation is simple and can be summed up in one word – Ireland. Here, in 2007 the penetration rate was an incredible 104 per cent, indicating that virtually every adult citizen was a member (and some were members of more than one union). Savings were at $19.7 billion and loans at $11 billion. By 2010 savings had dropped by 19 per cent to $15.9 billion and loans by 27 per cent to $8 billion (WOCCU, 2012a). Loan arrears increased from 6.5 per cent of total lending to 17.6 per cent (Carroll et al., 2012). The average dividend paid out in 2011 was just over 1 per cent. Clearly, if a country has a big credit union sector and then goes into deep recession, the sector will take its share of the pain (though the commercial banks are doing much worse). In Poland, savings have increased by 63 per cent and loans by 57 per cent over the same period, and from a low start other unions in Central and Eastern Europe are doing well. British unions are doing about the same business as they were before the crisis, though they are attracting small savers looking for a safe place to put their money.

In Latin America we see a loss of savings in 2008 (11 per cent) followed by a dramatic surge in 2009 (45 per cent) and continued growth (over 16 per cent) in 2010, which means overall a growth of 48 per cent over the period. In 2009 Crear reported that unions in Latin America were not feeling the effects of the crisis at all. The 2011 figures confirm this; there has been a very slight decrease in loans from 2010, but all other indicators are strengthening.

In North America, during the first year of the banking crisis, the unions recorded modest increases of 2.8 per cent in savings. Then in 2009 these leapt up by 13 per cent, and then again in 2010 by 5.6 per cent, making a 23 per cent increase over the three years. Clearly, customers were choosing to put their savings in a safer place than the big investor-owned banks. They also continued to keep up their level of lending; in 2009 when the banks were ceasing to lend to anyone they increased theirs by nearly 6 per cent. Over the three years lending increased by 9.5 per cent. The 2011 figures show a slight downturn in savings due to the recession, but all the other indicators are healthy.

It is the job of the central cooperative banks and credit union centrals to reinvest surplus cash from the local banks and unions, and in some cases they did so unwisely by buying investment products that lost much of their value. In Canada, SaskCentral posted a loss of over $45 million as it had a $51 million write-down on investments in asset-backed commercial paper (Birchall and Hammond Ketilson, 2009). Desjardins in Quebec also experienced significant losses; its return on equity in 2008 dipped to just

0.8 per cent, recovering to 10.4 per cent in 2009 (EACB, 2012). However, in 2009 Crear described the impact in Canada as 'relatively mild' (Crear, 2009, p. 3). For the USA, he reported that deposits had increased by $52 billion in a few months; press coverage had pointed out that the unions were a safer option than the banks, and so savings had flooded in. In 2008 loans by unions rose by $35 billion, while loans by the investor-owned banks declined by almost as much – $31 billion.

However, for the US centrals the situation was much worse. They had been investing heavily in the kinds of toxic assets that the American banking system had been so good at producing until the crisis broke. Their leaders are keen to emphasise that the losses were not due to a failure in corporate governance; at the time the investments were rated as low-risk products. However, the consequences were dire. Five corporate unions were put into conservatorship by their regulator, the National Credit Union Administration (NCUA, a federal body whose job is to regulate and insure the sector). These five represented 70 per cent of the entire corporate system's assets and 98 per cent of the investment losses (NCUA, 2010). The US Central Corporate Credit Union was hardest hit. In 2009 it received $1 billion in government aid, but despite this had to wind down its operations. In order to limit the damage, the NCUA created several special programmes. There was a liquidity guarantee programme to help keep the corporates solvent, a system investment programme, a corporate stabilisation fund to spread the cost to the unions of stabilising the system over a number of years, and so on. It created 'bridge' corporate unions to make sure that vital services to member unions were maintained. The distressed assets were put into separate asset management estates that the NCUA then resolved through a securitisation process.

As a result, member unions are now having to pay an increased insurance premium to a National Share Insurance Fund to help pay for the losses. We can see the damage done by looking at 2009 statistics for the federally insured corporates. Their total assets declined from $96 billion in 2007 to $60 billion in 2008, recovering to $71 billion in 2009. Total capital declined from $6 billion in 2007 to minus $2.6 billion in 2008, recovering slightly to minus $2.3 billion in 2009. These statistics do not include Federal Central, which was in liquidation at the time. The NCUA Annual Report for 2009 includes a figure of $35 billion for the assets of this failed central, but it does not make it clear how much of this is still toxic (NCUA, 2010).

There is a new problem: the losses caused by mortgage defaults by borrowers hit by a decline in the housing market. The NCUA has created an affordability relief programme for mortgage-holders, and an Asset Management Assistance Centre is managing the assets of closed unions. Fifteen unions were liquidated in 2008, and another 16 in 2009. Some were able to transfer to other unions, but others were closed down. However, this is not a large number, and it affects only those that are particularly exposed to the property market.

Like the Asian region, Oceania's savings rate dipped in 2008 (by 12 per cent), increased dramatically in 2009 (by 36 per cent) and then kept on increasing, so that over the period they increased by nearly half (49 per cent). A similar story can be told of loans. First they dropped by 14 per cent, then they surged ahead by 40 per cent and then again in 2010 by 24 per cent. The increase over the whole period was by nearly half (49 per cent). In 2009, Crear warned that in Australia the investor-owned banks had begun to seek retail savings as the securitisation market had ceased to function, increasing interest rates on deposits and putting pressure on credit union margins (Crear, 2009). However, the figures for 2011 show a huge leap forward in all aspects of the credit union movement, from financials to membership and market penetration. Clearly, here the unions are not just weathering the financial downturn but taking a lot of business from the investor-owned banks.

In general, the credit union movement has not been badly affected by the crisis, except in the region where the whole crisis began: North America. In some regions 2008 saw a dip in savings and credit but the recovery was rapid, and almost everywhere since then there has been continued strong growth. However, credit unions focus on a low to middle-income client group that makes them vulnerable to recession, and so the economic downturn that has followed the financial crisis is leading to a slowdown in their rate of expansion.

THE IMPACT OF THE CRISIS ON BANKS OWNED BY OTHER TYPES OF COOPERATIVE

Banks owned by other types of cooperative have been protected from the crisis because they carry out a very restricted type of business. However, in Japan the farmer-cooperative owned Norinchukin Bank lost $8 billion on investments and securitised products, making it the biggest loser in Asia from the crisis. The bank had continued to buy toxic assets, while other banks disclosed losses, because the assets were cheap, and its managers underestimated the severity of the crisis. How did this disaster come about? The Norinchukin Bank is the fourth biggest commercial bank in Japan, serving the 32 million members of over 5000 fishery, forestry and agricultural co-ops. Twenty years ago it had a reputation for being the best fund manager in Japan, and it avoided the crisis of the 1990s. It was relatively small at that time, and invested mainly in government bonds and lending to farm-related businesses. However, reform of farming began to affect the business, with government getting farmers to pool land in order to qualify for subsidies. After the consolidation, other banks came into the market and also began to lend to farmers. In response to the competition it invested heavily in US asset-backed securities, including the now notorious sub-prime mortgages. When the crisis broke, much of the paper it was holding proved worthless, and it lost at least $10 billion. It had to raise Y1.9 trillion ($20 billion) through share sales to its farmer members, but then it bounced back with a net income for 2009 of Y29.5 billion.

THE IMPACT OF THE CRISIS ON BUILDING SOCIETIES

During the crisis, UK building societies benefitted from being seen as a safe haven for people's savings. In the first half of 2008, nearly £6.3 billion of customer money flowed into their savings accounts, compared to just £3.8 billion for the same period in 2007. A report from an Oxford University research centre says:

> the mutual building societies were generally less scathed by the financial crisis than were banks in general and demutualised building societies in particular. Indeed, converted building societies proved to be more vulnerable the further they moved away from their traditional model (Oxford Centre, 2009, p. 12).

None of the demutualised institutions has survived as an independent institution, and two have failed and been taken into state ownership. Building societies have not received capital injections from the government, while the investor-owned banks have experienced serious capital shortages to the extent that government assistance has been needed on a large scale. However, as a result of the financial turmoil, building society profitability was significantly lower in 2008 than in previous years, and some building societies reported large losses for the first time in many years (see Table 6.7). Some societies (Cheshire, Derbyshire, Scarborough, Barnsley and Catholic) sought refuge through mergers, and one (Kent Reliance) formed a new company with a venture capital group, with its members holding a majority share of the assets. None of this is surprising given the enormity of the crisis in the banking and financial system, the serious recession, declines in property prices, and a generally weak housing market.

The Dunfermline Building Society was the only one to fail. It was unusual in having done a lot of commercial lending. It collapsed with losses of around £26 million – from its high-risk commercial loan book and some

Table 6.7 UK building societies during and after the crisis

Year	No. of societies	No. of depositors (thousand)	No. of borrowers (thousand)	Total assets (£billion)	Deposits from shares (£billion)	Deposits and loan balances (£billion)
2007	59	460	2941	330.3	206.8	98.4
2010	49	n/a	2569	309.5	210.8	73.5

Source: BSA (2012), reordered.

toxic assets. It was broken up and Nationwide took on the deposits and solid mortgage business, with the UK government providing Nationwide with £1.6 billion to cover the excess of deposits over assets being absorbed. The rump of the society was then put into administration. The lesson that other societies have drawn is that Dunfermline failed because it stopped behaving like a mutual! The supporters of the mutual model point out that, of the former building societies that were demutualised in the 1990s, not one has survived as an independent business. Two have been forced into public ownership, and a third is part of a group 43 per cent owned by the state. They changed the business model and paid heavily for it.

AFTER THE CRISIS

Before the crisis customer-owned banks were competing successfully against investor-owned banks. During the crisis they were not badly affected except in the area where the crisis originated – the USA. Only in a few places have their central banks had to accept government assistance, and, rather than being allowed to fail, weaker societies have mainly been taken over by stronger ones. Most of the losses incurred have been made up very quickly, within a year or two, and all the indicators are that they have bounced back and are growing again. There must be something about the customer-owned business model that makes it so strong. The next chapter will make more systematic the advantages and disadvantages of these banks to their customer-members and to the wider society.

NOTES

1. They were slightly but insignificantly higher than for savings banks, which seem to have similar advantages.

7. The comparative advantages of customer-owned banks

So far we have recounted the history of customer-owned banks and reviewed the evidence concerning their performance before, during and after the banking crisis. At various points we have noted that they have comparative advantages and – sometimes – disadvantages, when compared to other kinds of bank. In this chapter we provide a more systematic understanding of the advantages and disadvantages, using an analytical framework provided in the author's previous work on member-owned businesses (Birchall, 2010, 2012d).

A FRAMEWORK FOR UNDERSTANDING BUSINESS ADVANTAGE

Banks can be divided into different types according to their ownership structure, which then has significant consequences for the way they are governed and who benefits from their activities. Many people, when they think of how banks are owned, assume that there is only one type that is worth considering; the *investor-owned bank*. It is a simple concept; entrepreneurs propose the bank, people with money to invest buy a proportionate share in ownership, and they elect a board of directors to oversee the business on their behalf and hire professional managers to run it. Such a bank can be argued to be uniquely efficient and effective, because its governance is simple; owners all want the same thing – their return on capital in the form of share value and dividends – and boards and managers are given a clear mandate to do whatever it takes to deliver 'shareholder value'. It is often contrasted with the *state-owned bank* that is owned by citizens in general and governed by elected politicians, and that, while it may be good at persuading people to make deposits (government being seen as the ultimate guarantor), may have difficulty persuading borrowers to pay back.

There are several other ways of organising the provision of banking. The simplest form is the *individual moneylender* who appears in the history of cooperative banking as a rogue who thrives on the vulnerability of people in need. It is possible to imagine a benevolent individual who lends in a fair way without exploiting the borrower; for instance, the website Zopa brings together people who are willing to lend and people who need capital, but it has an explicitly ethical dimension. The problem is that when poor people have no collateral and there is no alternative the moneylender is in a monopolistic position. The borrower does have informational advantages, being in a better position to see how risky the loan will be. To make up for this, the lender demands high interest and monitors the loan closely, sometimes with threats of punishment if the payments are not made on time. A variant on this is found in relation to lending for production. When a business such as a family farm relies on another business to supply inputs or market the farm's outputs, the supplier or marketer is in a strong position to offer credit that then ties the farmer into a monopoly relationship. We might call this a *supply chain moneylender*.

The investor-owned bank, often called a 'commercial' or a 'private' bank is now regarded as the norm but it was not always so. When commercial banks first began, they were often *family firms*. The advantage of this type is that its governance is simple, and the relationship between the owners tends to create high levels of loyalty and trust. The disadvantage is that it is difficult to raise capital as outside shareholders are not allowed. *Partnership* is a similar type that was popular in the early days. It enables a group of wealthy people to find productive use for their capital while retaining some control over the operation. Governance is straightforward because they share the same aim – to maximise profit. There is also a *philanthropic bank*, usually called a savings bank. The governance structure of this type is more complex, being designed for one group of people to meet the needs of a different group. It is not really owned by anyone, because trustees are appointed who look after the business on behalf of the customers (Hansmann, 1996).

A *customer-owned bank* is another distinct type of ownership. We can identify the essential elements of this type from its history. It began in order to avoid market failures associated with other types, particularly the monopoly supply of credit by individual moneylenders and supply chain moneylenders. It also began in order to rectify another market failure that is often overlooked – a failure to supply. Banks are unwilling to do business with people who are on low incomes or living in isolated areas because it is seen as risky or too costly, and so there is no way of making enough profit for their shareholders. When they are small, customer-owned banks do not have serious governance problems, but when they grow, ownership tends to be dispersed among large numbers of people whose interests may be heterogeneous. This means they have to rely on an elected board and a professional management that makes them look like investor-owned banks. However, their directors are mandated to deliver customer value rather than profit. Member shares are set at a level that allows low-income people to join, and they receive a limited interest and are not usually sold at market value. Dividends to members can be seen as patronage refunds rather than profits; they adjust the price customers have paid for the goods or services down to cost plus expenses. They tend to allocate voting rights by person or by amount of use made of the business rather than by level of investment. In all of this they are 'people-centred' rather than profit-centred.

What does it mean to be a member of a customer-owned bank? There are three aspects: *ownership, control and benefit* (Birchall, 2004). Ownership rights mean that one has power to decide if a business continues to exist, is sold off or wound up. This is why even when members do not have any control over a business it cannot be sold without their permission. In the case of UK building societies, boards and managers had to campaign among members to get them to vote in favour, even though the members had never before been consulted and many were unaware that they were members (Birchall, 2001). Ownership usually gives control rights, even if these are attenuated by rules and practices that allow boards to operate with very little input from members. At the minimum, members have the right to vote on new appointments to the board and to approve annual accounts. As the recent example of the UK's Equitable Life shows, they can organise to censure or remove boards that they believe are failing to serve their interests. Ownership also confers a right to share in the benefits accruing from the business and also to have a say in how these benefits are allocated.

The advantages to their members of customer-owned banks can be summarised under these three headings of ownership, control and benefit. Disadvantages can also be summarised in this way and are sometimes a direct corollary of the advantages. Because, as we have seen, cooperative banks and credit unions tend to federate and to create jointly owned central banks and subsidiaries, we have to add in the advantages and disadvantages that come from being part of a larger system. Finally, there are significant benefits to the wider society from having a customer-owned banking sector.

ADVANTAGES DERIVED FROM OWNERSHIP

It is useful to identify the advantages derived directly from ownership, as these apply even if there is minimal member involvement in decision-making. They are intrinsic to the particular ownership model.

1. It Prevents Market Failure

Ownership of the means by which a good or service is produced prevents ownership by a different interest group that might exploit the economic weakness of individual members. Another way of putting this is that without the customer-owned bank existing there would be market failure. As we have noted in the historical chapters (Chapters 2–5), at the founding stage for each of the different types of customer-owned bank this was important. There was the danger of monopolistic or oligopolistic supply by moneylenders. Even when there was more competition among suppliers of capital, there was the danger of 'lock in'; here suppliers could exercise control over producers through supplying credit. This was particularly serious for small farmers who relied on short-term credit to tide them over for the season. In the nineteenth century, cooperative banks in Europe, followed in the twentieth century by credit unions worldwide, provided small businesses with the credit they need when commercial banks were unwilling to lend. In the less economically developed countries, these ownership advantages are as relevant now as they were in Europe during the 1860s.

2. It Prevents a Conflict of Interest between Owners and Customers

Economists have long ago identified the relationship between a bank's shareholders and its customers as an 'agency problem'. Ayadi et al. (2010) explain this in their recent report on cooperative banks. Equity shareholders may prefer a higher risk profile for the institution than would depositors due to the fact that they have limited liability. Their potential for profit is unlimited, while the potential for losses is limited. Depositors do not share in the profits, but they do share disproportionately in the risks, given the limited scope of deposit insurance. In customer-owned banks this particular agency problem is avoided, since the owners and customers are the same people. There is no separate shareholder interest and the banks can be expected to work in the interests of their customers (Michie and Llewellyn, 2009). As John Kay (*Financial Times*, 25 April 2006) puts it, they have a comparative advantage in establishing trust. This is particularly the case where there is a long-term relationship, where the obligations entered into in the contract cannot easily be spelled out, and where it is costly for customers to exercise their right of exit (see Hansmann, 1996).

In fact, in a retail bank there is no need for outside shareholders. All that is needed is a mechanism for bringing together those who wish to save money with those who need to borrow it; the bank merely recycles their money. This argument was put strongly by supporters of UK building societies during the demutualisation debate of the 1990s (Drake and Llewellyn, 2001). In this view, investors are merely 'middlemen' who take the profits while adding little value to the business. A recent report for Rabobank spells out what it means when customers are put at the core of the business. There is a long-term focus on customer value. Healthy profitability is necessary but it is not a goal in itself. The banks operate in local retail markets, so have access to stable sources of funding in customer deposits. Their balance sheets are more solid on the liabilities side. Centred on relationship banking, they produce strong local ties and networks. They are better equipped to assess creditworthiness, so have higher lending levels than their competitors. In the banking crisis, this customer focus means that they have invested in fewer complex financial products, and have been more careful in their use of securitisation (Groeneveld and de Vries, 2009).

3. It Provides an Efficient, Low-cost Model of Banking

Customer-owned banks have a 'dual bottom line', focusing on customer value as well as equity. They can use their comparatively low costs and abundant capital and lack of a profit maximisation constraint to pursue expansion (Fonteyne, 2007). They only need to remunerate the part of capital that is in member shares, and then not generously. Because they do not have to pay external shareholders, they can reduce the margin between the interest rates they charge to borrowers and pay to savers (Oxford Centre, 2009). They can even decide to sell products at below market price, incorporating the anticipated profits into the products (what we might call a cost-price mechanism). Consequently, they are able to attract a large share of retail deposits, so experience comfortable liquidity, with high deposit to loan rations. In good times they become net lenders in interbank markets. In bad times, the reserves can be built up to cushion banks against poor performance; the banks simply do not distribute as much dividend to members, or they adjust their prices upwards so as to extract more surplus (Hesse and Cihak, 2007). It is true that they cannot issue shares in order to raise capital easily and quickly, nor can they rely on the limited amount of capital raised through member shares. However, they allocate virtually all their earnings to reserves that are then used to finance further growth. The larger customer-owned banks are able to issue various forms of hybrid capital, and the national banking federations can attract capital via listed subsidiaries (Rabobank, 2011).

4. It Provides No Incentives to Risk-taking

After the banking crisis it is more obvious than ever that customer-owned banks are less risky than investor-owned. Why should this be so? They are not under pressure to maximise profits, a pressure that in investor-owned banks often leads to risky business practices such as insecure lending and the sale of complex products that pass the risk on. They are more highly capitalised than their competitors. They are under less short-term pressure and are more inclined to adopt a longer-term horizon in their business decisions and lending policies. It is less easy for them to raise external capital independent of their members, and so they avoid reliance on wholesale markets. They are not subject to the pressure from investors for immediate returns, and so a longer-term focus results. Their business strategy is all about relationship building; a number of studies find that cooperative banks are more willing to establish a long-term relationship with their clients, especially with SMEs (Ayadi et al., 2010). They have been found to have a more stable stream of earnings than other types (Hesse and Cihak, 2007) because they are able to use their reserves as a buffer. They have been found to have a better loan quality and lower asset risk than other banks, which is also a source of stability (Iannotta et al., 2007).

It is when customer-owned banks stray from their natural business model that excessive risk-taking begins. Even then, they are better able to cope with losses through the mutual support network provided by their national federations. Unlike the 'too big to fail' investor-owned banks, the biggest cooperative banks have been found to be better able to smooth out their gains and losses during the peaks and troughs of the business cycle (Groeneveld and de Vries, 2009).

ADVANTAGES DERIVED FROM CONTROL

What do we mean by member control? While ownership is a category – a person is or is not an owner – control is a variable, in that there can be more or less control by members. Clearly, in all but the smallest businesses members cannot expect to be in full control, as they cede most decisions to a board of directors who then delegate some discretion to managers. By member control we mean enough of a curb on directorial and managerial authority to ensure that the business is run mainly in the interests of members and under their ultimate direction. There are several advantages that customer members gain from keeping this kind of control over their bank.

1.   It Guarantees the Advantages that are Derived from Member-ownership

In theory, the advantages that are derived from ownership are intrinsic; they apply even if the members do not control their banks. There are advantages to member ownership even if there are failings in governance. However, these intrinsic advantages are not guaranteed for long if boards take decisions that are not in the interests of members. The first advantage of member control is, then, that it guarantees the advantages that are derived from member-ownership.

2.   It Aligns the Interests of Members with those of Boards and Managers, and so is Linked to Business Success

There is strong evidence that effective member control is linked to business success. In a study of several hundred agricultural cooperatives in India, Shah found that success could be explained not in relation to the environment the cooperatives were working in, but more directly in relation to governance. His theory is that there are three conditions for success: the purpose of the organisation is central to the members; the governance structure ensures patronage cohesiveness; and the operating system finds competitive advantage in the relationship with members. To achieve these conditions the members have to be in control of governance (Shah, 1996). Far from being a check on the success of the customer-owned banking model, member involvement has been one of the drivers of its success worldwide. A key to this is the high level of trust that member-owned businesses generate.

3.   Member Control Lowers Risk-taking and so Makes the Business More Durable

The more members are involved in governance, the more likely it is that the organisation will avoid excessive risk-taking. The problem in the customer-owned banks that lost money during the crisis was partly one of inadequate member control; they did not understand the riskiness of the investments that were being made on their behalf.

4.   It Provides Informational Advantages to the Bank, Enabling it to Lend to Lower Income Groups

Fonteyne (2007) points out that the fact that the customers are also members, and are involved in decision-making, should provide it with an informational advantage. Ayadi and her colleagues (2010) agree; the strong local presence and the proximity of the banks enables them to have a better understanding of the needs and the risk profiles of their customers, and ultimately to mitigate the problem of asymmetric information. This in turn enables them to provide credit to lower income earning individuals and businesses with no or little collateral, because they are able to reduce the transaction costs associated with screening borrowers as well as monitoring and enforcing repayments. In other words, these institutions effectively prevent opportunistic behaviour on the part of borrowers (Hansmann, 1996).

5. It Increases Opportunities to Pursue Ethical Aims as Well as Shareholder Value

The involvement of members creates opportunities for them to pursue other aims than just business success. They can express ethical aims in the way the business is run. For instance, the UK Co-operative Bank has been a market leader in ethical trading, being the first bank to offer free current accounts, pledging that it will not lend to companies its customers regard as unethical, and so on. We have noted in Chapter 5 that, as a wholly owned subsidiary of the Co-operative Group, it has had a supportive board that during the 1980s and 1990s was prepared for it not to make much profit (Birchall, 2005). Contrast the totally unethical way in which bankers in the investor-owned sector have behaved in recent years, and the disastrous effects their behaviour has had on the world economy.

ADVANTAGES DERIVED FROM BENEFIT

The advantages to be gained by members sharing in the benefits of customer-owned banks are not difficult to understand; together they can channel the value added from the business to themselves rather than to investor-owners or to 'middlemen'. Member-owned businesses more generally operate a kind of cost-price mechanism, first charging members a market price for their goods and then, after each trading period, calculating a patronage refund that returns to them any surplus that has been made. In banking this is less obvious, as many cooperative banks and credit unions have rules that allocate surpluses to reserves first, before any can be distributed to members as a refund. The 'inter-generational endowment' limits the benefits to existing members.

However, dividends are only one of the benefits that customer-owned banks may provide. Customers benefit from the convenience of having a more extensive branch network, and less drastic rationalisation than if they were tied to an investor-owned bank. Those living in rural areas benefit from access to banking facilities they would not otherwise have. Small firms benefit from the relationship with the bank as borrowers. A number of researchers have argued that larger banks are less capable of processing and transmitting the softer forms of relational information through their hierarchical structures. Locally based banks are in a position to better respond to the needs of small, local enterprises than are larger, less regionally focused banks (Ayadi et al., 2010).

ADVANTAGES DERIVED FROM FEDERATION

Customer-owned banks are not alone. They nearly always form federations, which means that for a full understanding of their advantages we have to consider them as a system. We have described such systems in previous chapters. Academics have classified the European cooperative banking networks in interesting ways. Desrochers and Fischer (2005) identify three types, atomised, consensual and strategic. In each country the advantages of federation will vary with the degree and type of integration. In some countries there is no business federation at all. However, the leaders of most customer-owned banks have found the impulse to federate irresistible, both as an interest group and as a business group.

Integration as an interest group brings benefits such as political influence (that brings a more sympathetic legal and fiscal environment), economies of scale in education and training, a wider sense of community with similar banks, and a common business strategy. Integration as a business group enables cost-effective provision of common services such as IT support, data processing, training, accounting, marketing, product development and representation. It also provides the opportunity to develop a common brand. If the integration reaches the stage of having a central bank, this enables the group to centralise excess liquidity, redistribute it, place surpluses in financial markets, and run a consolidated asset-liability management policy (di Salvo, 2003). It also enables the setting up or purchase of subsidiaries to offer insurance, asset management, investment banking and information technology expertise that local banks could not afford.

The central also cuts down on risk. Local banks have the disadvantage of serving a homogeneous, locally based clientele, but the centrals can expand the range of business, thus making the group's collective income more stable. In highly integrated groups they share risks through various mechanisms such as common deposit insurance or a central fund for liquidity support. Frequently, the federal body is granted supervisory powers that provide a common set of standards for local banks to aspire to. It also provides management consultancy and training that keeps up the quality of local banking. The centrals may also represent a risk if they diverge from the customer-ownership business model and pursue other objectives. Over-centralisation may also damage the autonomy of the local banks and compromise their ability to respond to local needs (Ayadi et al., 2010).

Note that among building societies in the UK there is no central bank, which means that when a society gets into trouble support has to come from one of its neighbours; it has to merge with another society. However, during the banking crisis in some cases this has not been enough, and new methods have been found to raise the necessary capital, such as mergers, the issue of preference shares or even the handing over of the business to a joint venture with the member share being held in a holding company. This is a weakness, as it means gradually a few large, national-level societies have predominated and localness has gone.

DISADVANTAGES DERIVED FROM (DILUTED) OWNERSHIP

These are just some of the arguments that have been made for the advantages of customer-owned banks (see Table 7.1 for a summary). However, these rely on the banks being able to realise their potential. They are also affected by the comparative advantages of other types of bank, which also may or may not be realised. There may be disadvantages from customer ownership that outweigh the advantages, and these will be considered next, again in relation to the three key elements of ownership, control and benefit.

1.   Ownership May Not Be Very Rewarding

Customer-owned banks tend to be owned by large numbers of people, each having a small, often nominal shareholding. Traditionally, cooperatives have set the shareholding at a low level so as to encourage poorer people to join. They have not rewarded this shareholding with anything other than a nominal interest rate, and when they leave members receive par value for it. Sometimes, in order to raise more capital, they offer loan stock (also known as preferred shares or B stock) that does not carry voting rights and is rewarded with fixed interest. This is all according to cooperative principles that have been carefully drawn so as to emphasise

Table 7.1   *The advantages and disadvantages of customer-owned banks to their members*

Derivation	Advantages	Disadvantages
Ownership	– prevents market failure – prevents conflict of interest between owners and customers – provides an efficient, low-cost model of banking – provides no incentives to risk-taking	– ownership may not be very rewarding – ownership is only partial – it may be difficult to incentivise managers – it is difficult to manage capital
Control	– guarantees advantages from member-ownership – aligns interests of members with those of boards and managers – lowers risk-taking so makes the business more durable – provides informational advantages to the bank, enabling it to lend to lower income groups – increases opportunities to pursue ethical aims as well as shareholder value – has intrinsic value to members who enjoy taking part and having a sense of control	– governance problems (see Chapter 8)
Benefit	– channels the value added to members rather than to investors – provides convenience of a more extensive branch network – provides access to banking facilities in remote areas – provides relationship banking to SMEs	– effective government regulation cuts down on benefits versus the investor-owned model – competition leads to isomorphism or greater risk-taking
Federation	– varies with degree and type of integration – provides economies of scale in purchasing, information and communications technology (ICT), marketing, training, product development – provides political influence – provides a common brand – provides ability to manage liquidity – enables mutual guarantees against risk and internal supervision, and so on	– problems managing the relationship between local and central banks – centrals getting out of control via subsidiaries and joint ventures – locals having to accept the discipline of common standards and brands

the primacy of users over investors, but it means ownership is not directly rewarding (Birchall, 1997, Ch. 7).

2. Ownership Is Only Partial

In addition, part of the ownership is held in common and so current members cannot appropriate it. Managers are custodians of this endowment, and current customer members can use it. This is a major challenge to the governance system, since it reduces the members' incentive to oversight, while increasing the need for it. As a result, members may be reluctant to subscribe more capital and so the bank has to raise money through building up reserves or taking on debt. Members only have weak financial incentives to take part in governance, and the low level of member investment can lead to lack of loyalty to the business. If the reserves become larger than they need to be to finance the business strategy, or if the potential value of the business in the shares market is much higher than the realisable value to the members, they will have an incentive to unlock the potential value by converting to investor-ownership or selling the business.

3. The Business Model May Not Be Able to Incentivise Managers

One disadvantage is that in a competitive market for bank managers, customer-owned banks are disadvantaged. Investor-owned banks can align the interests of their managers with those of the shareholders by issuing performance-related share options. On the other hand, in the customer-owned banks employees are more likely to be involved in decision-making, they have higher job security, and the chance to work in their own region or community. They are close to the customers culturally, share in the profits and receive valuable training (Fonteyne, 2007). In general, they do have flatter pay scales, so it is more difficult to attract talent. It helps that they have subsidiaries that are investor-owned, because here they can hire the best staff. However, after the banking crisis these supposed disadvantages become quite ironic; the lack of incentives for managers to take risks so as to increase the share price, and the lack of expertise in sophisticated markets can now be seen as advantages of the customer-owned business model!

4. It is Difficult to Manage Capital

In a crisis, investor-owned banks can raise capital by issuing new shares, but cooperatives cannot do this. For this reason, in the Swedish banking crisis of the early 1990s the cooperative banks were demutualised. On the other hand, if the crisis is sufficiently serious no banks can raise capital and they have to be bailed out by governments. Cooperative capital is stable. But is it equity or is it a liability? In 2004, the International Accounting Standards Board clarified this by allowing member shares to be classified as equity when there are restrictions on their withdrawal. This is important, but it does not add to the stock of capital. There are other ways of raising funds from members. Rabobank is particularly disadvantaged by having no member equity at all (membership is free), but it gets round this by issuing deeply subordinated shares to members via a joint stock entity on which dividends can be paid. Many of the Italian Banche Popolari have a mix of member and investor shares, with a quotation on the stock exchange. However, this causes controversy, as investors have to be paid at a much higher rate than the members. Elsewhere there are legal restrictions on the amount that can be paid out on member shares. For instance, in Switzerland Raiffeisen can only pay up to 6 per cent. In Italy the credit cooperatives are required to add 79 per cent of annual profits to reserves and 3 per cent to a solidarity fund, which does not leave much left to reward the member shares.

This inability to raise capital easily affects prospects for growth. Organic growth is possible through reserves, but big acquisitions have to be paid out of debt or through joint stock subsidiaries. However, as we have already noted, a buffer of reserves is a good thing! Low payout ratios are also a good thing. But if the bank has an excess capital base there is a temptation to expand into unfamiliar business areas just to make use of it. Other banks face shortages and have to issue non-voting equity shares. As Ayadi et al. note in their report on European cooperative banks,

> co-operatives face fundamental challenges in managing their capital. They cannot shed excess capital, fully rely on the capital they have, or raise capital as needed, especially in times of crisis as they need it (Ayadi et al., 2010, p. 48).

On the other hand, experts agree that the knowledge that capital cannot easily be replaced acts as a check on risky behaviour. After the banking crisis, this lack of access to outside capital can be seen as a strength not a weakness.

5.   Customer-owned Banks May Be Less Profitable Than Their Competitors

Ayadi and her colleagues (2010) have reviewed the evidence and found that cooperative banks tend to operate more or less as efficiently as commercial banks. However, one common finding in the literature is that they are more cost-efficient but less profitable. The evidence is mixed on whether low profits are due to operational inefficiencies, a lack of capital market discipline or simply an unwillingness to enhance current profits by giving up customer value. Are we to take this disadvantage seriously? Not if we consider the dual bottom line with which cooperatives operate. The purpose of the business is not to maximise profits but to maximise returns to members.

DISADVANTAGES DERIVED FROM LACK OF CONTROL (GOVERNANCE PROBLEMS)

The attenuated ownership rights described above lead some commentators to predict problems of governance in cooperatives because their members are not incentivised to participate. Also, the growth in size of banks and their tendency to form very large, complex federal bodies militate against direct participation. Deposit insurance has made the banks less risky and so the incentive of members to monitor them is diminished. In developed countries, though the tasks of providing a safe haven for savings and the opportunity to borrow have stayed the same, the nature of the communities that the banks serve has changed enormously. We will be pursuing the issue of governance in Chapter 9.

DISADVANTAGES DERIVED FROM (LACK OF) BENEFIT

Under conditions of market failure the advantages of customer-owned banks to their members tend to be obvious. However, if governments step in to regulate markets, or if markets that were failing have become more free (sometimes as a consequence of the action of cooperatives, sometimes as a policy of economic liberalisation) then it will be difficult for customer-owned banks to justify their existence over investor-ownership. During times of intense competition, the dual bottom line tips over in favour of profitability, and cooperatives will emphasise this aspect in order to survive. Through competition there is a tendency towards 'isomorphism', that is, to copy the business techniques of other types of bank, so that they become indistinguishable from each other. If competition is intense and profitability declines, customer-owned banks may go further and neglect their core business in favour of more profitable, and riskier, opportunities, such as setting up branches in other countries or going into investment banking. During times of crisis, though, the cooperative business model shows its advantages and we can expect customers to find membership more attractive. The disadvantages that come from a perceived lack of benefit are, therefore, more apparent during the good times than the bad.

DISADVANTAGES FROM FEDERATION

The benefits of federation are obvious. However, there is a down side, as was seen in the recent crisis where centrals in some countries lost very large amounts of money in unsafe investments. The systematic nature of the federation means that primary banks have to make up the losses. More generally, there is a problem in managing the relationship between the centre and the periphery. It causes new *agency problems* in the relationship between local and national representatives and managers. In highly integrated systems the central institutions have stronger incentives than local banks to safeguard mutual resources, such as a shared brand name, or a pooled reserve fund. The locals may resent their lack of autonomy. The most successful systems, such as Desjardins Group in Canada, have managed to balance these different interests.

THE BENEFITS TO THE BANKING SYSTEM

So far we have been identifying the advantages to members, but there are wider benefits to the banking system in general from having a customer-owned banking sector. The most obvious one is the diversity that different types of ownership bring to a market sector. From an evolutionary point of view,

> the ability of society as a whole to respond to changing conditions depends on the responsiveness of its constituent organisations and on the diversity of its organisational populations (Hannan and Freeman, 1989, p. 3).

Diversity is important because it affects the capacity of a society to respond to uncertain future changes. Different types of banks are a 'repository of alternative solutions to the problem of producing sets of collective outcomes' (Hannan and Freeman, 1989, p. 7). If we see the global economy as a kind of evolutionary, adaptive system then we can expect one type of business to thrive at the expense of another. However, if one type dies out completely then the stock of existing solutions will have declined. This almost happened with the UK building societies in the 1990s, but around

30 per cent of the sector survived and, as we have noted in Chapter 5, they are now showing that they have some inherent advantages over investor-owned banks. They are more risk-averse and so more trusted by consumers for relatively simple transactions such as residential mortgages and savings, and they have built-in advantages from not having to remunerate a separate group of shareholders (Drake and Llewellyn, 2001).

Research carried out by Which in 2001 estimated that if every remaining building society had converted, the costs to consumers would have added up to £30 billion over ten years (cited in All-Party Parliamentary Group, 2006, p. 16). Nationwide Building Society, in its evidence to a parliamentary enquiry, said

> Not only does our presence in the market, challenging the banks in savings, mortgages and retail banking, help provide a competitive benchmark, but we also believe we champion the interests of all consumers and keep the banks under scrutiny to ensure transparency and fairness (cited in All-Party Parliamentary Group, 2006, p. 16).

An international study carried out in 2003 backs up this point. It found that the size of the mutual sector in most countries had a direct influence on the size of the banks' profits, finding that 'the profitability of the banking sector is inversely proportional to the market share of mutuals within the banking sector' (All-Party Parliamentary Group, 2006, p. 17). In a comparison of the cost of mortgages across Europe, low prices were largely associated with a strong mutual share of the market. For each 10 per cent of the market taken by mutuals, the average customer was found to receive a benefit of around ten basis points per year (cited in All-Party Parliamentary Group, 2006, p. 17).

The benefits of diversity are not just the preserve of customer-owned banks. The savings banks also have a distinct business model. They are not really owned by anyone, but trustees hold them on behalf of the public interest. We will be investigating their relative advantages and disadvantages in Chapter 8. Another advantage of customer-ownership is greater stability in the financial sector. The stability and low level of risk that we have already identified as advantages for members also have implications for the public interest. Countries where the cooperative model is strong are less badly affected during a crisis than countries where the model is absent. Another advantage to the wider economy is the smoothing of the economic cycle. If banks create reserves during the upturn in the economic cycle they can release these during a downturn and help avoid recession. Investor-owned banks have no incentive to do this, and they tend to reward their owners (and managers) excessively during the good times and then ask for bailouts when the going gets tough. As the current Spanish banking crisis illustrates, this is also true of savings banks that are owned by nobody but controlled by politicians. The bursting of a property bubble in Spain has been made worse by the banks continuing to lend on dubious surety so as to delay the downturn. If we have banks that are prepared to create reserves in good times and unlock them in bad times, this becomes a public good.

As Ayadi et al. (2010) explain, there is a conflict between what is optimal for the entire economy and what is optimal for a bank's owners and managers. For the owners of an individual bank, disclosing and selling its reserves in good times is always more profitable than keeping them. They have a fiduciary duty to maximise profit for shareholders, and they are also under pressure to keep up the price of their shares in the stock market. It would be socially valuable if bank managers and owners were not interested in disclosing and selling the reserves they may have built up. Allen and Gale (2000) argue that this is the case with savings banks, public banks and cooperative banks; they are not just profit-oriented, and because of their institutional and legal design they cannot be sold at their full value. Thus, their managers can be expected to create reserves in good times and unlock them if there is a need to do so.

CONTRIBUTION TO LOCAL ECONOMIES

There are several advantages of customer-owned banks to local economies, particularly in low-income countries and disadvantaged regions of higher-income countries. The most obvious advantage is financial deepening, the ability to provide people on low incomes with banking services they would otherwise not be able to access. Without a safe place to put their savings and the chance to borrow, the poor are locked into that same cycle of poverty that so challenged Raiffeisen and Schulze in Germany in the 1840s. This affects not just them but the whole local economy of which they are a part.

Another advantage derives from the main purpose of the banks as an intermediary enabling saving and lending. Sometimes savings banks gather up savings from within a local economy but invest them outside in government bonds, or they gather savings from rural areas and invest them in faster-growing urban areas. In contrast, customer-owned banks foster local economic development by mobilising savings, and lending these out to individuals, families, farmers and small businesses in the same area. The provision of banking services in less well-populated areas also helps to stabilise the local economy by persuading people to remain in the area. The banks' ability to develop real relationships in the long term with local businesses is absolutely crucial, as it enables them to lend at low risk to people that other banks would not touch. They also provide a tax base for local government. Because they belong to their local communities, they are not going to leave and reinvest in more profitable areas.

Ayadi et al. have reviewed evidence from several studies that show cooperative banks in Europe have had such a positive effect on local economies. Their own research shows that they have a significant pro-growth impact in Austria, Finland, Germany and the Netherlands. In Germany they have a self-reinforcing effect; more growth enhances activity, which in turn increases growth further. In Austria and the Netherlands, however, a different pro-growth dynamic is at play: cooperatives continue to operate in areas experiencing low growth and so help to limit the damage (Ayadi et al., 2010). One reason why cooperative banks have this effect is that they are particularly good at lending to SMEs in the locality in which they are based.

Another important advantage to local communities is the way financial cooperatives enable the sending home of remittances from migrant workers. They are very important in Latin America, where in six countries they amount to more than 10 per cent of GDP. They contribute to the standard of living of some of the poorest people in the most remote areas. Without the remittance system organised by WOCCU, they have to rely on sending money by human couriers, or by post, or by commercial money senders that charge high fees. It began in 1995, when WOCCU helped a credit union in California to send money transfers to unions in El Salvador (Birchall, 2004). Now the international remittance system transfers vast amounts; in 2006, \$267 billion was sent worldwide, of which \$61 billion went to Latin America (WOCCU, 2012b).

Perhaps the most important advantage to wider communities is the loans given to support local businesses. Take the situation in North America, for instance. In Canada, the English-speaking credit union sector is the second largest lender to small businesses, with a market share of 18.3 per cent. In the Quebec region, Desjardins has a 27.9 per cent share of business credit, including 26.5 per cent in the SME segment and a 42.7 per cent share of agricultural financing. Desjardins is large enough to have its own venture capital subsidiary, which partners with 300 businesses, helping maintain nearly 35000 jobs (Desjardins, 2012a). In the USA, business lending is limited to 12.25 per cent of total lending for most unions, though loans of less than \$50,000 are not counted against this limit. Particularly important are the community development credit unions that serve low-income, minority and other excluded populations.

The evidence for the effects of financial cooperatives in developing countries is also impressive. Projects that are designed to strengthen the cooperatives can use the same network to provide agricultural extension, small business development, micro-insurance, and value chain work with farmers. The aim is to integrate the provision of credit with a wider goal of increasing people's incomes. They have to make sure that they do not undermine people's discipline in paying back loans, by resisting the temptation to pour donor funds into the cooperative. If they keep the core savings and loan function separate, then the wider approach works well. We have to recognise that credit alone does not solve the problems of small farmers and micro-entrepreneurs.

CONCLUSION

This listing of the advantages and disadvantages of customer-owned banks shows that on balance the advantages far outweigh the disadvantages. Yet they are more than just a list; they all act together in a systemic way that amplifies the individual advantages. As a recent Rabobank report describes it, a high level of market share in savings, high capital buffers, mutual support mechanisms and long-term strategies combine to create a strong alternative-banking model (Rabobank, 2011). Taken together, these advantages to customer-members and to the wider society should lead to governments creating a sympathetic regulatory system. However, the regulators are often ignorant of the customer-owned bank model and regulate as if it were investor-owned. The regulator may push them to provide a similar return on equity as investor-owned banks, and this may lead to more risky activities (Fonteyne, 2007). Inappropriate supervision and regulation can push them off course, making it harder for them to build on their inherent advantages. This is a subject we will be exploring further in Chapter 9, but first we need to find out if other types of bank also have the same advantages.

8.   Some alternatives: savings banks and micro-finance institutions

Before we accept at face value the argument put in the last chapter, we need to test it out against a strong counter-argument. The *focus on customer-ownership may be misguided*; there may be other ways of achieving the same ends that include some but not all of the features of cooperative banks, credit unions and building societies. A recent report by Ayadi and her colleagues (2009) distinguishes between banks that have a single bottom line, focusing on short-term profit at the expense of everything else, and banks that have a dual bottom line, focusing on profit but also on social goals. They do not distinguish between customer-owned and non-customer owned banks, but between *stakeholder rather than shareholder owned* banks. There are strong similarities between cooperative banks and savings banks. They are both organised in networks of affiliated, but decentralised, organisations. They are not set up to maximise profit but to provide a service; the customer-owned banks serve their members, the savings banks, the local economy. Thus they are both 'stakeholder banks' (Ayadi et al., 2010; Cuevas and Fischer, 2006).

How useful is this approach when compared to the customer-ownership approach taken in this book? To find out we have to investigate the savings bank model further. What is a savings bank? It is a business whose primary purpose is to provide a safe place for people's savings. It is not mutual, as it is not owned directly by the depositors. It is, as Hansmann describes it, a 'non-owned' institution (1996), which is why its ownership structure is hard to describe. As usual in complex business organisations, a board of directors governs it but they are not elected directly from among the owners. There are two types of ownership structure, depending on whether the bank's constitution is private or public. In the private type, ownership is held 'in trust' by some or all of the board members who are designated as trustees. They oversee the organisation on behalf of a wider constituency who take no part in governance. They are effectively self-perpetuating, as new board members are invited to join as they are needed. In the public type, a wider group of 'members' are the owners, and they elect the board. This wider group are elected or appointed by other bodies that have a recognised interest. They are there to represent employers, employees, depositors, local or central government.

In Germany, for instance, the savings bank is a public law institution with no private owner. Two-thirds of its executive board are appointed by the local municipality and one-third elected by the employees. In Norway the committee of representatives consists of employees, depositors, public appointees and holders of primary capital certificates. In Spain a general assembly is formed from stakeholders, including employees, representatives of depositors, local and regional government, founding entities and community interest groups. In order to prevent the bank being 'captured' by politicians, public bodies are limited to no more than 50 per cent of voting rights (Manghetti, 2011). The opaque and uncertain nature of the ownership and control structure of savings banks is a weakness that has made them – at various times and places – vulnerable to conversion into investor-owned or publicly owned banks.

The origins of the idea are disputed, as it seems to have evolved at around the same time in several countries. In France a savings bank was established in 1765 in the town of Brumuth. There was one in Hamburg, Germany, in 1778, in Berne, Switzerland, in 1787 and in England in 1799. In 1810 a bank was founded in Ruthwell, Scotland. By 1816 the idea had reached the USA with the founding of a bank in Boston, from where it spread rapidly to Baltimore, New York, and other east coast cities. The listing of places and dates does not make for a very interesting story, and so the founding of the savings bank movement is generally credited to the Reverend Henry Duncan, minister of Ruthwell in south-west Scotland. He 'invented' the savings bank under circumstances that were remarkably similar to those that stimulated Raiffeisen and Schulze a few decades later. When he became minister of Ruthwell he immediately began trying to improve the lot of his desperately poor parishioners, buying flax for women to spin in their cottages and employing men to turn his land into a model farm or to work on the roads. He revived a local friendly society and imported grain at wholesale prices. Then he decided to set up a parish bank. He laid his plans well, first founding a local newspaper through which he could argue the case and recruit supporters. Local landowners backed him readily; they liked the idea that the poor could save to meet future needs because they would then not be so dependent on parish poor relief.

Duncan had rare talents. He had spent three years working in a bank in Liverpool before deciding to become a minister, and so he combined both the impulse for philanthropy and business experience. The idea was simple. People could open a savings account with just six pence. Deposits were held at a local commercial bank where they received 5 per cent interest, the savers receiving back 4 per cent. The remaining 1 per cent was used to provide a charity fund, tiered interest for long-term savers and a sum for administering the bank. Duncan ran the bank himself, and instead of taking a salary used the money due to him to build a school in the parish. The business model was easy to replicate. Within five years of the first bank opening, there were savings banks throughout the UK. The following year they began to spread to Europe and the United States. During that first year at Ruthwell, the total savings amounted to £151. Ten years later in the United Kingdom the total had reached over £3 million (Lloyds TSB, 2012).

The history of this form took a new direction with the founding of a postal savings bank in England in 1861. From then onwards governments began to take an interest, and the linking of postal services with savings became common. Depending on their origins, the banks reflected either the influence of private philanthropy or state sponsorship. Gradually, savings banks expanded from the focus on savings to become providers of retail banking in general. Like the cooperative banks and credit unions they developed a decentralised distribution network and focused on areas of the country that were otherwise unbanked. In continental Europe, like the cooperative banks, they now have a significant market share (see Table 8.1). The latest figures are from 2006 and some countries do not supply market share, but the general conclusion must be that in several European countries these banks are a serious alternative to investor-owned and cooperative banks.

In size of assets they are strongest in Germany and Spain. In Germany, the savings bank finance group has 431 *sparkassen* in membership. They are independent local banks with shareholders who are mainly local authorities. Along with government, they are part owners of a set of seven *landesbanks* that do commercial banking and provide the sparkassen with central services. In Spain there are 46 *cajas de ahorras* that have competed successfully with the investor-owned and cooperative banks so that they now have over half of the market. They are private foundations but there is a lot of political influence in the way they are governed. They have recently undergone a drastic reorganisation through mergers into a much smaller number of cajas.

This model has spread from Europe throughout the world. The World Savings Banks Institute is the global representative trade body for what it describes as 'savings and retail' banking, representing 'savings and socially committed retail banks or associations thereof' worldwide (WSBI, 2012). It has 113 members in 90 countries, divided into 37 members in 31 countries in Africa, 23 members in 15 countries in the Asia Pacific region, 37 members in 30 countries in Europe, and 16 members in 13 countries in

Table 8.1   Savings banks, top ten by market share of assets in 2006

Country	Name	Market share of assets (%)	Market share of non-bank deposits (%)	Market share of non-bank loans (%)	No. of savings banks
Germany	Sparkassen Finanzgruppe	35.5	38.7	38.1	474
Spain	Confederacion Espanola de Cajas de Ahorros	39	50	46.9	46
Malta	Bank of Valletta plc	41.2	46	37.1	1
Portugal	Associacao Portuguesa de Bancos de Poupanca e Caixas Economicas	27.2	34.9	27.2	3
Russia	Sberbank	26.5	Not provided	Not provided	1
Slovakia	Slovenska Sporiteina AS	18.2	21	Not provided	1
Austria	Osterriechischer Sparkassenverband	17.5	17.3	17.2	57
Czech Republic	Ceska sporiteina as	22.1	22.6	23	1
Hungary	Orszagos Takaarekpenztar (OTP)	17.6	20.7	13.2	1
Bulgaria	DSK Bank plc	13.6	Not provided	16.2	1
EU total		19	24.7	21.2	951

Source: ESBG (2012), reordered and simplified.

the Americas. In form it is similar to the World Council of Credit Unions, but without the latter's social mission and conviction that there is one model of banking; the institute is quite an eclectic grouping, reflecting the diverse origins of this type of bank. Out of 113 members, at least 22 are postal banks, several others are clearly national state-owned savings banks, while others are state development banks. The Lloyds Banking Group in the UK is a member despite being investor-owned, presumably because it inherits some of the savings bank tradition in its 'TSB' arm (WSBI, 2012).

The savings bank model has been vulnerable to conversion into other types. In Italy in 1990 they were converted to investor-ownership, while in France in 1999 they became part of the cooperative sector. In the UK during the 1980s nearly all the savings banks were merged into the Trustee

Savings Bank (TSB) that was then sold by the government to Lloyds Banking Group. The TSB part of the group has now been sold on to the Co-operative Bank. In Germany during the 1990s there was a great deal of pressure for the savings banks and their second tier of landesbanks to be privatised, as they were seen as being publicly owned. They fought off these attempts, but the EU insisted on government ending its guarantees to the landesbanks because it was seen as unfair competition. In Spain, the pressure has been not so much to convert the banks but to limit the amount of influence politicians can have in their governance; this is now down to 50 per cent. The uncertain ownership structure of the savings banks can be a disadvantage, leading in some cases to much greater instability than we find in the cooperative banks.

PERFORMANCE OF THE SAVINGS BANKS BEFORE AND DURING THE FINANCIAL CRISIS

Before the crisis, studies of the comparative performance of European savings banks with cooperative and investor-owned banks showed no significant differences. Ayadi et al. summed up their study by saying 'their financial performance is not inferior, and possibly even superior to that of other types of banks' (Ayadi et al., 2009, p. 12). A summary of the evidence undertaken by Manghetti (2011) also shows they had no significant difference in performance compared with other banks. However, they did show some serious weaknesses. He shows that European Savings Group market shares grew over the ten years to 2007 in France, Spain, the Netherlands and Sweden, were stable in Germany, declined slightly in the UK but declined drastically in Italy, Belgium and Austria. Most savings banks registered a constant relative decline in direct deposits. In some countries they disappeared, while in others they joined large financial groups.

During the boom years, according to European supervisory authorities they had several weaknesses. They had a structural weakness in governance, with insufficient division of internal authority; this was the same weakness as investor-owned banks showed before the crisis. There was a contradiction between their short-term commercial targets and their longer-term social aims. There was a structural weakness in capital, and so a lack of stability; it was difficult to attract private investors, so their capital increased less than their assets. Their activity was concentrated in long-term investments such as mortgages and loans to the real estate sector, which carried dangers if the property market were to collapse. The traditional funding strength from retail deposits was not enough to tackle

Finance in an age of austerity

liquidity risks. Manghetti (2011) found that in some countries, such as Norway and Italy, they were able to compete by respecting the old values, but in Spain they did not respect their lending principles.

These are serious charges, and unfortunately during the crisis they have been shown to be true. At first, reports were optimistic. Ayadi et al. (2009) said the current financial crisis had affected the savings banks less than most other banks. They predicted that this 'crisis resistance' would improve their image and serve to strengthen political support. Their explanation for the stability of the savings banks was that, like the cooperatives, they had stuck to their traditional business model. However, the German savings banks were indirectly affected by the crisis because they were co-owners of the regional banks (*landesbanken*). The landesbanks were in trouble from the start. Sachsen, the regional state-owned bank in Saxony, had to be rescued by a consortium of savings banks with a loan of $23.3 billion, and there was a similar bailout of IKB Deutsche Industriebank. Then, as the crisis got worse, several more had to take state aid. They had been caught out by the collapse of the market in securities backed by sub-prime mortgages, and were caught holding a lot of US sub-prime debt. However, they were not just victims of an American-led disaster. They had actually pioneered the use of off-balance-sheet conduits since 1998. They had had government guarantees that had enabled them to borrow more cheaply than other banks; they got high ratings, and so could take big risks.

In 2001 the EU insisted the government withdraw these guarantees, and by 2005 they had been phased out. However, critics charged that the banks had continued to act in the same way, partly out of habit, partly in order to compete with the investor-owned banks. They did not have the experience to assess these risky securities, partly because their boards had a high proportion of politicians on them. Their losses were 43 per cent of the total losses incurred by German banks, and almost double their market share based on total assets. The prescription for recovery is that the landesbanks should develop a closer relationship with the savings banks, offering banking services to SMEs and providing them with the kind of services that DZ provides to the cooperative banks.

In Spain, the cajas were badly hit by the crisis, because they had lent extensively to the residential and commercial property markets in a bubble that burst. In 2009 there began a major reform to tackle excessive fragmentation, excess capacity in branches and staffing, and write-downs of balance-sheet losses of €52 billion. They needed a bailout to replace the lost capital, and 38 banks merged, reducing the numbers from 45 to 17 (Manghetti, 2011).

Then in 2011 a different kind of crisis occurred in South Korea. Here, there are around 100 savings banks that cater for low to middle-income people. They only have about 2 per cent of the market, and so the turmoil has not threatened the rest of the economy, but the crisis does illustrate some of the weaknesses of the model. Seven banks were suspended due to their weak financial standing; they had been caught out by heavy exposure to another declining real estate market. The government has closed several banks and is in the process of selling others. There are allegations that executives made payments to government officials to avoid or delay closures and restructuring, but now the bigger banks have stepped in to take them over. Now there are stricter lending rules, and the regulator wants savings banks to return to providing financial services to low-income individuals and small businesses rather than extending loans for risky construction projects. Critics say they focused on growth while ignoring their role as finance providers for the working class (Lee, 2012).

A SYSTEMATIC COMPARISON

Table 8.2 provides a summary of the advantages and disadvantages of savings banks to their customers. The list is similar to that provided for customer-owned banks in Table 7.1. The obvious differences are in bold, and this shows graphically that there are many more similarities than differences. However, the differences are important. As we have argued above, the problems of governance have proved to be more acute, with recent savings bank failures in Spain and Korea. As we have already noted, if customer-owned banks do not involve their customers in governance they are de facto non-profits, and almost indistinguishable from savings banks. The differences between the two business models are only shown up in sharp relief when the customer-owned banks really capitalise on the strengths that come from membership.

The advantages of savings banks to the wider society are similar to those of customer-owned banks. They also contribute to local economies and help to smooth out economic cycles. Their greater vulnerability to risk-taking means that they may not provide as much stability in the financial sector as do the customer-owned banks. The strongest argument in their favour is the argument for diversity. In his foreword to a study of savings banks, David Llewellyn says

> It is economically and socially beneficial to have dual-bottom line financial institutions. It is the mix of different types of institutions that is as important (if not more so) than the merits of any particular ownership structure or business model (Foreword to Ayadi et al., 2009, p. 5).

Table 8.2   The advantages and disadvantages of savings banks to their customers

Derivation	Advantages	Disadvantages
Ownership	– prevents market failure – prevents conflict of interest between owners and customers – provides an efficient, low-cost model of banking	**– unclear who owns the bank** – difficult to incentivise managers – difficult to manage capital **– incentives to risk-taking if governed by politicians!**
Control	**Customers have limited control**	– governance problems (see Chapter 9)
Benefit	– channels the value added to customers rather than to investors – provides convenience of a more extensive branch network – provides access to banking facilities in remote areas – provides relationship banking to SMEs	– effective government regulation cuts down on benefits versus the investor-owned model – competition leads to isomorphism or greater risk-taking **– appropriation hazard – governors take the benefits?**
Federation	– provides economies of scale in purchasing, ICT, marketing, training, product development – provides political influence – provides a common brand – provides ability to manage liquidity – enables mutual guarantees against risk and internal supervision, and so on	– problems managing the relationship between local and central banks – centrals getting out of control via subsidiaries and joint ventures – locals having to accept the discipline of common standards and brands

Note: Differences from customer-owned banks are in bold.

This means that we should value both cooperative banks and savings banks as valid ways of doing business that do not just have intrinsic advantages but contribute to an *eco-system* of banking. Diversity ensures stability because different types of bank respond differently to their environment, and have their own distinctive goals and occupational cultures. From this point of view the market share of one type of stakeholder-owned bank is not as important as the diversity that each type brings to the sector.

THE DISCOVERY OF MICRO-FINANCE

Mohammed Yunus discovered the importance of credit to poor people in the same way that Schulze and Raiffeisen did, by observing the lives of the poor at first hand. As a professor at Chittagong University in Bangladesh, he began his work with an intimate study of a neighbouring village, Jobra. As he explains in his autobiography,

> I decided I would become a student all over again, and Jobra would be my university. The people of Jobra would be my teachers (Yunus, 1999, p. 5).

He realised that the cause of their poverty was that moneylenders had trapped them in a system of abuse that kept them in poverty. It worked in different ways. There were usurers who charged high interest rates on loans. Then there were traders who advanced loans against standing crops with the right to buy the crop at a predetermined price that was lower than the market rate. There were middlemen who supplied materials to craftspeople who then sold the product back at a predetermined price; in one case a woman made bamboo stools that, when the trader had bought them, left her two US cents a day to live on. One method of repaying was to work for the creditor as a bonded labourer, which is a kind of slavery. When land was advanced against a loan, if the borrower was late with a payment the creditor had the right to buy the land at a predetermined price.

Yunus was amazed by the small size of the loans that had this effect, and by the inability of the formal banking system to meet people's modest needs. He was convinced, as were Schulze and Raiffeisen before him, that people remained poor not because they were stupid or lazy but because 'the financial structures that could help them widen their economic base simply did not exist' (Yunus, 1999, p. 11). He also realised that they had the best possible reason to pay back a loan; they might need another loan in the future, and being so close to subsistence their need would be serious. In 1976 he lent $27 to 42 people in the village but realised that this was not enough; the problem needed an institutional rather than a personal response. After much experimentation, in 1983 the Grameen micro-credit system began. It was an outstanding success. By 1998, $2.3 billion was being lent to 2.3 million families, and the system was being replicated in 58 countries worldwide. In banking terms, it worked because the costs were not excessive, and the default rate of less than 1 per cent was much lower than for conventional bank lending. Grameen had found a way of enabling financial deepening that conventional banks could not match, and that could be replicated with only minor variations in many different countries.

There were several new elements. Business was done through a small group of members who monitored and stood guarantee for each other's loans, rather than on an individual basis. The loans could only be accessed by women, or by men through their womenfolk. This is because women had proved much more reliable both at making a living and spending it on the family, particularly benefitting children. The organisation was not split down into autonomous local societies that then federated at national level, but remained one national bank with branches. The emphasis was on seeking out the very poor, and not mixing them in with better-off members as credit unions do. It also made use of a wider range of business types, including investor-owned subsidiaries and NGOs; both Raiffeisen and Schulze set up supply and marketing associations as separate coopera-tives, so that in comparison their systems could be seen as more purely cooperative.

The Grameen system proved to be astonishingly successful in Bangladesh; by 1995 it had over two million member-borrowers, nearly all of them poor women, in over 30 000 villages. It was replicated all around the world, but then some development specialists began to find flaws in it. Their evaluations showed that programmes were donor-driven, interest rates were inadequate, costs were very high, and savings mobilisation was weak. The gap between high and low performing programmes was wide. They largely depended on donor funding and, unlike other alternatives such as cooperative banks and credit unions, never became sustainable. This meant that even though they targeted poor women, they never reached enough of them to be successful (Seibel, 1998). When government was the donor, the governance structure did not provide any incentives to keep costs down or make profits, and politicians interfered, making politi-cal appointments and keeping interest rates too low. Once again, as in the so-called 'co-operative credit societies' in India and China, the bank was seen merely as a conduit for donor funding.

A catastrophic flood in Bangladesh in 1998 also caused a rethink. Even though 80 per cent of borrowers still paid on time, the bank lost touch with the other 20 per cent. The rigid set of rules for repayment had not taken into account the precarious life of the poor and the impact of natural disasters. The movement's motto changed from 'The poor will always pay back' to 'The poor will always pay back once their situation improves' (Dowla and Barua, 2006, p. 72). As soon as the bank introduced flexible loans, the debtors came back. A loan insurance programme was introduced, the bank moved away from group to individual loans, and products were extended to include retirement pensions and higher educa-tion loans. There was a new emphasis on savings, with open access savings accounts and incentives for branches to encourage more deposits (Dowla and Barua, 2006). The bank's leaders realised that if they were to become self-sufficient and independent of donor funding they needed to balance savings and loans, just as Raiffeisen had done 140 years before.

Is the Grameen bank a credit union? It has some features in common with Raiffeisen's system, being partly owned and controlled by its members through elected representatives. It focuses resolutely on savings and credit services within local economies, and does not stray far from narrow retail banking. Like Schulze, Yunus and his colleagues have set up separate companies to meet related needs such as for supply and marketing of textiles, but the reach of Grameen is wider, with initiatives in education and healthcare, and in new technologies such as cell phones and the internet. The values of the new movement are also similar to those of the old. There is an emphasis on the formation of moral character, the need for trust among members, and also a determination to remain politically neutral. This can be seen in the way Grameen in Bangladesh has managed its relationship with governments, aid agencies and the World Bank, though replications in other countries have not always been so independent.

We can illustrate some of these similarities and differences if we compare Grameen II to the Sanasa Movement in Sri Lanka. Sanasa has many similarities with this new version of Grameen, such as the emphasis on member education and self-sufficiency at the local level combined with careful acceptance of financial and technical help from aid agencies and NGOs. The movement has set up its own central bank and several subsidiaries. It has remained free of government influence, except in one instance in the 1980s when the government insisted Sanasa dispense funds from a national 'Million Houses' programme (Birchall and Simmons, 2013, forthcoming). This led to societies being set up just to get access to the loans, and for a time damaged the movement; only by rigorously grading societies by quality and closing down the bad ones could Sanasa recover. This story is similar to the story told by Yunus about a government policy in Bangladesh of giving housing loans. Grameen negotiated over the terms of this and was able to offer 'shelter' loans to its members without compromising the quality of its work (Yunus, 1999). Table 8.3 summarises some similarities and differences. Comparing Grameen I to Grameen II, we can see that the movement is becoming more and more like the credit union movement.

OTHER MICRO-FINANCE INSTITUTIONS

In the business of financial deepening, there are three main alternatives to member-owned credit unions: government-owned banks, NGOs

Table 8.3   Similarities and differences between Grameen Bank and Sanasa

Features	Grameen 1	Grameen 2	Sanasa
Purpose of the society	'Credit first'	Savings and credit	Savings and credit
Clientele	The very poor, women	Individuals	Individuals
Type of integration	National, with branches	National, with branches	Local to national in federation
Terms under which loans given	Group-based mutual guarantees	Individual contract	Individual contract, but common bond
Help from the aid industry	Reliance on donor and government funding	Attempt to become more self-reliant	Self-reliant, except for technical help
Ownership	Government + members	Government + members	Members only

and investor-owned banks (Table 8.4 summarises their characteristics). Government-owned banks can be effective, providing they are given commercial targets and made immune from political interference; Bank Rakyat (People's Bank) Indonesia is a good example.[1] It is 70 per cent government owned, and is the most profitable bank in Indonesia. It does not do group lending but targets a broad low-income market segment, with individual lending backed up by risk-assessment technology. It emphasises self-reliance through savings mobilisation, and full financial self-sufficiency (Seibel, 1998). However, examples of government-owned banks that serve the poor in an effective and sustainable way are few and far between. There is too much temptation for politicians to get involved, to fix interest rates, and make political appointments.

NGOs do not have a good reputation in micro-finance. In the words of one development expert 'They have come to be more tolerated than admired' (Fisher, 2002, p. 331). They have done useful and innovative work in small areas, but have found it difficult to scale up so as to have a wider impact, and have not been able to become financially self-sustaining. Fisher says:

> Many doubt the ability of NGOs to manage the provision of micro-financial services, and alternative organisational structures like financial companies and banks are regarded as preferable (Fisher, 2002, p. 331).

Table 8.4   Characteristics of different ownership types in micro-finance

Advantages	Credit unions	NGO micro-finance	Government banks	Investor-owned banks
Ability to reach the poorest	Medium – high if targeted	High – the main aim	Low – capture by elites?	Low – poor seen as risky
Ability to raise incomes	High – a main aim	Low – problems in scaling up	Low – unless well managed	Medium – creating wage employment
Ability to scale up	High – can grow rapidly	High – with donor support	Low – unless by imitation	Low – except by expansion
Sustainability	High, if democratic	Low, depends on donor funds	Depends on government priorities	Low, if not profitable
Organisational flexibility	Medium	High – but donor pressure	Low – depends on government	High – in search of profits
Governance rights	One member, one vote	Stakeholder based – like savings banks	Political appointment	Voting by level of investment
Democratic accountability	High – interests aligned	Varies – high to low depending on leaders	Low and erratic – clientalism	Low –poor alignment of interests
Attitude to profit	Distribution to members	Non-profit	Low priority	Distribution to investors
Identity of borrowers	Members	Clients	Citizens/voters	Customers
Savings or credit?	Both – in balance	Credit – but emphasis changing	Savings	Credit

However, NGOs are useful in working at a local level to help the emergence of financial cooperatives, and then to support the development of federations and apex cooperative banks.

Investor-owned micro-finance companies are becoming more popular. It might be expected that investors will be wary of lending money to people on low incomes because of the high risk of default. However, new computerised loan appraisal and risk management systems have cut down on the risk, and the high interest rates that such companies can charge make the return profitable. Lending tends to be restricted to small businesses, and there comes a point where high interest rates become usurious and we are back to where we started, with people being in debt to moneylenders.

CONCLUSION

In summarising the advantages and disadvantages of different types of bank and micro-finance institutions, a note of caution is needed. We should not fall into the trap of comparing an ideal model of one type with a realistic model of another (Groeneveld and Llewellyn, 2012). This is something that many economists have done in the past, and it has led them to favour the investor-owned model. In advocating for customer-owned banks we have to be careful not to make the same mistake. When we compare the actual workings of different types of bank we find that they all have problems with their governance. The aligning of the different interests of the providers of capital, the customers, the elected directors and the managers of any complex business organisation is difficult and unsatisfactory. When the public interest is taken into account as well, the problem just gets worse. We will be devoting part of the next chapter to this issue of governance.

NOTE

1. Not to be confused with Bank Rakyat Malaysia, which describes itself as a cooperative bank.

9. Regulation, governance and the need for member participation

Banks are regulated; they have to work within a legal and fiscal environment created by government, and are granted powers to do different kinds of banking. The regulator acts on behalf of the public, which includes looking after the interests of customers, but also the wider interest of citizens. Banks are also supervised in order to ensure compliance with the regulation, and also honesty and stability in the system. It can be done by governments if there is no alternative, but is better done by the sector itself, through audit unions and central federations. For self-supervision to become possible, it requires a mature movement that cedes real powers to the centre, that submits to the mutual disciplines of agreed rules and standards, and that contributes towards a mutual insurance fund that can be drawn on if things go wrong. Governance is the running of the business, which can mean either control over day-to-day decisions or strategic decision-making, depending on the level of competence and independence management has reached. Governance provides a strategic direction for the business, a check on managerial powers and representation of member interests. However, it does not guarantee the public interest; that is the job of government. In all but the most atomised of customer-owned banking sectors, governance works on two levels; the group as a whole and the individual primary society. Table 9.1 cross-references five levels of activity with the three types of cooperative sector suggested by Desrochers and Fischer (2005).

THE QUESTION OF SUPERVISION

For regulation to be effective there has to be effective on-going supervision of the banks. It is often assumed that governments will do this, but in Europe and North America there is a long tradition of government allowing cooperative bank groups to supervise themselves. The national or regional union supervises the primary banks, while they provide a governance structure that makes sure the central bank acts in their collective interest. The system tends to work well because the mutual guarantees

Table 9.1   Type of customer-owned banking system by type of regulation, supervision and governance

Type of system	Atomised	Consensual	Strategic
Government regulation	Strong involvement or neglect	Negotiation with apex federation	Apex body interacts to create environment
Government supervision	Strong involvement or neglect	Light touch	Given over to the apex body
Mutual supervision	Not much, except sharing of good practice	Audit federations	Supervision of primary societies by apex
System governance	Not applicable	Independent governance of primaries	Inter-dependent governance
Primary society governance	Of individual societies	Of individual societies plus central guidance	Levels permeate each other

they offer provide incentives for the primary banks to watch over each other, while the powers they give to the centre allow it to watch over them, and their representative governance structure allows them to keep control over the central bank. Governments recognise that the system is, to a large extent, homeostatic. Clearly, where self-monitoring works it is more efficient, but it requires strong member governance. It can also be more effective; the few outright failures that there have been in cooperative banks occurred during the 1980s in Argentina, Colombia and Peru under a regime of direct supervision.

Who pays for supervision? The short answer is that it is the supervised that should pay for it, since they are the beneficiaries. However, there is a public good involved, since everyone benefits from having a stable and safe banking system, particularly one that reaches down to the poor. For this reason, if the customer-owned sector cannot yet afford it, supervision can be subsidised by government or by donors, as in new sectors such as Vietnam and Poland. The main question is one of sustainability. Supervision is an on-going activity that is particularly unsuited to short-term project funding!

THE QUESTION OF GOVERNANCE

Regulation and supervision are about external relationships, while governance is about the internal relationships between members, the board and the managers. In customer-owned banks that are not fully mutual, they are also about the interests of customers who are not members. In the literature on corporate governance there is a tedious debate about the relative merits of cooperative versus investor-owned business models. It has usually sided with investor-ownership because of the supposed difficulties of getting a widely dispersed set of members to govern cooperatives, and because managers are less subject to the disciplines of the market. We do not really need to engage in this theoretical debate anymore; the banking crisis has seen to that. The investor-owned business model has failed! The secret is out: the banks operate only in the short-term interests of their shareholders and managers. However, we should not rush to the opposite side and argue from the theoretical advantages of customer-ownership.

Groeneveld and Llewellyn say:

> It is tendentious to compare the actual behaviour of a co-operative bank model with some mythical ideal form of shareholder value model . . . in practice both forms operate imperfectly and, in the world of the second best, no safe conclusions can be drawn regarding the superiority of one form over the other (2012, p. 7).

But customer-owned banks do have some built-in advantages. The dispersed ownership by members tends to lead to a longer-term orientation and a risk-averse view of the business. There is a focus on retail banking, on long-term relationships, and on putting the interests of members first. Customer-owned banks are better equipped to assess the creditworthiness of customers because they tend to be small and based in a particular locality. This means they tend to be stable, with good liquidity and sound asset quality. Because there is no separate group of investors needing attention, they aim to maximise customer value. They deliberately accumulate capital, which cannot be appropriated by anyone and should be seen as an intergenerational endowment. Managers are disciplined by member governance, but more powerfully by the need to compete in the market alongside other bank managers. Profit is a necessary condition but not a goal in itself, and local banks can exercise influence on their national banks and federations in order to keep the system working in the interests of its customer-members. Governance has a dual structure, with members having ownership rights over primary co-ops, and primaries over secondaries. Groeneveld and Llewellyn (2012) say that these are not just theoretical advantages in governance. In fact, the practice is more persuasive than the theory. Agency theorists have speculated that in a customer-owned bank there would be greater scope for managers to extract more than they should from the system. Not in practice.

In cooperatives, good governance is really important. In a large study of Indian agricultural co-ops undertaken in the early 1990s, Tushaar Shah found a strong link between governance and business success. He studied hundreds of agricultural and credit cooperatives in different states, and found that the 'design principles' on which they were built were crucial. He identified three conditions for success: the purpose of the organisation is central to the needs of the members, the governance structure ensures patronage cohesiveness and the operating system finds competitive advantage in the relationship with members (Shah, 1996). Under the right governance, cooperatives will not only survive but will be replicated by people who are in similar circumstances and want to gain similar advantages for themselves. They will take the organisational design that works in one place, try it out in another place and modify it as necessary. This hints at an evolutionary theory of cooperation, in which forms that work survive and are replicated, while others – no matter how hard they are promoted by governments – will fail.

What are the causes of failure? Boards may not be sufficiently independent from managers. Employees have a greater incentive to participate than other members, so a customer-owned bank may in practice become a kind of worker cooperative. Local politicians can get involved, and have an interest in turning them into semi-public organisations. Small groups of members could, in the absence of checks from the wider membership, take over on behalf of some ideology. Fonteyne (2007) suggests that these dangers can be avoided through measures such as better disclosure standards, a strategy of reconnecting with stakeholders, an increase in member investments and higher dividend payouts, with greater incentives to take part in governance. He believes a legal duty should be imposed on to cooperatives to organise members independently of management. Other more traditional measures would include reforms to improve board member effectiveness, and to introduce independent oversight of a board. All of this, ultimately, comes down to the question of member participation. Will members participate? If not, can they be persuaded? And who will do the persuading?

At this point it is useful to see how governance problems have been tackled in a related area of business: mutual life insurance. Corporate governance is a problem in mutuals for much the same reasons as it is in large cooperative banks; they contain large numbers of members who have heterogeneous interests and who face high costs in trying to influence decision-making. Because their interest is so widely dispersed, there is no equivalent of the large institutional shareholder in an investor-owned company that can oversee its business. A recent review of the governance of life insurance mutuals in the UK confirmed that in some mutuals this was a serious problem (Myners, 2004).

The review came about because of the governance failures implicit in the demise of one of the largest mutuals, Equitable Life. In 2000 Equitable lost a court case that meant it had to honour an agreement to service high interest-bearing life insurance policies entered into many years previously when interest rates were much higher. In the subsequent financial crisis it had to sell off parts of the business and cease to write new policies. An inquiry into the collapse by Lord Penrose found that there had been 'ineffective scrutiny and challenge of the executive of the Society', the board had insufficient skills, was totally dependent on actuarial advice and 'was never fully advised of the financial implications of the decisions that were said to be open to them'. Crucially, the board itself was:

> . . . not subject to effective external scrutiny or discipline. Policyholders were effectively powerless, and the Board was a self-perpetuating oligarchy amenable to policyholder pressure only at its discretion (Penrose, quoted in Myners, 2004, p. 113).

To make matters worse, not all customers were members, only those who had with-profits policies.

Rather than tackling the underlying problem of the lack of member participation, Penrose recommended that the Financial Services Authority appoint an expert to a board who would report back to the authority. The Myners Review commissioned research that found that members valued their membership and had a very positive view of mutuality. They had high levels of trust and believed mutuals could deliver superior performance. The majority were not interested in taking part in governance, but there was a substantial cohort who were interested in becoming engaged, suggesting that 'while engaging members may be difficult, it is certainly not impossible' (Myners, 2004, p. 102). The review went further than Penrose, recommending that mutuals find ways of connecting with their members, and calling for their trade associations to provide best-practice guidance in member relations. It set out detailed principles for fair and accessible voting procedures, and called for mutuals to be obliged to notify members of major transactions and to have to seek their permission for very major changes. Many of their recommendations have been implemented, and the situation is now much improved.

THE QUESTION OF MEMBER PARTICIPATION

Member participation in governance is vital for the continued alignment of the interests of customers, managers and boards. There is very little evidence for what proportion of members is active, but it is usually quite small. A study of Irish credit unions found only about 2 per cent of active members. There were more – 5–8 per cent – in the European cooperative banks, but here the percentage of customers who are members is also low and highly variable (Ward and McKillop, 2005). In the absence of member interest, boards can quickly become self-perpetuating and not much different from the boards of savings banks.

Agency theorists point out that monitoring is a costly activity, and that members must be incentivised to bear these costs. There is a free-rider problem, since everyone seeks to benefit from the monitoring costs of others. Expertise is likely to be low, and this also increases the costs of learning. The sanctions that individual members can exercise are weak, and so members need to form coalitions in order to get things done, and that is also costly in time and effort (Fonteyne, 2007). However, coalitions can form more cheaply now, through use of the internet and social media (Birchall, 2012c). Individuals who are disappointed by their experience of 'voice' can exercise the other option of exit (Hirschmann, 1970) but this is not very effective in disciplining boards and managers unless large numbers are involved. Also, exit is costly for the individual if the bank is the only one operating in a rural area, or among a particular income group. Yet the conclusion from two experts on the European cooperative banks is that they 'have sufficiently active, involved and qualified members to limit these agency costs' (Groeneveld and Llewellyn, 2012, p. 18).

How much member participation is enough? Customer-owned banks do not need mass participation. For governance to work, they need a small group of active members who are prepared to interest themselves in the business, to stand for elections to boards and to represent members in general. They need a larger group, from which these activists can be drawn, that know enough and care enough about the business to vote intelligently for their representatives. They then need to keep in touch regularly with members in general, partly because it is good business to do so, but partly because some of the inactive members might be persuaded to become more active.

Of course, governance by members is not the only issue. There needs to be a mix of skills on a board of directors, and there are good arguments for including top managers as board members and co-opting people with particular skills as non-executive directors. However, this argument can be used to exclude people from the board whose main purpose is to represent members. A few years ago, an ordinary member of one UK building society tried to get elected. The board reacted swiftly to persuade members not to vote for him on the grounds that only they could determine the mix of skills necessary. They were used to selecting their own candidates and then asking the members to vote simply to approve their choice. Other building societies have taken the opposite view and sought out someone to represent members on the board. However, the idea that there may be competition among members for election to the board is one that they are not familiar with.

Member participation cannot be left to chance, but has to be orchestrated. First, it needs specialist staff whose task it is to keep up the quality of governance by fostering member participation. The experience of consumer cooperatives in the UK is that the membership promotion staff have to be given enough authority within the business to make it work. They are not just a subgroup of a public relations office, but are a dedicated team dealing with all aspects of membership and governance (Co-operative Commission, 2001). Second, member participation needs committed boards whose members are prepared to foster new leaders who may eventually challenge their own dominance, and this requires value-based leadership. Third, it needs a management team who are also prepared to be challenged and made accountable not just to the board but also to the members. The rewards from all this are tangible; they include increased customer loyalty and greater commitment by staff, both of which contribute directly to business success (Shah, 1996).

In the UK and other countries that have a unitary board there is a particular problem – a lack of opportunities for members to serve. Countries that have a dual board, with a supervisory board electing a management board, provide more opportunities. Even when there is a unitary board, a member council can be convened to enable members to exercise their voice and to come to a more considered view on the bank's business strategy and performance. However, if the members lack real decision-making power they may decide it is not worthwhile.

CURRENT ISSUES IN REGULATION, SUPERVISION AND GOVERNANCE

There are four issues that customer-owned banks have to face. First, there is the need to deal with the tightening of government regulations in the aftermath of the banking crisis. Second, there is a crisis in supervision of subsidiaries and the growth of hybrid forms of ownership, mixing member-shareholding with investor-shareholding. Third, in rapidly growing but poorly integrated credit union systems there is a crisis of effective supervision and governance. Fourth, in countries where government interference has led to deformation, there is a crisis of confidence leading to collapse of the system, or reform, or both.

Financial Regulation after the Banking Crisis

Policy-makers are searching for ways of preventing a repeat of the behaviour that led to the banking collapse in 2008. They are concerned that if the system is not reformed a similar crisis could occur again; some people say without reform it is bound to occur again. People are also searching for a way to reconstruct the banking sector so that it fulfils its obligations to the 'real' economy. Banking is not just one sector among others; it is the foundation on which an economy is built. Without sound money, a safe place to put savings and a way of providing credit for business development, the rest of the economy suffers. Some critics are content to suggest ways of regulating the existing banks so they return to doing what they did before the crisis, but without taking such large risks (Milne, 2009). The focus is then on finding ways of strengthening the existing regulatory system. Lawrence White, drawing lessons from the S&L crisis of the 1980s, advocates pricing government deposit insurance according to the know riskiness of a particular bank (White, 1991). Joseph Stiglitz advocates having well worked out methods for taking a bankrupt bank into administration so that the losses are borne by the shareholders and bondholders before the taxpayer has to bail the bank out (Stiglitz, 2010). Others are more radical, wanting to restructure the banks so they provide either 'narrow' retail and commercial banking or the much riskier investment banking, but not both.

Some would go further and advocate mutualising the banks that are currently in public ownership, so that the banking sector benefits from diversity (Michie and Llewellyn, 2009). Going further still, advocates of cooperative banking argue that it is not just diversity that customer-ownership brings to the mix, but an 'altogether different way of doing banking'; as we found in Chapter 7 there are specific advantages that are unique to cooperatives. Giovanni Ferri (2012) explains that the ownership structure of banking tends to determine its business model. Banks will behave as their corporate makeup dictates – their behaviour is already predicted in their organisational 'DNA'. A corrective is not enough and we need to change the purpose for which bankers do business. Customer-owned banks have a different DNA than their investor-owned competitors that makes them inherently cautious, risk-averse, yet committed to serving low-income customers, SMEs and local economies. In fact, the characteristics of a new, more risk-averse global financial system have been part of the DNA of cooperative banks from the start (Groeneveld and de Vries, 2009).

If we accept the argument made in Chapter 7 for the inherent advantages of mature customer-owned banking sectors, it follows they only need to receive light-touch regulation and supervision from governments. Supporters say the regulators need to appreciate the distinctive nature of the cooperative, yet they are not hopeful; in the past the regulators have been proved woefully ignorant. Writing in 2007, Fonteyne found that Basel II had no mention of cooperative banking, despite this type having such a large share of the European market (Fonteyne, 2007). Will Basel III be any more informed? At a recent conference in Venice, academics and cooperative bankers together signed a declaration, saying:

> It is particularly troubling to observe that the new regulatory framework for financial institutions poses a serious threat to the viability of European local and cooperative banks, thus jeopardizing a key ingredient for the economic recovery and the future financial stability of our continent (Venice declaration, 2012).

They were worried that the regulators' 'one size fits all approach effectively penalizes the banks that contributed the least to the onset of the crisis and proved to be the best at mitigating its effects'. It is the new requirements for information that are proving to be damaging. The cooperative bankers argue that inappropriately detailed requirements will impose costs that will damage the competitiveness of smaller banks. In the USA, regulators have recognised this issue by exempting community banks from some of their requirements.

The International Co-operative Banking Association (ICBA) has found another potentially damaging issue. Basel III has declared that it is necessary to strengthen banks' 'stable and safe' Tier 1 capital. This should not be a problem for customer-owned banks. They have millions of members who each subscribe to a member share that until now has been considered to be cooperative capital. However, the regulators are concerned that member shares are not stable, as members can withdraw them at any time; they look more like deposits than shares. The ICBA explains that this goes against the whole idea of the cooperative, which should not be judged as if it were an investor-owned bank. The variability of capital is 'linked to the deep nature of the cooperative banking model' (ICBA, 2012, p. 6). The member shares are not really redeemable at will, because cooperatives do have an unconditional right to refuse to redeem member shares. Also, this ignores the importance in the cooperative model of reserves that cannot be shared out. As we have noted, in cooperative banks and credit unions there are clear rules that state a proportion of profits should be allocated to reserves. This is another capital buffer that supplements member shares.

This issue first raised its head in relation to a decision by the International Accounting Standards Board to reclassify member shares as liabilities. Following the adoption of this new standard, many cooperatives have changed their rules to make it possible to refuse to redeem member shares, and to introduce a level below which capital would not be allowed to fall. Basel III will be implemented in January 2013, and cooperatives have a ten-year delay for member shares to be excluded from Tier 1 capital. The issue will remain controversial.

Diversification and Hybrid Ownership Structures

In the more mature cooperative systems of Europe, there is a growing distance between the banks and their members (Rabobank, 2009). Decisions are increasingly being made at the centre. However, the evolution towards a more centralised structure is not complete, and is more pronounced in some countries than others; for instance, the Dutch group is one of the most centralised, while the Italian is still the most decentralised in Europe. There are still choices to be made about the relative weight to give to governance between the local and central banks. In response to the pressures of increased competition and globalisation, the banks have been internationalising and creating complex new subsidiaries that make it hard for the members to understand what is going on. Rabobank estimates that about 25 per cent of European cooperative banks' net revenues is derived from outside their home country (2009, p. 18). Banks have either acquired foreign banks or entered into strategic alliances. For instance, Raiffeisen International (a subsidiary of Raiffeisen Austria) has set up a large number of retail operations in Central and Eastern Europe, largely through acquisitions of formerly public banks. Credit Agricole and Credit Mutuel recently acquired banks in Italy, Greece, Poland and Germany. Rabobank has made strategic acquisitions and new business start-ups, and now has 603 offices spread over 46 foreign countries. In almost all cases they have not converted the foreign banks to a cooperative model, nor have they offered membership to customers. The banks have to answer the question of whether their diversification into corporate and investment banking is justified, and whether they should be chasing business in other countries. When they do so they could agree to limit themselves to strategic alliances with other cooperative banks and credit unions.

As well as governance issues, there may be good business reasons for restraint. The French cooperative banks suffered during the banking crisis because of losses made by their subsidiaries. This has made them less resilient to the financial turmoil. Also, it has led to a 'hybridisation' of the sector that biases decision-making towards the apex of the structure, and the interests of outside investors (Ory and Lemzeri, 2012). Rabobank has had a difficult time with its overseas operations. In 1999 the bank made a decision to cut back its investment banking and overseas business, and to phase out lending to 'non-core customers outside the Netherlands' (Rabobank, 2009, p. 38). If cooperative banks are not very good at investment and corporate banking and at expanding beyond their borders, then perhaps they should concentrate on their core business and, at the same time, make it easier for local members to monitor their banks and maintain a high quality of governance.

The same kind of choice faces credit union leaders around the world, as they make the transition from the small, local, volunteer-run unions of the Raiffeisen system to the much larger, more professionalised unions that now dominate the system in North America. Seen from the perspective of those who want to compete with the big commercial banks this is an inevitable evolutionary step forward. Seen from the perspective of those who value member participation and hands-on governance it is a mistake. This issue is often presented within the credit union movement as a dilemma, in which one has simply to choose between the two options. However, this does not take into account the strength that comes from federation. Designed properly, a federative system can provide both market share and closeness to members. It will still be a compromise between antinomic principles, and so will not satisfy everyone.

Regulation and Supervision of Fast-growing Credit Union Sectors

There are particularly acute issues of regulation in developing countries. Cuevas and Fischer (2006) say that the technical details of regulation are well known and there is a consensus over how to supervise what they call cooperative financial institutions (CFIs). Yet there is disagreement over whether the legal framework should be under general cooperative laws, specialised credit union laws or wider banking and micro-credit laws. Many CFIs are registered under laws that use the Indian Act of 1904 as a template. However, this is flawed because the Indian Act took a German regulatory law that was based on self-help and changed it into a promotional law, making cooperatives instruments of development policy (Cuevas and Fischer, 2006). This influenced laws in Asia and English-speaking Africa, and then from the 1960s onwards, Latin America. The cooperatives were a way of channelling state and donor funds to farmers, and often the laws were drafted without their makers bothering to consult with the sector. The legal framework must take into consideration that the credit union is not an instrument of state policy but a way of solving problems of market failure through risk sharing and self-governance. It has a fragile governance structure that needs to be kept in equilibrium. It naturally seeks alliance with others, and so it is the sector rather than the individual union that needs regulating.

Following the failure of this kind of government-promoted CFI, the 1980s saw a loss of interest among donors and international development agencies. A new NGO movement began to promote its own version of micro-finance. The problem was that the CFIs were included under the micro-finance category, and proposed laws to regulate the micro-finance sector overlook their very different features. It is possible to provide one law for both; Cuevas and Fischer (2006) say that Mexico in 2001 achieved this, and that such a dual-law system is one possible model for the future.

There are now three distinct legal frameworks: a CFI specialised law, a cooperative societies' law and a financial institution or banking law. The most common combination is a cooperative societies' law and a banking law. The wisdom of this dual regime is the subject of intense debate, and as Cuevas and Fischer warn, not all choices are equally good. On the one hand, the dual regime can be seen as a transition towards a unified regime with supervision under a banking authority. On the other, the dual regime is damaging to the unity of the sector, and leaves the smaller unions without protection. CFIs can be caught out from two directions. If they are incorporated under a country's banking law, then they run the risk of having to comply with inappropriate regulations designed for investor-owned banks. If they are incorporated under a micro-finance law, they may have to comply with regulations designed for micro-finance organisations supported by NGOs. Some argue that a specialised law is needed for CFIs, and this is being promoted in Africa. Others argue for a dual regime as in Brazil. The only alternative not liked by anyone is the original cooperative law regime.

The World Council of Credit Unions has provided a blueprint for a universal credit union law. We might think this will solve the problem, but it may not suit everyone. Cuevas and Fischer point out that the regulatory framework in Europe shows that regulation evolved with the systems themselves; 'adapting to the evolution of the system and always encouraging its development while ensuring its stability'. They go on to say that in Europe,

> in all countries where the CFI sector is a significant player, the regulator has not attempted to put the institution into a straitjacket designed for another

institutional form, as has increasingly been the case in developing countries (Cuevas and Fischer, 2006, p. 38).

There are some basic principles that apply to any regulatory regime. The regulatory structure should focus on the system, not just the individual CFI. It should focus on the member–manager conflict rather than on a shareholder–depositor conflict that, in customer-owned banks does not exist. It should make the regulation proportionate to the size and complexity of the business, with simplified reporting standards for small credit unions. It should recognise the nature of cooperative capital that is both variable and redeemable. It should recognise, too, that alliances between cooperatives are not oligopolistic attempts to fix the market but organisational tools to help serve the market. Regulators should recognise that customer-owned banking groups have the capacity to regulate themselves through deposit insurance, and a commitment to merge failed banks into successful ones, which is a kind of 'institutional insurance'.

The Reform of Government-controlled Credit Cooperatives

There is a particularly difficult question concerning financial cooperatives in countries where they have been taken over by governments and made to serve political purposes. In Chapter 3 we have described the situation in India with the credit cooperative societies and their superstructure of district and state banks. Can this system be reformed and restored to its members? If not, it is better if it collapses altogether so something new can grow out of the ashes? Should it be reclassified as a government-owned banking system so that real financial cooperatives are not discredited by association? The problem is that a system of farm credits is still needed and so if the Indian system does collapse we need to be sure something takes its place. On the other hand, if it is shored up by World Bank funding and continues to operate under government control it occupies the market niche that credit unions would normally occupy, and so prevents the emergence of genuine cooperatives.

The debate about how to reform the Indian rural credit cooperatives has several dimensions. There is a need to strengthen the administrative capacity of the second and third-tier banks that supervise the primary societies, and of the state governments that supervise the banks. State laws have to be reformed so that the parallel systems of regulation and supervision by the national bank (NABARD) and the states do not get in each other's way. The managerial competence of the banking staff has to improve, and new technology brought in to make the system more efficient. Accounting standards have to improve and a realistic assessment made of the likely losses from non-performing loans. World Bank funding has been made conditional on all of these happening.

However, along with these reforms there is a need to restore the primary societies to their members. We can see how this is done from the example of successful reforms such as in the Tanzanian coffee cooperatives. Here, the registrar cleared out existing board members and held elections for new boards. At the same time, a process of community development was carried out to empower the ordinary members (Birchall and Simmons, 2010). In India, all of this will be needed on a massive scale, but also the laws will have to be changed to prevent politicians from coming back to dominate the new boards. It will be difficult because the ordinary members have always seen the system as being government-owned and have had nothing much to do with it.

In China the situation is similar, and all the reforms mentioned in relation to India are also relevant. However, it would be a mistake to see the reform process merely as a set of technical and economic issues. The problems are essentially political and so the main priority is to reform corporate governance. In China, the cooperatives are 'owned' in practice by local government and the Communist Party. A recent study found that fewer than 5 per cent of members have ever attended a members' meeting, and those who have attended are local councillors or party officials. No amount of technical support for micro-finance lending methods will help, because these owners directly influence the decisions of managers over loans (Ong, 2006).

There is a further problem faced in systems where the cooperative bank is a subsidiary of another type of cooperative. In a recent research project in Sri Lanka, all our key informants told us that the multi-purpose cooperatives (MPCSs) are effectively government-controlled. The then registrar of cooperatives admitted that half of the MPCSs were loss-making. Yet they continue to survive. Officials from the Asian Development Bank told us that they had recently tried to persuade the MPCSs to separate out their rural savings banks from their much weaker retailing businesses, but that they had failed. They were worried that the depositors in the banks may be at risk (Birchall and Simmons, 2010). In South Korea, the agricultural cooperative system is extensive and consists of two parts: the agricultural marketing arm and the bank. The marketing department has always made a loss and has been subsidised by profits from the bank. In 2012 the government recognised that this was not good practice by modern banking standards, and changed the law to separate out the bank. It is expected that this will lead to drastic cuts in the services provided to farmers. However, in 2011 the marketing department made its first ever surplus and so the system may adapt. In Japan a similar system exists, with the Norinchukin Bank nested within a larger group of farmer-owned businesses. We have noted in Chapter 6 the serious losses made by the bank during the financial crisis of 2008. Again, the lack of a firewall between the bank and the other businesses was a serious concern, though the farmers have made up the losses and the system now looks to be sound.

CONCLUSION

A hidden question lurks within this discussion of regulatory, supervisory and governance systems. How much can be expected of members? Are they prepared to participate, and if so, under what circumstances? Can participation be fostered, and if so, how? To answer these questions we have to delve more deeply into theories of human motivation. The question of member participation is so important that it is worth taking a chapter to explore it in more depth. The next chapter will do this, using insights from a wide range of behavioural sciences.

10. What motivates members to participate?

Are we really cooperators or are we self-motivated individuals who are just pursuing our interests through cooperatives? To answer these questions we need to review the evidence about *cooperation* provided by behavioural scientists. Then, to sharpen the analysis so as to understand what makes people cooperate in some activities but not others, we need to switch to the more active concept of *participation* and review the evidence about what motivates people to participate in governance of cooperatives.

Twenty years ago it would have been difficult to get started answering these questions, because the experts were better at explaining why people do not cooperate than why they do. Their basic mistake was to begin from a very limited set of premises: that humans are rational, self-interested individuals looking to maximise their own utility, who calculate in every situation whether it is worth cooperating. Political scientists were wedded (many still are) to a rational actor model of participation that predicted people would not vote; the argument was that one vote counted for very little and the cost of voting would always make it rational for people to stay at home. Nor would they take part in collective action, because again it was more rational not to participate: people would realise that in a large group it was possible to 'free-ride' on other people's actions while sharing the results. They would only take part if the group were small enough for their contribution to be essential, or if they were incentivised by personal rewards that lowered the cost of participating (Olson, 1965). The problem was that people participated far more often than the theory predicted, and so some political scientists began to expand the idea of personal 'preferences' to include altruism (we reward ourselves for being good to others), or wider incentives (we reward ourselves for working for a cause that we consider valuable) (e.g., Margolis, 1984).

Psychologists used to suffer from the same problem (and again, some still do). The dominant approach was that there are two types of motivating factor: extrinsic and intrinsic benefits. As a researcher wanting to explain people's participation in some group activity, you began by expecting extrinsic benefits such as career advancement, development of marketable skills and, of course, monetary payment. Then, if these did not explain everything you included enjoyment, intellectual stimulation, social benefits, increased self-confidence and so on (Ryan and Deci, 2000). Again there was an explanation shortfall, and so some psychologists added in a desire to act on the basis of principle, and to meet the normative expectations of a group to which a person belongs (Lindenberg, 2001). However, the theory was still individualistic, and could not easily deal with motivations that come from membership of a community that provides a strong collective identity (Lakhani and Woolf, 2005).

We might expect that evolutionary theorists would provide a more rounded view of human nature. After all, our ancestors lived until very recently in small bands of hunter-gatherers with collective hunting of game and shared care of children that have made us into a uniquely cooperative species. But again the assumption of individualism and self-centeredness has – until recently – dominated our understanding. First, biologists rejected the idea that groups have much to do with evolution; it is the fittest *individuals* that survive and pass on their genes, not the fittest groups. They were so keen to demonstrate what groups do *not* do that – until recently – they failed to theorise the crucial importance of groups in helping individuals to survive and replicate themselves. They were determined that altruism, even within the group, did not make much evolutionary sense. Second, in his famous book *The Selfish Gene*, published in 1976, Richard Dawkins shifted our attention away from people to genes as the basic drivers of evolution (2006, third edition). He argued that we are machines created by our genes – our task is to carry them around and give them a means to copy themselves. They are the only unit of selection, and they have only one task – to survive and copy themselves. They are, in this sense, completely selfish.

Dawkins concluded that, because these basic building blocks of the human being are selfish, we have to teach people altruism; it does not come naturally. An altruistic act is one that tends to make the altruist more likely to die, while the non-altruist is more likely to survive. This means the non-altruists will have more children and after several generations will overrun the altruists. Dawkins admitted that genes mutually co-evolved and cooperated in the creation of 'survival machines' to carry them around. The making of a human body can be described as a cooperative venture; a gene that cooperates well with other genes will have an advantage. However, the dominant metaphors in the book were all about selfishness and competition.

In the second edition of his book Dawkins modified his view to some extent, adding two chapters that acknowledged new evidence from game theory showing that people are much more cooperative. He had no choice but to do this, because in the interval between the two editions a revolution was taking place in our understanding of the human capacity to cooperate. People working from just about every angle – evolutionary biology, economics, anthropology, psychology and even neuropsychology – have begun to develop a much deeper – and more optimistic – understanding of the human propensity to cooperate (Mansbridge, 1990).

HOW COOPERATIVE ARE WE?

It is easy to understand why people cooperate in situations where it is mutually beneficial to do so and where everyone gains from it. There are many instances where the choice of whether to cooperate is 'non-zero-sum', meaning one person's gain is not necessarily another person's loss. By cooperating together people can be better off than if they did not cooperate (Wright, 1994). Also, through developing exchange of goods through trade we have built up a complex division of labour, in which nobody can be self-sufficient. We are all heavily dependent on others to live and so in our everyday lives we have to cooperate – there is no alternative (Ridley, 2010). These points are amply illustrated in the early history of cooperative banks and credit unions; it made sense to cooperate for mutual benefit.

However, there are many situations in which people do not cooperate when it would be beneficial for them to do so. In 1968 Garrett Hardin wrote a paper called the 'Tragedy of the Commons'. He described how livestock owners graze their animals on common land knowing it is being overgrazed but unable to do anything about it. If they limit their usage others will just increase theirs. Though everyone will in the long run be worse off than if they agree to limit their usage, there is no incentive to cooperate (Hardin, 1968). The tragedy applies to any resource that is free for anyone to use, but has limits to its use before it degrades or disappears. This is not true in a world in which there is more of a resource than humans need. There are commons that do not degrade with use – the internet is a good example, as are open-source software and social networks. However, Hardin predicted severe problems with our most precious resources – land for grazing, fish stocks, water supplies for irrigation, forests. The problem can only be solved if an outside force – the state – can set and enforce rules restraining its use.

To understand the limits of human cooperation we have to start from this severe social dilemma. It can be modelled formally as a game called the 'Prisoners' Dilemma' (PD). Martin Novak calls this 'an enchanted trap that has ensnared some of the brightest minds for decades' (2011, p. 3). It goes like this: you and your accomplice are in police cells, having been charged with a serious crime. Each of you is offered a deal – if you incriminate the other while he or she remains silent, you get a reduced sentence of one year while the other gets a four-year sentence. If you both remain silent, you both get two years for a lesser offence. If you both incriminate each other, you are both convicted of the serious crime but get three years for pleading guilty. What is the best outcome? The terms used to describe these choices are *defect* and *cooperate*. If the other player defects you are better off defecting. If the other player cooperates you are much better off defecting. And this is the dilemma – no matter what the other person does, it is better to defect. The problem is that if both persons follow this line of reasoning, you both defect and are worse off than if you had both cooperated. The best strategy for each individual leaves both worse off. It gets worse. Imagine that individuals trying to survive and reproduce play out prisoners' dilemma (PD) over generations. If the dominant strategy of defect is correct, natural selection opposes cooperation, because cooperative individuals will gradually die out and the population will eventually consist only of defectors. The greater good is undermined.

If the story ended there we would not be able to explain the great outburst of cooperation among people all over the world that has resulted in the creation of – among other things – cooperative banks. However, the story continues with the evolutionary biologist, Robert Trivers, who wrote a paper on 'reciprocal altruism' (1971). Previously, PD theorists had thought of PD as a 'one shot' game in which the temptation to defect was overwhelming. Trivers was the first to establish the importance of the repeated (iterated) PD for biology, discovering that one way of escaping the dilemma was to repeat the game! Frequent interaction leads to commitment. It explains the behaviour of cleaner fish that team up with others if they have proved reliable in the past, explains why vampire bats share a meal of blood with others that are not kin, and it explains something that had puzzled biologists for ages: the way birds put themselves at risk by warning other birds of danger. Cooperation grows out of the 'tit for tat' logic of everyday interactions.

There are three types of reciprocity. First, there is *direct reciprocity* between two people who have an ongoing relationship and who exchange goods or services over time, sometimes at market value but sometimes with delays and only rough equivalence. Second, there is *generalised reciprocity* between several people who reciprocate but not necessarily to the one who last did them a favour, and not necessarily in full. Third, there is *indirect reciprocity* between many people who know each other by reputation. This last type must be important in explaining exchanges between people who do not know each well but cooperate in the governance of member-owned businesses such as cooperative banks. It is this willingness to engage in indirect reciprocity that is the key to member participation. We will come back to this point below when discussing the idea of social capital.

In the game that was developed to model the PD, the two players have the choice of cooperating or defecting and they can respond in different ways to the choices made by the other; they can develop strategies. But what strategy is best? Do we cooperate until someone defects and then refuse to cooperate ever again (the Grim strategy), or just for a while (the Grudger), or should we be nice and forgive the occasional defection (Tit for two Tats)? In the late 1970s, Robert Axelrod provided the answer through a competition he organised, not between real people, but between populations of decision-making units each following their own strategy in an iterated PD within a computer. He advertised for game theorists to submit strategies that could be pitted against each other. In the first round, 14 strategies were submitted by the theorists, plus one he added that was purely random. Two hundred and twenty-five games were played, each having 200 moves. Surprisingly, the eight nice strategies beat the seven nasty ones; it seems cooperation can be quite robust. Even more surprising, the winning strategy was the simplest – tit for tat – submitted by Anatol Rapoport. Tit for tat begins by cooperating, and then on every subsequent move it does what its opponent has done in its previous move. This means it is both good at punishing defection and forgiving in restoring cooperation as soon as possible. In the parlance of game players, it avoids being a sucker or a meany. In a second tournament, with 63 entries, Maynard Smith submitted tit for two tats, which is more forgiving. It would have won the first tournament, but did not win the second because some deviously nasty strategies were also submitted – it came in at 24th. Tit for tat won again (Axelrod, 1984).

Axelrod then collaborated with the evolutionary biologist Bill Hamilton on the idea of an evolutionarily stable strategy (ESS). The problem for tit for tat was that in the first tournament if the other 13 strategies had been nasty it would not have won; it needed a mix of cooperators and defectors to show its advantages. Axelrod ran the 63 strategies over again, with the points gained being counted as offspring. Some strategies went extinct, and then eventually at around 1000 generations, stability was reached. Again, the nice strategies did well, though the very nice ones went extinct (Dawkins may have been right about altruism). Some nasty ones did well and then declined steeply. The evolution game was played six times and tit for tat won five, with another nice strategy winning the sixth. When all the nasties were extinct, there was no way to distinguish between the nice ones, they all cooperated. Even when the payoffs were altered to give defection a strong advantage, it was found that tit for tat can survive through clustering. These findings have important implications for any organisation that relies on a high level of member participation. Customer-owned banks provide an opportunity for people who want to cooperate to cluster together to produce an environment that is stable, highly cooperative and resistant to those who act out of pure self-interest. The fact that the banks have lasted so long – some for 150 years – is evidence that this strategy can work.

Why is tit for tat such a good strategy? We have to understand that no best rule exists independently of the strategy of the other player. Tit for tat avoids unnecessary conflict, yet is provokable in the face of defection; it forgives the other immediately the other cooperates, and it has clarity (so the other player can know what you are likely to do). Tit for tat out-performs every other strategy almost all the time, including much more complex ones. An even nicer strategy, tit for two tats, can score higher, provided it is not up against a really bad strategy, such as Tester, which is designed to look for, and punish, softies. But those that are very unforgiving score badly as they set off a series of mutual recriminations. In Axelrod's tournament, many entries were too competitive for their own good; it pays to be optimistic about whether the other will cooperate. However, too much optimism is also dangerous; one nasty strategy called Tranquilliser cooperates, lulls its opponent into a false sense of security and then defects. So it also pays to be retaliatory. We can see this balancing act working itself out in the rules that cooperatives adopt. They are forgiving of members who get into financial difficulty, but only up to a point. They expect members to attend meetings, and sometimes disallow a loan if they do not. The rules of the early cooperative banks and building societies may seem to us very draconian, with their fines and expulsions, but they were playing 'tit for tat' and ensuring the organisation's survival.

The message from these behavioural scientists is a cautiously optimistic one. The Russian geographer and anarchist philosopher Peter Kropotkin foresaw it over 100 years ago. In his book *Mutual Aid: a Factor of Evolution* he said:

> The cunningest and shrewdest are eliminated in favour of those who understand the advantages of sociable life and mutual support (Kropotkin, 1902).

This explains how high levels of cooperation are being achieved through customer-owned banks and other cooperative businesses. Large numbers of people who begin as strangers to each other are able to form cooperatives and defend themselves against defectors. In keeping score, building up reputations, avoiding exchanges with known defectors, and generally playing tit for tat, they are creating and sustaining institutions that have a highly cooperative equilibrium.

AN OPTIMISTIC VIEW OF OUR CAPACITY TO COOPERATE

The evidence from game theory is reinforced by evidence on the evolution of the human species that confirms this optimistic view of our capacity to cooperate. People have an inbuilt tendency to want to join groups. This is not the same as saying the fittest group survives, but that our culture builds on an evolved human nature to make us highly sociable. Frans de Waal sees humans from the perspective of someone who is an expert on our nearest relatives – chimpanzees. His argument, developed over several books, is that the view of human nature as self-centred and individualistic is simply wrong. He says 'There never was a point at which we became social' (de Waal, 2009, p. 4). We have been group living forever; we started out interdependent, bonded and unequal, coming from a long line of hierarchical animals for which life in groups is a survival strategy. He points out that group-oriented individuals leave more offspring, and that solitary confinement is the worst punishment humans can face! De Waal identifies a powerful driver of our 'groupiness' in our ability to feel empathy. He thinks it probably evolved through parental care. Like our cousins the chimps, we are capable of three levels of understanding: emotional contagion, which means we pick up other people's emotions; empathy, which means we feel how other people feel; and sympathy, which means we understand what they need and try to provide it for them. It was sympathy that led Raiffeisen and Schulze to set up cooperative banks, and it was the inbuilt tendency to groupiness that led so many people to replicate them.

Michael Tomasello adds evidence from child development. He finds that humans are both quantitatively and qualitatively unique in the way we are adapted for acting and thinking cooperatively in cultural groups. We have a set of 'species-unique skills and motivations for co-operation' (Tomasello, 2009, p. xiii). The underlying psychological process is shared intentionality, 'the ability to create with others joint intentions and joint commitments in co-operative endeavours'. This is structured by processes of joint attention and mutual knowledge, underpinned by the cooperative motive to help and share with others. We teach each other things, which is a form of altruism. We imitate others in the group simply in order to be like them. Human children are equipped to participate in 'cooperative groupthink' through a special kind of cultural intelligence. They have special skills, which arose through *gene-culture co-evolution*. Comparing human children and chimpanzees, Tomasello finds that children from one year old are already cooperative and helpful in many situations. They do not learn this from adults – it comes naturally. Later, at around three years of age, they begin to make judgements based on reciprocity and internalised norms. There are two types of norm – for cooperation and conformity – so children seek out the accepted way to behave. They want to know how the 'game' should be played and this is where norms of fairness come into play. They play tit for tat, starting out altruistic and then making judgements based on other children's responses. Tomasello's work is of obvious importance in helping to explain why humans have taken so readily to the establishment of cooperatives. He says that apes work in 'I-mode', while humans work in 'we-mode'.

Because we are so sociable and want to conform to the group, we soon develop a sense of fairness and obligation. De Waal (2009) argues that morality is not a cultural veneer on top of a more selfish human nature, with people being nice on the outside and nasty on the inside. It is an outgrowth from the social instincts that we share with other animals. There is compelling evidence on this from recent advances in game theory. The *ultimatum game* is a one-shot anonymous game in which one subject is allocated a sum of money and has to decide how much to give to another, who has to agree to the gift or both lose. Researchers who still believe in a 'rational actor' model of human nature expect the recipient to accept any amount at all because this makes him or her better off. The results show that the modal offer is 50 per cent, and responders frequently reject offers below 25 per cent. They would rather get nothing than accept something they feel is unfair. This is where customer-owned banks have a huge advantage over discredited investor-owned banks. People have an innate sense of fairness, and they are choosing to put their money into those banks that they feel are likely to be fair to them.

When we make moral judgements, both our cognitive skills and our emotions are fully engaged. Matt Ridley (1997) suggests that the origins of human morality lie in reciprocity. We have an 'exchange organ' in our brain, able to calculate the costs and benefits of exchanges, and we have become remarkably good at finding and punishing cheats. Emotions are problem-solving devices for settling the conflict between short-term expediency and long-term prudence in favour of the latter. They enable us to make credible commitments to others, and to alter the pattern of rewards from exchanges so that we are not always selfish. They are mental devices for ensuring commitment. For instance, when we feel rage we are motivated to punish transgressors. When we feel guilt this makes cheating painful and in a sense we punish ourselves. Contempt and shame are other ways of keeping people committed to fair exchange relationships. Relationships are dominated by a sense of fairness, and virtue enables us to find other trustworthy people to exchange with (Ridley, 1997). All of this helps explain the emotional energy that people bring to volunteering in and governing credit unions. It also explains why customers who feel let down by 'greedy bankers' are so vindictive and are likely to want to punish them if they get the chance.

As well as needing to know the reputation of others, we want to have a good reputation ourselves. Novak says that reputation is a collective resource (2011, Ch. 2). Its advantages are clear, and it explains the evolution of cooperation and the big brain – we need the brain's massive processing power in order to make judgements about whether people are worth cooperating with! Reputation even helps explain the evolution of language – we need to communicate through gossip. It stimulates moral systems that generalise norms of behaviour such as the Golden Rule. We can see how important reputation is in different types of bank by observing how managers and board members behave. One of the criticisms of investor-owned banks, particularly in the USA and UK where they caused the crisis, is that their directors and top managers do not seem to care what others think of them. They have been accused of arrogance and of being cut off from normal citizens by the huge salaries and bonuses they award themselves. The reputation of bankers is at rock bottom, and it will take many years before they are trusted again.

On the other hand, there is strong evidence that customer-owned banks still have the trust and confidence of citizens; studies of the UK building societies have consistently found that they are much more trusted than the investor-owned banks. Now customers are switching in large numbers to customer-owned banks. In the USA the credit unions are growing strongly, whereas in the UK it is the building societies, the Co-operative Bank and even the small credit union sector that are benefitting. We will be discussing this phenomenon in the final chapter.

WHAT MOTIVATES PEOPLE TO PARTICIPATE? SOME INSIGHTS FROM MUTUAL INCENTIVES THEORY

Beyond these theories of cooperation, we need a more specific theory of what motivates people to participate in customer-owned banks. How do people come to participate? How do they start, and then continue and sometimes drop out? When Richard Simmons and I began working on this question, we searched the literature for generalisations that could be put together into a general explanation (Simmons and Birchall, 2005). We came up with a 'participation chain'. There are three links in the chain, resources, mobilisation and motivation.

The first link is the prior *resources* that potential participants bring to their decision whether or not to participate. Research has shown that these include the amount of time, money, skills and confidence available to potential group members, and also the state of their health (Verba et al., 1995). In principle, the more individuals have these resources, the more likely they are to participate.

The next link in the chain is the *mobilisation* of participants. Research has found that *issues* are important catalysts of participation. The more people are concerned about issues that they feel can be tackled by collective action, the more likely they are to participate. The less interested they are in the issues being tackled by the group, the more likely they are to stay at home or refuse to join an internet group. *Opportunities* to participate are also important. The greater the number and variety of types of opportunity to get involved, and the more often these are presented, the more people are likely to begin to take part. Finally, research has pointed to the importance of *mobilisation attempts* (Klandermans and Oegema, 1994). While a few people seek out opportunities themselves, most people have to be asked, and they are more likely to say 'yes' if the person asking is known to and trusted by the participant. This means social networks are important. Attempts to mobilise customers are particularly important in the European cooperative banking system, where customers can choose whether or not to take up membership. Rabobank decided on a strategy to increase membership, and the number of members rose from 550 000 in 2000 to 1.7 million in 2008, an increase from 6 per cent in 2000 to nearly 20 per cent by 2008 (Ayadi et al., 2010).

The third link in the chain is the *motivation* to participate. Here we want to draw on a theoretical model we call the 'mutual incentives theory' (MIT) of motivations to participate (Simmons and Birchall, 2005). First, it is 'mutual' because it does not assume that people are inherently cooperative or selfish, but that their motives are a blend of self-interest and concern for others. Motives vary depending on the circumstances – in some circumstances people are more selfish, in others they are more concerned for others. To find out what mix of motives they have, instead of just theorising, we have to ask people. Second, the theory is mutual because it recognises that in a community group, online network or cooperative there is no need to contrast the interests of oneself and of other people, because the mutual structure of the group allows us to pursue our own interests by cooperating with others. By becoming part of the group, we cease to define our interests in purely individual terms and begin to think in terms of collective goals. MIT draws on two general social-psychological theories of motivation that we call individualistic and collectivistic. It is important to stress that they are both about what motivates *individual people*. When we talk about 'collectivistic' motivations, we do not mean some kind of 'groupthink' but the way an individual person's motives for participating can be formed by a sense of being part of a group.

The *individualistic approach* is developed from social exchange theory (Homans, 1974). It assumes that people are motivated by individual rewards and punishments, and provides a set of generalisations about how they interact. First, the more people expect to receive benefits that are valuable to them, the more likely they are to participate. There are different types of benefit: extrinsic and intrinsic. Extrinsic benefits include more material factors, such as gaining access to a wider a social life, furthering one's career, developing marketable skills or being paid. Intrinsic benefits include subjective factors, such as personal enjoyment, the satisfaction that comes from having one's say and a sense of achievement. Second, people are put off participating by costs, which can range from financial costs to loss of time, tiredness, boredom and so on. The more costly people's participation becomes, the more likely they are to stop taking part. Just as there can be a wide range of benefits, there are lots of ways in which people experience participation as costly. There is a special type of cost called 'opportunity cost'. Here, people weigh up what else they could be doing with their time, and decide which activity is more valuable to them. The greater the opportunity cost of participation, the more likely people are to decide to do something else.

Another important factor is habit. After a while, participation does become something of a habit, especially if people are asked to do something regularly at the same time and in the same place. When people's costs begin to outweigh the benefits of participating, the theory predicts that they will not give up right away, but will continue to participate out of habit, at least for a time. Finally, there is satiation. This is a word that is usually used to describe having eaten too much. What it means here is that people who have got what they wanted out of participation will cease to take part because there is no further incentive.

In summary, the more benefits people get from participation, and the higher the value they put on these benefits, the more likely they are to participate. The higher the costs, the more likely they are not to take part. The benefits have to outweigh the costs. If the value of what they obtain through participation goes down – through satiation – they will eventually stop. But even if rational calculation tells them they should stop, they may keep going for a while out of habit. Finally, there is a strong relationship between what people expect to get out of their participation and their motivation to continue. If they are disappointed, or feel neglected, or feel that other people have gained but they have not, they will feel angry and cheated. When they stop taking part it will be very difficult – if not impossible – to get them going again.

The *collectivistic approach* is drawn from theories of altruism and cooperation. It interprets human behaviour very differently, assuming that participation can be motivated by three variables:

1. Shared goals: people express mutual needs that translate into common goals.
2. Shared values: people feel a sense of duty to participate as an expression of common values.
3. Sense of community: people identify with and care about other people who either live in the same area or are like them in some respect.

This approach generalises that the more each of these three variables is present, the more likely people will be to participate.

*   The stronger the sense of community, the higher the level of participation.
*   The more people share common values, the higher the level of participation
*   The more people have shared goals, the higher the level of participation.

This is good news, but there is more good news to follow. Each of these three variables affects the others as well as affecting the level of participation. The stronger the sense of community, the more people are likely to develop shared goals such as making the area they live in safe from crime, or using the internet to coordinate car sharing. The pursuit of shared goals tends to make people care more about each other, so that a group of people who set out with a desire to 'get things done' tend to develop social bonds as well.

Shared values take longer to develop. A sense of duty to participate will carry people through bad times when they would otherwise give up. More positively, if people find that they care about the same things – fair trade, or the environment, or other people with similar problems – this will strengthen participation. People who come together to fight for people like them – such as those with mental health problems, or people with learning difficulties, retired people or consumers – may begin with the belief in the rightness of what they are doing, and then develop social bonds and shared goals with like-minded people.

FINDINGS FROM TWO RESEARCH PROJECTS ON COOPERATIVES

MIT has not yet been applied to customer-owned banks, but it has been applied to public service users (Simmons and Birchall, 2005), area committee members of the UK Co-operative Group (Birchall and Simmons, 2004), and housing cooperatives and consumer cooperatives in the English Midlands (Simmons and Birchall, 2004). The study that is most relevant to the banks is that of the Co-operative Group, one of whose subsidiaries is the UK Co-operative Bank. We carried out a questionnaire survey of an estimated 500 members of the area committees of the Co-operative Group, and 448 replied (about a 90 per cent return). As a 'control' group, we also took a random sample of members who had chosen to receive regular information from the group but did not want to be more active (98 sent back our questionnaire – a 36 per cent return).

On *individualistic incentives*, we assumed that the higher the cost to participants, the lower would be the level of participation. To our surprise, few respondents said the costs of participation affected them; 55 per cent of participants and 45 per cent of non-participants said that *none* of the costs we suggested to them applied. However, 20 per cent of non-participants – a significant minority – did say that financial costs were important to them. There was an underlying issue for the most active participants in this regard too. Of the 10 per cent of participants who said financial costs were important, the majority were from the most active categories. To encourage participation, cooperatives have to convince non-participants their costs will be met in full, and to compensate the most active participants more generously.

The development of *habit* is important, as it means people have stopped calculating what they might get out of it, and just carry on participating. In our study only a quarter of participants said they acted out of habit, but they include a type we identified in another study as 'habitual participants' (Birchall and Simmons, 2007). For them, regularity and predictability of events and interactions are important.

Benefits are the opposite of costs, and so we can expect that the more people benefit, the more they continue to participate. Benefits can be subdivided into *external* (material) and *internal* (subjectively perceived) types. To our surprise, only a small minority (16 per cent) of participants said 'external' benefits were important to them. This was even more surprising because area committee members were paid an honorarium of £500 a year (plus further increments if they participated at Regional or main board levels), and received a 10 per cent discount on purchases. However, some members pointed out that if they calculated the payment at an hourly rate they would be receiving no more than a fraction of the UK minimum wage! Few participants saw these financial benefits as an incentive. They preferred to think of them as a buffer against the hidden costs of participation, and as recognition of their commitment. In this respect, they were important.

By comparison, many more respondents considered 'internal' benefits to be important to them, particularly the sense of having 'a valuable learning experience', 'a sense of achievement', 'a chance to have my say' and 'enjoyment'. If cooperatives want to increase participation they should concentrate on these more internal rewards. Participants' motivations seemed clear-cut; the benefits outweighed the costs, making continued participation more likely. However, the influence of these individualistic incentives was called into question by another unexpected finding; over 75 per cent of participants who expressed a preference said they would still participate *without* any of these incentives. They had collectivistic incentives that outweighed the individualistic ones. When asked, most participants stated they wanted to get benefits for the group as a whole (60 per cent) as opposed to individual benefits (1 per cent) – 36 per cent said they wanted both.

This brings us to the other side of MIT: *collectivistic incentives*. We measured these using an attitude scale. Non-participants scored significantly lower on each of these three measures than participants. It was not that they had no sense of community, shared goals or shared values, just that their attachment to them was weaker. Among participants, in a straight fight between our individualistic and collectivistic explanations, collectivism won conclusively. Some might argue that we were simply measuring what members wanted us to hear. However, depth interviews and observations at meetings confirmed that collectivistic thinking and discourse were dominant amongst participants. The influence of individualistic incentives was not necessarily unimportant, but it was secondary. What follows is that a strategy for participation should not only seek to provide individual internal benefits; first it should strengthen members' collectivistic incentives.

Area committee members did have a *sense of community*, although this did not often extend much further than general support for a Co-op shop in their own community, or support for the idea that there should be a shop where one had previously been closed. Sense of community was much weaker for non-participants. We recommended to the Co-operative Group strategies for strengthening members' sense of community that included providing a focus for community identity, and more opportunities for member interaction (Birchall and Simmons, 2003). For cooperative banks such a focus is found in the local branch and, in small cooperatives, in the primary cooperative itself. Opportunities for member interaction include educational events such as seminars and conferences, and also increasingly internet-based groups based on shared interests and values. For the Co-operative Group, in this respect size is an issue. It is one of the biggest cooperatives in the world, and it does not have the federal structure of most cooperative banks and credit unions. Instead it has to operate with a decentralised three-tier system of 50 area committees, eight regional boards and a main board. It should be easier for banks with the two-tier system based on primary cooperatives and central banks to anchor themselves in identifiable local and regional communities.

When it comes to developing *shared values* cooperatives have a natural advantage, in that the values and principles set out by the International Co-operative Alliance provide clear guidelines (Birchall, 1997). At the time when we did the research, the Co-operative Group was giving increasing emphasis to these values and principles, even in its business planning. The emphasis on fair trade and ethical consumerism was popular with members. If they want to build on this motivational driver, customer-owned banks have to emphasise the 'cooperative difference', which rests on how members differentiate the cooperative from other types of bank. Size is not as important a limiting factor here, as values and principles can extend and be shared across long distances. However, it depends upon sustained leadership and commitment from the very top of the organisational hierarchy, reproduced at local level by employees in the bank's branches.

Members' commitment to *shared goals* depends on the sense that the organisation as a whole is working towards the same objectives and 'pulling in the same direction' as members, and that committees are effective – they are able to 'get things done'. In our study, many area committee members did have some sense that the organisation and its members were 'moving together'. There was a clear demarcation between the work of the areas, which was mainly advisory, and the regions, which was much more concerned with decision-making and budgeting. Our evidence shows that area committee members understood this, and that their aspirations were not unrealistic. A more significant problem was members' sense of effectiveness; some were frustrated by their sense that they lacked real influence. Cooperatives have to find ways of involving members in governance that are realistic about the limitations but also convincing that the members' views will be taken into account.

We expanded our analysis to consider the other factors at work in the 'participation chain'. The first link in the chain examined participants' *resources*, such as money, time and skills. In the study of the Co-operative Group, as in the other studies we carried out, *money* did not show up as being a necessary resource. Cooperatives are good at involving people who are not very well off; paying their expenses, and making them feel valued. *Time* also showed relatively little effect, either on whether participants got started or on the quantity of their participation once they were involved. However, participants with children were less likely to participate for more than five hours per month. We found that childcare commitments did not stop people participating at the local level, but they did prove a barrier to becoming a higher-level representative. Another issue was compensation. We felt that there was a strong argument for boosting annual fees given to board members to the level that would be lost by an average earner. In this way, it would remove some of the barriers to those who have to be in paid work, and might help to bring younger people and more women into the higher levels of governance.

Skills derived from educational qualifications did not show up as important in whether co-op members got started or not – non-participants were actually more likely to have educational qualifications than participants! However, skills derived from previous experience were important. Eighty-five per cent of participants, but just 52 per cent of non-participants, had previous experience. *Confidence* has related effects. Participants reported much higher levels of confidence than non-participants about their ability to participate, and they also had much more confidence that they personally could make a difference to getting things done (see Simmons and Birchall, 2005 for statistics). Amongst participants, confidence also correlated strongly with the extent to which members participate; confidence was related to previous experience. It follows that more effort needs to be made to build up the capacity of non-participants who do not have the experience and skills of current participants. This means putting more investment into education and training activities, and incentivising people to take advantage of them.

On the *mobilisation* of members, participants were significantly more engaged than non-participants on *issues*. Here the customer-owned banks have a significant advantage, because they can confidently claim to be good for the local economy and to provide an ethical alternative to discredited investor-owned banks. In the study, participants were also much more likely than non-participants to feel that the Co-op provided them with enough *opportunities* to participate, and to say their initial experience of these opportunities was positive. However, non-participants were particularly keen to see more localised opportunities for participation. We also found that participants were much more likely than non-participants to be subject to face-to-face *recruitment efforts*, and that the recruitment agent was usually known to the participant through existing social networks. Our findings showed that face-to-face recruitment methods were more effective. Non-participants were more likely to have been contacted through written material, while participants were more likely to have been asked by someone they knew. The obvious 'recruitment agents' are the staff, many of whom will be familiar to, and trusted by, the customers.

DIFFERENT TYPES OF PARTICIPANT

Up to this point we have talked as if participants are all the same. Yet it may be that some types of person participate more than others. For example, in previous research (Simmons and Birchall, 2004) with public service user groups and cooperatives we found that some groups were imbalanced in their age profiles, with older people more likely to participate than younger people. Indeed, people over 50 years of age were sometimes twice as likely to participate as those under 50. Similar trends also show up in research on participation and social capital (Putnam, 2000). There are two potential reasons for this: a 'generational' effect, whereby older and younger generations have different attitudes to participation, and a 'life cycle' effect, whereby participation is something people 'come to' in their later years. Social capital theorists until recently discussed the 'doomsday scenario', suggesting that once the current generation of participants passes on, few people will replace them from the younger generations. However, the enormous boom in 'joining' that the internet has generated is already confounding these predictions. More recent analyses suggest that the dip in participation experienced in the 1980s and 1990s (blamed on the 'Me-generation') has passed and that younger people (the new 'We-generation') are much more participatory, though in completely new and unanticipated ways.

There are more subtle ways of dividing people up into different types of participant. In previous work we have divided group members up according to their answers in our surveys using cluster analysis. This allows us to typify participants and non-participants according to their key motivations. In one of our studies, of people connected to housing and consumer cooperatives, three generic clusters of participants and two of non-participants emerged (Simmons and Birchall, 2004).

Amongst non-participants, there are first *unmotivated people*. They perceive the costs of participation to be higher, the benefits to be lower, and score lower on collectivistic motivations across the board. They are likely to be more negative about joining a group, and to feel unconfident about coming forward to participate in its governance. Second, there are *marginal non-participants*. These members are much less negative, and do not perceive the costs of participation to be particularly high, but currently lack strong enough positive motivations to come forward. However, with the right encouragement they might be persuaded. Amongst participants, there are first *campaigners*. These members are quite highly committed and active. They are 'doers', who take responsibility on committees and as office-bearers, and tend to seek change rather than defend the status quo. Second, there are *footsoldiers*. These members are also quite committed and active, but are happier to contribute in a different way, volunteering to provide 'support functions' for the group (such as communications and publicity). Finally, there are *marginal participants*. These members are relatively uncommitted and inactive. They are much less motivated, perceiving the costs to be higher and benefits lower, and their collectivistic motivations are almost at non-participant levels; this suggests that it would not take much for them to decide to stop.

In any group of people working together there will be these kinds of differences. The above types are merely suggestive and in other studies we found a different set that also included *fatalistic non-participants*, and participants who felt their job was as *scrutineers*, making sure the campaigners did the job properly. Whatever the mix, it is important that groups contain different types of people who can all contribute at different levels of intensity and in different ways. It is also important to understand that some participants are not very different from some non-participants: marginal participants and marginal non-participants score very similarly on the collectivistic scale. This means that anyone trying to foster group action over time must try to retain and recruit participants.

CONCLUSION

Taken together, these insights from theories of cooperation and participation show that people can be persuaded to participate in customer-owned businesses, provided the directors and managers of those businesses want them to, and have a member participation strategy. The new communications technology and human nature are both on their side.

11. Customer-owned businesses – the wider picture

Apart from banking, are there other types of business owned by their customers? Of course there are. They can be found wherever people have needed to organise the supply of some good or service for themselves. Table 11.1 lists the types that have become well established, and in the final row adds in banking to show the similarities with these other sectors.[1] The closest sector to banking is insurance, since many banks offer a range of insurance products and insurance mutuals often also provide savings products; the term 'bancassurance' indicates that in some countries the two sectors are beginning to merge. Another closely related sector is agricultural supply, which in the Raiffeisen system in Europe grew up in parallel with the banks. Similarly, consortium cooperatives (sometimes called shared service co-ops) for small business people and retailers grew up in parallel with the supply of credit by the urban Volksbanks. Utility co-ops have sometimes been founded alongside banks supplying credit to farmers. Consumer cooperatives have set up banking departments that sometimes have grown into separate cooperative banks.

CUSTOMER-OWNED RETAILERS

The idea that consumers might organise to meet their own consumption needs reaches back to the earliest stages of the industrial revolution. However, it presupposes that a monetised economy has developed in which people rely at least partly on buying what they need in a market. They also have to have enough income to support the new business. They also need to find a method of governance that will ensure the business runs in the interests of the members, and a method of distributing surpluses in a way that is fair and provides an incentive to do business with the 'co-op' rather than with its competitors. Although the earliest experiments date back to the 1760s, this is why the official history of the consumer cooperative begins with the Rochdale Pioneers in 1844; like Raiffeisen and Schulze for the cooperative banks, they promoted a business model that would succeed and be copied all round the world (Birchall, 1994).

Table 11.1   A suggested taxonomy of customer-owned businesses

Market sector	Type of business	Supplies	Type of customer
Retailing	Consumer cooperative	Food, clothing, pharmacy, funeral, travel, banking, etc.	Individual
Insurance	Friendly society, mutual insurance company, consumer cooperative	Life, health, accident, fire, property, personal indemnity insurance	Individual and commercial (including other types of customer-owned business)
Utilities	Utility cooperative	Water/sewerage, biofuel, telecoms, electricity	Individual, commercial
Primary producer	Agricultural, fishery, forestry supply cooperative	Inputs to businesses owned by primary producers	Commercial, plus some individual consumption
Small business sector	Consortium cooperative, retailer-owned wholesaler	Inputs to a variety of businesses, e.g., taxi drivers, dentists, small retailers	Commercial
Banking	Cooperative bank, credit union, building society, SACCO	Savings, loans, mortgages, current accounts, investment services, etc.	Individual and commercial

The catalyst for action was a depression in the weaving industry that left people destitute. It was only a few years before the famine of 1848 in Germany that led to the development of the banks. In Britain during the eighteenth century, weaving had been a proud trade, decentralised in well-built industrial villages and employing whole families in a mixture of self-employed weaving and small farming (Thompson, 1968). Within two generations they had been reduced to destitution. The first blow was a supply chain monopoly; small masters gave way to large merchants who cornered the market in supply and marketing of cloth and were able to use their monopoly power to force the earnings of the weavers down. The second blow was the growth of a factory system with its mass production, extreme division of labour, and a deskilled workforce. Combined with this loss of status and income came rapid urbanisation and serious public health problems and epidemics; in 1848, when the Pioneers' store was just beginning to establish itself, the average life expectancy in Rochdale was just 21 years. Reports from the poor law commissioners of the time describe how, in the recession of 1841–42, 60 per cent of workers were unemployed. The irony was not lost on the commissioners that blanket weavers had had to sell their own blankets and sleep on straw (Thompson, 1968).

The Pioneers were helped by the under-developed nature of the retail trade at the time. A revolution in industry and urban living had not yet been matched by a revolution in distribution, and town dwellers were dependent on weekly markets. High-class grocery was a skilled trade, but working-class people relied more on family-owned general stores that were few in number, poorly stocked and charged high prices to offset the risk from giving credit (Davis, 1966). A new working class was taking shape whose demands were simple and easy to estimate, but the industry was inefficient and in need of new methods of organisation (Jeffreys, 1954). The Pioneers virtually invented retail management via branch stores, and through cooperative wholesaling and manufacturing were able to organise distribution much more effectively than their competitors.

They laid down some basic principles that would ensure both business success and democratic control by consumers. The 'dividend principle', by which surpluses were distributed regularly to members in proportion to their purchases, ensured their loyalty. The principles of giving no more than a fixed and limited return on shares, and of one person, one vote, regardless of the size of shareholding, meant the business could not deform into one owned by investors. The low cost of entry, combined with an open membership principle, meant that all but the poorest could afford to join. New members were welcomed, because the larger the membership the lower would be the expenses and the higher the dividend (Birchall, 1994). All of these created an incentive for member participation in governance. There was a prudent principle of cash trading that, though it had the effect of excluding the very poor (who relied on weekly credit from small shopkeepers), ensured that the business would survive in bad times. Finally, there was a principle of supplying only good quality products, which meant that at a time of almost universal adulteration and short measures the cooperatives could be trusted to work wholeheartedly in the interests of consumers (Holyoake, 1907).

We know quite a lot about the Pioneers (Birchall, 1995). Out of the 28 men who attended the first meeting only eight were flannel weavers, though half were associated with the trade. The rest were skilled artisans and small-business people, and so they were not the poorest; as one historian described it, they were moved more by idealism than by hunger (Bonner, 1970). This is understandable, since poverty leaves little energy for institution-building. It is a pattern that was to recur in the setting up of the cooperative banks and credit unions; people on middle incomes setting up a society to benefit the poor, not as a matter of charity but of mutual aid. There is an even more direct parallel. A trade depression in 1847–48 nearly ruined the experiment, but the Pioneers had a stroke of luck; in 1849 a Rochdale Savings Bank collapsed and many people rushed to join the Co-op because it was the only safe haven for their money. It had not been designed as a savings bank but it developed into one, and this partly explains why the European model of cooperative banking never caught on in Britain; the 'Co-op' had filled the same niche.

The movement grew rapidly. By 1881 there were 547 000 members in 971 societies with sales of nearly £15.5 million. By the end of the nineteenth century there were over 1.7 million members in 1439 cooperative societies, with a turnover of more than £50 million a year. By 1914 there were over three million members in 1385 societies (some smaller ones had amalgamated), with a turnover of £88 million, which in those days was a very large amount of money (Birchall, 1994, p. 65). The cooperators had also expanded their business vertically into the wholesaling and production of the goods they needed. Starting from nothing in 1863, the Co-operative Wholesale Society had by 1914 become a massive business in its own right, with a turnover of £35 million, with retail societies, productions worth £9 million a year and a workforce of over 22 000 (Redfern, 1938). The Scottish CWS had grown along similar lines and had sales of £9.5 million by 1914. As well as being among the largest wholesalers in the world, CWS and SCWS had become major growers, manufacturers and importers, bringing to the British consumer the benefits of cheap food from abroad and cutting out the 'middle man' throughout the supply chain.

There were several background conditions that help explain this success. Until multiple chains and department stores began there was a lack of real competitors; the chains only began in the 1870s and the department stores in the 1890s, giving the cooperatives 'early mover' advantage (Jeffreys, 1954). Demand was growing. There were more and more customers (population doubled between 1851 and 1914), and wages were more than keeping pace with prices, growing by 35 per cent by the end of the century. A revolution in railway transport coincided with the growth period, making it possible to supply towns and villages cheaply and reliably, while the development of steam ships led to import of cheap food (Burnett, 1989). It has been estimated that in the ten years from 1877 the price of food in a typical working-class family dropped by 30 per cent (Redfern, 1938). There are more specific reasons for this period of growth. The invention of the branch store led to horizontal integration, and that of the wholesale society led to vertical integration. The needs of co-op members were easy to estimate and so plans could be laid that seemed ambitious but were based solidly on a guaranteed market.

At around the same time as the Rochdale Pioneers were opening their store, similar experiments were being carried out in other countries, but it was only when promoters in each country discovered the Rochdale 'system', with its dividend on purchases, that their own movements began to take off. In Switzerland, existing societies converted and by 1904 there were 204 of them, with their own wholesale society and national union. In France, by 1907 there were 2166 societies, with over 600 000 members. Religious and political divisions inhibited the Belgian movement, but even so, by 1905 there were 168 societies with a national federation. In Italy, by 1904 there were 1448 registered societies, with around a third as many again unregistered. In Germany, by 1905 a central union of consumer cooperatives had 787 societies in membership, along with 260 attached to the credit banks; their wholesale society was explicitly modelled on the English CWS. In Russia, by the 1905 revolution there were nearly a thousand societies with 300 000 members. After this, a more liberal political climate led to rapid growth, so that by the time of the Bolshevik revolution they had become a vital part of the supply chain. Other Central and Eastern European countries also established small, but nationally federated cooperative sectors, and some can boast cooperative-type stores as old as that of the Rochdale Pioneers. In Japan, cooperatives began in 1879 (Kurimoto, 2010), and by 1907 there was a society 'in every town of any importance' (Vacek, 1989, p. 1033). By the time of World War I, all the countries of Western Europe and Scandinavia, Russia and several countries in Central and Eastern Europe had well-developed consumer cooperative sectors. The largest was still the British movement with three million members, but the Germans, with 1.7 million members, were not far behind.

In Britain, the movement grew steadily during the interwar period, and by the start of World War II it consisted of 1100 societies, controlling 24 000 stores, and having 40 per cent of the market in butter, 26 per cent of milk, 23 per cent of grocery and provisions, and 20 per cent of tea, sugar and cheese. It employed a quarter of a million people in retailing and another hundred thousand in manufacturing and distribution. With 155 factories, the CWS was one of the biggest businesses in the world (Birchall, 1994). In all countries with established cooperative movements this was also a time of steady expansion. Because they were dealing in basic commodities, cooperatives tended to stand up to the shocks of economic depression and mass unemployment. In times of trouble, member loyalty tended to increase, even if for a while their total spending went down. During the interwar period the idea reached North America. In Canada, it took root most firmly among the mining communities of the Atlantic Provinces, where it combated the monopoly supply of goods through company stores. In Nova Scotia, like the credit unions the consumer co-ops were aided by the adult education system developed by the Antigonish movement that stressed the importance of cooperatives to the local economy (Fay, 1938). Despite setbacks in countries taken over by totalitarian governments, by 1937 the International Co-operative Alliance had in membership 50 000 consumer co-ops with nearly 60 million members.

After World War II, the movement in the UK continued to expand. It was at the forefront of innovations such as self-service and supermarkets, but these hid underlying structural problems. With over 1000 societies, a range of different-sized shops, many of which were too small, and with a lack of integration between societies and their wholesalers, the movement was losing ground to the multiple chains. In the post-war period, at first consumer cooperatives were ahead of the field, opening self-service stores and supermarkets. In the UK their market share reached 11 per cent of retailing. Then they became seriously challenged by competition from multiple chains that had grown partly by copying the Co-op's methods. There then began a long and often dismal struggle to persuade local societies to merge and form regional societies, to divest themselves of their wholesaling and manufacturing businesses which by now had become a liability, and to reshape themselves along similar lines to the multiples, who did not go further back in the distribution chain but used their buying power to gain market power over manufacturers.

By the end of the twentieth century, in Britain mergers had reduced the original 1000 societies to around 40, and faced with some of the most effective and efficient multiple retailers in the world the movement's market share had declined to just 3 per cent. The German movement also faced stiff competition, and by 1965 it had just 8.6 per cent of the market (Brazda, 1989). Here the response was similar. Instead of paying a dividend to members, co-ops began to offer rebates to all customers, thus weakening the vital connection between membership and economic returns. Similar too were the structural weaknesses of the sector; attempts to organise mergers were hampered by weak central direction and the resistance of small societies determined to keep their autonomy even at the risk of extinction. In the early 1970s, in response to mounting debts, societies began to convert to a conventional limited company form, and amalgamated in one central organisation, Co-op Zentrale AG, that by 1980 was back in profit. However, weak accountability structures and fraudulent management led to further drastic reorganisation until much of the sector had to be sold off.

A similar story can be told in other Western European countries. In Austria, a too rapid expansion in the 1970s led societies into a serious debt burden, and eventual amalgamation into one Konsum Austria. Stagnation and the concealing of the crisis from consumer-members led, in 1995, to the national society's – and therefore the whole movement's – bankruptcy. In the Netherlands, in 1973 the movement had to be sold off to the private sector. In France, in 1985 around 40 per cent of the movement was sold off, and now only a few small societies remain (Schediwy, 1989). Consumer cooperators in the Scandinavian countries also faced strong competition and the need to rationalise the number of societies, but they did a better job of it and kept a substantial market share. Two success stories are the movements in Italy and Switzerland. In Italy, we might have expected the gradual decline seen in other countries, but because of the relative backwardness of the retail trade during the 1980s the co-ops experienced 'expansion and growing social recognition' (Setzer, 1989, p. 853), though with only a small share of a fragmented retail trade.

The consumer cooperative sector in Switzerland faced similar challenges to that in the UK, but the national union took a tougher line than did the UK Co-operative Union, threatening weaker societies with expulsion if they did not merge and imposing disciplines such as a common logo. Its strong performance can be accounted for partly by the need to compete with another consumer co-op, Migros. This was started in 1925 by a complex character called Gottlieb Duttweiler, whose father had been a co-op manager and who, despite being a talented entrepreneur, admired cooperative values. He built a large retail chain, then turned it into 12 regional co-ops grouped into a federation. By the 1960s Migros had become a massive conglomerate, with its own production units, its own bank and an insurance company. Although it did not give the traditional co-op dividend, it specialised in low prices and used the profits to fund extensive adult education activities.

The best example of a successful consumer cooperative sector in the postwar period is, undoubtedly, Japan. Here, it was the consumer movement of the 1960s that really established a sustainable cooperative sector. It was a large-scale citizens' movement that arose in response to widespread food adulteration, misleading labelling and environmental pollution. Opposition from retailers held them back, sponsoring laws that forced cooperatives to become fully mutual (customers had to become members) and to stay within prefectural boundaries. It is significant that they were not allowed to set up their own bank. Despite these restrictions, the movement experienced sustained and rapid growth. Membership grew from two million in 1970 to 14 million in 1990, while turnover grew tenfold. Some reasons for success were the active participation of house-wives as members, a home delivery system organised through small 'han' groups of consumers, and a strong sense of being a social movement. They managed to succeed in doing what other movements had thought was impossible – to make large-scale organisation compatible with member democracy and with organisational efficiency.

Recently, the sector in the UK has begun a noticeable revival. Specialising in small supermarkets, it has begun to capitalise on its strengths rather than copying the competition (Birchall, 1987). It has brought back the dividend (using an electronic card), and through use of the internet is revitalising the idea of membership. The UK Co-operative Group now has over six million members, 106000 employees and 4800 retail outlets, and turnover of more than £13 billion. It is a cluster of businesses that include food retail, pharmacy, funerals, travel, farming, banking and insurance. It is the fifth largest food retailer in the UK and the leading convenience store operator. It owns the Co-operative Bank and Co-operative Insurance Society, which are now organised under one umbrella, the Co-operative Bank Group (Co-operatives UK, 2012). With the strong performance of the group and of some regional societies, market share has leapt to more than 9 per cent of UK retail trade.

In Finland a dramatic reconstruction of the sector has led to renewed growth under the title S-Group. In its core business of the supermarket trade, S-Group is now the market leader. In 2007 it opened its own cooperative bank. In Sweden, the sector is also reorganised under one strong federal body, and has a 21 per cent market share. Like the Finnish S-Group, it has a bank whose membership card is crucial for maintaining the relationship with members and delivering an extensive reward scheme. In 2007, for example, members received 7.7 million reward vouchers with a redemption value in discounts of around SEK 465 million (Birchall, 2009). In Italy, nine regional societies are now integrated in one group, Co-op Italia, which has become the largest supermarket chain with a market share in retailing of 18 per cent. In France, where consumer co-ops almost disappeared, the few that survived are doing surprisingly well. In Switzerland, Co-op Schweiz has succeeded in merging the remaining 14 regional societies into one, completely transforming itself from a decen-tralised, local society based union into a unified national retailer, with over two million members and a market share of around 17 per cent. Its rival, Migros, now has over two million members, over 80000 employees and a market share in retailing of 32 per cent. It also has Switzerland's fifth largest bank. In Canada, consumer cooperatives have also faced difficult times. However, there are still strong sectors in western Canada and the Atlantic region that have retained the traditional structure of local primary societies backed up by strong wholesale arms.

In Japan, the long economic recession, changing lifestyles and stiff competition from retail chains have meant that the cooperative sector has ceased to grow. With a steady increase in the proportions of women in paid employment and a change to a more individualistic lifestyle, the mainstay of the cooperative strategy, joint buying, has become less popular. However, non-store retailing is still sustainable because of a switch from joint buying to individual home delivery. The legal restrictions mean the system has remained decentralised, but this has made it easier for them to enter into agreements with producer co-ops to guarantee pure products that are locally produced. In this respect they are still way ahead of their competitors (Kurimoto, 2010). In Singapore, NTUC Fair Price has become the market leader with 57 per cent of the grocery market (Davies, 2005). It seems that when it comes to explaining the growth, decline and recovery of consumer cooperatives we have to consider carefully the conditions in each country.

The renaissance of the cooperatives is partly explained by the drastic restructuring of the last 50 years that has enabled them to compete through gaining economies of scale and being able to hire good managers. At first this led to a democratic governance deficit and a sense that, though the cooperatives could compete, they did not serve a clear purpose. Now a new generation of managers and directors have emerged who can see the potential of consumer ownership as a business advantage, and are keen to reconnect with members (Co-operative Commission, 2001). If they find ways of doing this cost-effectively, consumer cooperatives will continue to prosper and find a distinctive place in the retail market. In countries where they have set up their own banks, they will also contribute significantly to cooperative banking.

CUSTOMER-OWNED INSURANCE PROVIDERS

Mutual insurance was invented for the same reasons as customer-owned banking. It was a straight case of market failure through under-supply. People had to find ways of insuring themselves against common risks such as ill health, unemployment, old age and death, at a time when neither the state nor commercial insurers were willing to get involved. Like the banks, they developed through distinct historical traditions. There are three types of insurance cooperative: friendly societies, mutual insurance companies and insurers owned by other types of cooperative.

Friendly Societies

The history of the friendly societies goes back a long way. In Britain they began like the building societies, with a group of members, an alehouse and a moneybox. The members deposited a small amount of money each week in the box, and agreed to pay out of it the cost of being attended by a medical doctor, weekly sickness benefits and a death benefit to the family of any member who died; in modern terms, they provided health insurance, sickness insurance and life insurance. There are records of societies in Scottish ports in the seventeenth century, and by the end of the century the novelist Daniel Defoe could describe them as being quite common throughout Britain (Gosden, 1973). They were closely related to the savings societies that worked in the same way, enabling people to save to buy specific items such as clothing, boots and shoes. In France, mutual aid societies also trace their origins far back, to medieval guilds and workers' associations. Like the British friendly societies, the movement was self-generating. A historian comments 'neither the legislators, nor the philosophers, nor the learned have exercised any notable influence on their development' (Mabilleau, quoted in Aubrun, 1915, p. 7). It was the people's needs, their coordinated efforts and the publicity given by sympathetic supporters that caused the movement to grow.

In Britain, by 1801 it was estimated there were 7200 societies with 648 000 members out of a total working population of nine million (Gosden, 1973). Then, throughout the nineteenth century, growth was rapid and sustained, and it was accompanied by a remarkable development of new types of society that were designed to meet a wide range of needs. At this time, there was a high failure rate; societies could easily become financially exhausted and collapse. There was a particular problem with insurance; actuarial knowledge was undeveloped and statistical tables for calculating risk were unreliable. The societies charged a flat-rate contribution regardless of age, and as their members grew older and so liabilities grew over time, they found it difficult to attract younger members. However, like the banks they had the advantage of information about the members, which was useful in preventing moral hazard (members claiming more than they were entitled to in benefits). The sense of mutual obligation, combined with detailed knowledge of each other's situation, meant that members tended to limit their claims against the society.

The movement quickly began to benefit from federal structures; regional societies called 'orders' were set up, providing economies of scale for local groups called 'lodges' that maintained some local independence; a similar structure to that of the European cooperative banks. Gradually, the societies became more professional, moving from a system of equal contributions and locally determined benefits to the use of actuarial tables to calculate risk and centrally determined contributions and benefits. Just as the building societies worked out how to become permanent lenders for long-term mortgages, the friendly societies worked out the principles of modern insurance.

As members of societies emigrated to Australia, Canada, the USA, New Zealand, South Africa and the West Indies they took the idea with them. Returning emigrants also took the idea back into continental Europe. In France, after its recognition in law in 1852 the movement grew rapidly, increasing from around 2000 societies with 100 000 members in 1850 to 13 000 with 2.1 million members by the end of the century (Wisconsin, 2010). In Britain, by 1904 the movement had reached its peak. There were 5.6 million members in registered societies, plus an unknown number in small, unregistered societies. Out of a total of seven million workingmen, nearly all were members of friendly societies. A new form of society grew up, called a 'collecting society', that sold life insurance policies through local agents who collected weekly premiums. By 1903 there were 43 of these with nearly seven million members. As in the building society movement, at around the same time, some took advantage of their remoteness from members to neglect governance and charge high management fees. The United Assurance Company was the worst; there were problems of mismanagement and extravagance, culminating in 1883 in its collapse. In this type of society, members were almost excluded from governance (Hopkins, 1995). The friendly society movement also faced a growing challenge from commercial competitors. The Prudential Insurance Company had begun business in 1854, and by the end of the century 'industrial insurance' companies had grown into a gigantic industry with over 30 million funeral benefit policies outstanding, and a workforce of 100 000 to administer them.

In the USA friendly societies came to be called 'fraternal societies'. Like the British societies, they mainly provided sickness benefits, death benefits and medical care through society doctors, but they also had a wider welfare role: one historian says that, before the great depression of the 1930s, they were the leading providers of social welfare apart from the churches (Beito, 1990). By 1920, their National Fraternal Congress had 200 member societies with 120 000 lodges that were insuring nine million members. However, this was the tip of the iceberg, because most societies were local and not affiliated to the national congress; in Chicago alone there were known to be 313 fraternal organisations providing insurance (Siddeley, 1992). One historian estimates that altogether, 18 million people or nearly 30 per cent of all adults over 20 belonged to such societies. They dominated the health insurance market, helped resettle vast immigrant populations and were particularly popular among African Americans (Beito, 1990). Because they could micro-manage the administration of sickness benefits so as to avoid moral hazard, they 'provided an efficient delivery of working-class sickness insurance that commercial insurers could not match' (Emery, 2010, p. 5). There is a parallel here with the credit unions that used their knowledge of the character of the members to avoid default on loans.

In France, by 1915 there were nearly seven million members in 25 000 societies for mutual aid that had sickness benefits as their main activity (Aubrun, 1915). In contrast to Britain, most of the French mutuals encouraged women members and provided maternity benefits. As in Britain, societies were facing strong competition from large insurance companies that used actuarial tables to set their rates, and they were beginning to become more business-like in response. Like the German cooperative banks, they set up a three-tier system of primary societies, regional unions and a national federation. This enabled them to provide further services such as reinsurance, hospital and pharmacy services and sanatoria.

Given the importance of insurance against such basic risks as sickness, it would be surprising if the state had not intervened to make coverage more generous and comprehensive. Voluntary insurance can never cover everyone, and there is an argument that it should not do so because mutual insurance is character-building (Beito, 1990). There is also a counterargument that if it does not cover women or people on low incomes it fails a more important test based on criteria of equality of condition and social justice. Some mutualists believed that eventually mutual societies would evolve to cover all of people's risks, while others were beginning to see that the limits of mutuality might already have been reached.

When the state begins to take an interest there are four options. The state can use mutual and investor-owned insurers to deliver a statutory service, it can take over completely, it can provide comprehensive cover for part of the cost letting mutual or investor-owned insurers top it up, or allow a private market and provide residual cover to those who cannot afford any private provision. The first option occurred in Britain and France in the period from 1911 to the 1940s, the second in Germany in the 1880s and Britain in the 1940s, the third in France and some other European countries in the postwar period, and the fourth in the USA. In Australia, an attempt was made to set up a compulsory social insurance scheme in 1928, for which the friendly societies agreed to be the agents. However, it was abandoned through opposition of the medical doctors' association, and after World War II the societies agreed to become health insurance funds under a government national health scheme. Thus it came

Finance in an age of austerity

about that politicians, influenced by the medical profession, decided the future of friendly societies in each country, and in the resulting healthcare settlement they were either incorporated or completely shut out (Birchall, 2010).

Mutual Insurance

There are a variety of needs for insurance that can be met through customer-owned businesses. It comes in two major forms; 'non-life', which covers all sorts of risks to property and person, and life insurance, which is a payment to a beneficiary on someone's death. Non-life insurance began with the need to spread the risks from fire, and its origin can be traced precisely to the Great Fire of London in 1666 that destroyed more than 13 000 homes. There are two ways to mitigate loss by fire; one is to put the fire out and the other to restore the monetary loss. The first began in 1696; a society with the improbable title of 'Contributors for Insuring Houses, Chambers or Rooms from Loss by Fire by Amicable Contributionship' provided fire engines and crews to put out fires in houses owned by its members (Mutual Assurance, 2010). The idea spread to America, where Benjamin Franklin helped set up a volunteer fire-fighting association in Philadelphia called the Union Fire Company, which provided a model for many others. However, Franklin realised that insurance against loss was also needed, and in 1752 he set up a society called The Philadelphia Contributionship.

The first life insurance mutual was Equitable Life, founded in London in 1762. It was made possible by advances in the scientific understanding of risk undertaken by Charles Dodson, who calculated premiums using mortality tables and probability studies. This meant that the policyholder's premium could be fixed throughout the term of the policy and the amount paid on death was guaranteed (Equitable Life, 2010). However, it was in America that the mutual life insurance sector became fully developed. Commercial life insurance began in the USA during the colonial period, but companies rarely survived for long and sold few policies (Murphy, 2010). Suddenly in the 1840s it took off, for two reasons. First, there were legislative changes that allowed women to insure their husbands' lives and to benefit from the payout. Second, mutual life companies began to emerge that redistributed annual profits to policyholders rather than stockholders. They did not really need to raise large amounts of capital from a separate group of stockholders; if they grew quickly their size would soon ensure that they could meet claims out of their own reserves. Also, their mutual status reassured potential customers of their trustworthiness at a time when there was little state regulation. The mutuals grew quickly through aggressive advertising and were popular with policyholders because of the annual dividends they paid, not on capital but in reduced premium payments.

From the early part of the nineteenth century, the idea of mutual insurance spread throughout America, moving west with the population and becoming the normal way in which fire insurance was organised. Fire insurance then became bundled up with other risks and sold as home insurance. Auto insurance began that covered both damage to the vehicle and legal liabilities arising out of accidents. A variety of risks to the person began to be insured, such as accident and disability cover, designed to mitigate loss of earnings. A major innovation begun by the Equitable Life Assurance Society was the deferred dividend policy, whereby people could both insure their life and share dividends from an investment fund when they retired. By the end of the nineteenth century, the mutual companies and the fraternal societies dominated the business in life insurance. Between 1885 and 1905 the mutuals began doing business internationally; Equitable provided insurance in almost 100 countries, New York Life in almost 50 and Mutual in about 20 (Murphy, 2010).

In 1905 an investigation was made into the mutuals; it found that like in some of the collecting societies in Britain there were abuses such as excessive management costs, high expenses and political lobbying, and proxy voting was being used to frustrate control by policyholders. Legislation was passed to combat this, and another surge in the growth of mutuals began; while there had been 106 companies in 1904, by 1914 another 288 had been founded, and they continued to dominate the market until a demutualisation trend began in the 1980s.

Insurers Owned By Other Types of Cooperative

There is yet another important mutual insurance sector: member-owned insurance societies set up by consumer cooperatives and similar organisations. The earliest example is the Co-operative Insurance Society, founded in Britain in 1867 by the consumer cooperative movement to meet the needs of its societies for fire and property insurance, and then by extension to meet their members' needs for personal insurance. Thereafter, the history of the sector is really the history of individual secondary co-ops founded by a variety of sponsors: consumer cooperatives, farmer cooperatives, trade unions and churches. There are particular advantages to providing insurance this way. While a mutual insurance provider does not need large amounts of capital to get going, it does need to grow quickly if it is to gain the protection of numbers that makes its commitments less risky. This is best done through an existing organisation that can invest enough capital to get it over the initial period when it is not able to meet all its commitments and provide it with a guaranteed market.

We can track the growth of this type by membership in its trade body, the International Co-operative and Mutual Insurance Federation (ICMIF). In 1922 it had just 21 member co-ops. By 1999 it had over 100 members from 60 countries with nearly 9 per cent of the world's market for insurance. A survey in the same year showed that 15 per cent had a base in agricultural cooperatives, 29 per cent in trade unions and professional groups, 19 per cent in multi-purpose cooperatives from developing countries, 19 per cent in credit unions (18 per cent in other categories: Kennedy, 1999, p. 227). By 2009 this number has risen to 216 members worldwide. The members in turn represent over 400 insurance organisations with assets approaching $1 trillion spread across more than 70 countries. A further 1700 mutual insurers are indirect members through their national trade associations (ICMIF, 2010).

In virtually every developed country one or two cooperative insurers will be among the top ten. The Nationwide Mutual Insurance Company started as an auto insurer for Ohio farmers, and is now one of the largest insurance and financial companies in the world, ranked 108 in the Fortune 500 listing. It has almost $15.5 billion in statutory assets, and has more than 16 million policies. The Debeka Group provides life and health insurance mainly for civil servants; it is the top private health insurer and the fourth largest direct insurance company in Germany. Unipol was founded by one of Italy's cooperative federations, Legacoop, to meet its members' needs for insurance. It is now the fourth largest insurer with a market share of over 10 per cent. The Co-operators in Canada is the largest Canadian multi-product insurer. It is owned by cooperatives and credit unions, and provides a mixture of individual and farm insurance. The customer-owned banks are intimately tied into this sector; CUNA Mutual is a huge international insurer owned by credit unions, for whom it markets a wide range of products. There is more and more integration between the insurance and banking sectors; soon it may be impossible to identify them as a separate sector.

The boundaries between different types of ownership can never be taken for granted. In the insurance industry there have been periods of mutualisation and demutualisation. For instance, the UK-based insurer Standard Life was founded in 1825 as an investor-owned business, in 1925 it converted to a mutual and in 2006 it converted back again. The first move was towards mutuality. Early on in the evolution of insurance, several investor-owned companies in the USA and the UK, such as Standard Life and Equitable Life, decided to switch to mutual status, because it gave them advantages in the market; at that time, with little or no government regulation, customers did not trust the investor-ownership model. Then, with better regulation by governments, some traffic began to flow the other way: by the end of the 1970s in the USA 100 life companies and about the same number of non-life companies had demutualised (Franklin and Lee, 1988), and the 135 that were left had a market share of 43 per cent (down from 69 per cent in 1954 – Hansmann, 1985). The process was slowed by laws passed in the 1920s in New York State and several other states because of insiders benefitting from windfall profits, and it only got going in the 1980s when deregulation of the industry took place.

In other countries demutualisation was not an issue and there was some movement in the other direction; in the 1960s several insurers in the UK converted to mutual form in order to 'escape from the attentions of the corporate raiders of the time' (Franklin and Lee, 1988, p. 89). In another twist to the tale, in the 1970s several insurance companies in France and Germany, and auto insurers in several states in Canada, were nationalised. In the UK the consumer cooperative-owned CIS had to fight hard against nationalisation of the whole industry.

The recent trend has been in the direction of investor-ownership, in the USA, the UK, South Africa, Australia and Japan, and the mutual sector is much reduced; in the UK it is down to 4.5 per cent of the market. The main reason given for demutualisation was to gain access to the capital that new investors bring in. It might be thought that, like the customer-owned banks, a business that recycles money to and from its customers cannot be in need of extra capital; one of the main advantages of a customer-owned insurer is that it merely invests money on behalf of its customers. Why then does it need capital from outside? Sometimes a mutual has to demutualise and seek new capital because it has got things wrong. For instance, the UK's largest mutual, Standard Life, suffered a reduced capital base when the stock markets fell between 2001 and 2003, and its board decided it could no longer provide the kinds of benefits with profits that policyholders expected from a mutual. It also needed to seek additional capital to meet its commitments, and so in 2006 it converted back to investor-ownership (Standard Life, 2010). However, as with the building societies and S&Ls, the main reasons for demutualisation are that the mutuals can enter new markets that are riskier than the ones they are in, and that the managers can benefit from enhanced salaries, bonuses and stock options. They were not very convincing arguments at the time, but after the banking crisis they look even weaker.

The Current Situation for Customer-owned Insurance

Surprisingly, demutualisation has not dented the sector as much as we might have expected. In 2007, the global market share of mutual and cooperative insurers (all the types we have been discussing so far) was still 22.6 per cent (ICMIF, 2010). Its share of the US market was 28.7 per cent, of Japan 41.6 per cent, of France 38.2 per cent, of Germany 43.5 per cent, of the Netherlands 25.8 per cent, of Canada 16.1 per cent, of Italy 13.6 per cent, and so on. Another way to look at the same figures is to list the top ten countries where the mutual market share is largest. At number one is Finland with a 71 per cent market share, followed by Germany with 43.5 per cent. Then follow Denmark, Japan, France, Norway, Austria, Iceland, Tunisia and the USA. This shows how dominant the sector still is in most countries in Europe and in Japan. If we look at the figures by region we find that North America, Europe and Asia/Oceania have similar shares of the mutual market (28 per cent, 21 per cent and 21 per cent respectively), with Latin America taking 6 per cent and Africa just over 1 per cent. The global market share is 20 per cent in life and 26.5 per cent in non-life business.

Is the mutual share growing or contracting? Between 2006 and 2007 it fell from 23.6 per cent to 22.6 per cent, not because of demutualisation but because of a reduced share of the fast-growing life insurance market. It seems, then, that from a global perspective the sector is now quite stable. The three streams (friendly societies, mutual insurers and insurers owned by other customer-owned businesses) have all flowed into one river of mutual insurance, and it is becoming harder to distinguish between them; in some countries they share the same trade association and they all work in the same markets. They are all now represented internationally by one trade body, the ICMIF. Increasingly, there is a confluence of insurance with banking, so that the category of mutual insurance is increasingly being relabelled as 'mutual financial services'.

CUSTOMER-OWNED UTILITIES

There are some sectors in which governments have a strong interest in making sure a service is provided, because there is a vital need to be met, because it has made a service compulsory for all citizens, or because the sector is a natural monopoly and politicians do not want consumers to be exploited. Examples include healthcare, education, utilities and leisure services. In these sectors customer ownership is sometimes found, but the public sector is often dominant because governments choose not just to fund the provision but also to provide it. Producer groups also have an interest and are sometimes reluctant to let consumers own and control the organisation that delivers the service, preferring to own it themselves, or to part own a hybrid form that also includes consumers and employees. If the governance is likely to be contentious, the stakeholder groups may prefer to leave governance to a set of trustees in a non-profit (Hansmann, 1996).

One service that has historic links with agricultural cooperatives and cooperative banks is utilities. The term refers to the supply of goods that rely on a fixed distribution system such as pipes, lines or cables, and so the business sectors that are referred to as utilities are water supply, electricity, gas, telecommunications and some forms of transport. There are natural monopolies involved, because the costs of installing the system that carries the utility are usually large, and once it is built there are high barriers to entry. Also, because the commodity is often vital for human life and consumers cannot do without it, they cannot avoid purchasing it even at a high price. It is vital that the organisation that owns the distribution system is accountable to the public, otherwise it will charge monopoly prices and enrich its owners unfairly, and may stop short of providing the service to people in rural areas or on low incomes if this is not profitable. Where private companies are allowed to be the owners, there is likely to be demand from the public and from other business interests for heavy and persistent regulation by governments (Birchall, 2010).

There are obvious theoretical advantages in customer-owned utilities. If consumers are supplying themselves it does not matter that there is a monopoly. If they make a profit they can redistribute it in lower prices, operating an automatic cost-price mechanism that, like other consumer co-ops, excludes the 'middleman'. There may be disadvantages if they cannot raise capital as easily or as cheaply as their competitors, but where they have succeeded in becoming established they usually receive low interest loans or other favourable treatment from government (NRECA, 2010). What opportunities have there been to compete in these sectors? First, there are situations where there is no distribution system at all, a local economy is only just reaching the stage where it is needed and governments choose to offer the monopoly to a customer-owned business; this happened in the 1880s in Finland in water and telecoms, and in the 1930s in the USA in electricity supply. Second, there are opportunities to deliver energy to a distribution system that allows competing suppliers; consumer-owned businesses now supply wind-generated electricity in Denmark, and solar and hydro-powered electricity in Switzerland. Third, there are situations in which other types of business have failed and consumers have created their own solutions; this happened in water supply in Bolivia.

Water Cooperatives

Probably the earliest consumer-owned utilities are the water cooperatives that supply rural areas in Finland. Here, local government took responsibility for providing water and sewage facilities to urban areas, but because the rural areas had sparse populations and there was a long tradition of self-help, towards the end of the nineteenth century consumer co-ops became the preferred option. Now, as well as 400 municipal utilities, there are 902 cooperatives. Some are quite large, serving more than 10 000 people, and they supply rural areas and small towns. Not many countries have followed Finland's lead, but water cooperatives are important in Argentina, Chile, Colombia and Bolivia. Here, the provision of water has been surrounded by controversy over what sort of ownership structure works best. During the 1990s, the World Bank supported privatisation to large transnational water companies, but the UN came out against such privatisation because private companies had found ways of excluding poor people. The UN Development Report for 2003 said that local communities and firms were the best providers, and that it was the government's role to build their capacity (UN, 2003).

In Santa Cruz, Bolivia, a consumer cooperative known as Saguapac has been providing the city's water since 1979. Saguapac is a true consumer cooperative, and all 96 000 domestic customers are automatically members. It has been copied elsewhere in Bolivia and has proved to be efficient and effective (Birchall, 2003). How does it compare with other forms of water delivery? It is one of the best-run water companies in Latin America, with a low level of water leakage, a high level of staff productivity and universal metering. It has a low average tariff and high collection efficiency. It is also efficient in its use of foreign loan finance for investment, out-performing two private companies (Nickson, 2000). Its cooperative structure is the main reason for its good performance; the cooperative shields managers from the kind of political interference that weakens municipal water companies, it allows for continuity in administration, and the electoral system works against corruption.

Electricity Co-ops

During the 1930s, electricity co-ops began to be developed in rural USA. As in Finland, the idea of cooperation had become deeply rooted in rural areas through agricultural and credit cooperatives. President Roosevelt's New Deal programme brought these into partnership with the government in a drive to develop the rural economy. Power companies were uninterested in supplying electricity to farmers; they were uncertain about the demand and wary of committing the huge amount of capital investment needed to create a transmission system. The government offered low-interest loans to electricity co-ops and established four public power companies to generate electricity from federal dams and offer it at low prices to the cooperatives. By 1953 more than 90 per cent of US farms had electricity. Now there are 864 distribution co-ops and 66 generation and transmission co-ops in the system, providing power to 12 per cent of the population (42 million people) in 47 states. They have 42 per cent of the distribution lines, and deliver 10 per cent of the power used in the USA each year (public bodies deliver 16 per cent and private companies 74 per cent); they are predominant in rural areas and their share of the market seems assured (NRECA, 2010).

The American model of rural electricity co-ops has been exported to the Philippines, Bolivia, Costa Rica and Bangladesh, where it leads to notable improvements in the quality of life and local economic development (Birchall, 2010). How does it compare with alternatives? In the Philippines, the cooperatives achieve 95 per cent revenue collection, and their performance compares well with neighbouring private utilities. In contrast, public companies do not have a good track record; there are technical failures, losses of power due to deteriorating networks, poor management, inability to make consumers pay their bills, and sometimes corruption. Private for-profit companies have experienced the same disincentives that prevented them from electrifying rural USA. The trade body, the National Rural Electric Co-operatives Association, says 'our experience has demonstrated that a focus on serving the consumer results in the most efficiently run systems'. Cooperatives have the advantage of being consumer-driven, putting the key stakeholder in the centre of the business, being able to access capital but keeping bills affordable, and helping people find new ways of making a living (NRECA, 2010).

Electricity co-ops are also important in Brazil, Chile and Argentina. In Denmark they have been leading the way in development of wind farms. Here, like in the USA, in rural areas the consumers own the networks. The cooperative model guarantees accountability to consumers, has price transparency and a non-distribution rule that means profits are returned to consumers in lower prices. Despite privatisation, cooperatives remain a popular option. Denmark leads the world in wind power, and cooperatives have played a surprisingly large part in its development. The idea is not new; even in the 1930s there were 30000 windmills, some of which were producing electricity, and so when modern turbines began to appear they were not seen as controversial. Local communities became involved on the principle that they should own their own power source, and then when schemes became larger and moved offshore ownership was opened up to the whole population. Between 1978 and 1994 co-ops captured over 50 per cent of market share, but this has now fallen to around 23 per cent as landowners and larger investors have entered the market. By 2004, no new wind farms were being planned, but the sector had become established: 150 000 families are members of wind-energy cooperatives, owning over 3000 turbines (Birchall, 2009).

Denmark is also a world leader in district heating networks which now account for over 50 per cent of space heating, and allow cheaper, low-grade fuels to be used. The decision was made 30 years ago to invest in district heating rather than individual connections to natural gas networks. From 1986 onwards, the emphasis was put on combined heat and power plants which were more efficient and allowed for fuel flexibility; natural gas, biogas, woodchip, straw, bio-oil and even solar thermal can be used, and excess heat from power stations can be circulated to city heating grids. In order for the new system to work, local authorities were given the power to force consumers to connect to the system, and this was counterbalanced by a commitment to the consumer control and price transparency that cooperatives provided. Of the 430 district heating companies in 2001, 85 per cent were cooperatives (though they only account for 37 per cent of the heat sales because the larger ones are owned by local authorities). They are recognised as being more efficient and responsive to consumers than the local authority district heating systems (Birchall, 2009). Switzerland provides a twist in the same tale; here there are around 50 solar energy co-ops that provide an opportunity for consumers to invest. Some are also developing small hydropower schemes.

Telecoms Co-ops

In Finland, the development of telephone networks began at the same time as the water co-ops. The telecoms company Elisa Oyj was founded in 1882 and soon became dominant in the rural market (though it was demutualised in 2000). Another 27 local telephone associations banded together in the Finnet Group, which has a mobile phone network called DNA Finland, and a market share of 18 per cent of the fixed telephone lines (Birchall, 2009). Again, to find the next example we have to make a leap of the imagination from Finland to Latin America, where Argentina has 130 telecoms co-ops.

Transport Cooperatives

There is not much evidence of consumer ownership of transport systems such as roads and railways. The collective action costs of start-ups have been too high, it is difficult to exclude non-members, and also consumers do not form a coherent interest group. It is possible to envisage a quasi-membership organisation that owns a rail network, but it would have to be multi-stakeholder based and non-profit (Birchall, 2002). However, there is one area where consumer ownership has begun to thrive. Car sharing cooperatives began in Switzerland and Germany during the 1980s as a way of enabling people to cut down on their car use and make better use of resources. One example is Mobility, a Swiss car sharing cooperative that provides over 2200 vehicles at 1000 stations throughout Switzerland. It has 80 000 customers, including more than 2100 businesses. Members of the cooperative can book online and use various types of credit and ID cards to gain access to a vehicle without having to use keys. The idea has spread throughout Europe, and there are several such cooperatives in Canada and Australia (Birchall, 2009).

CUSTOMER-OWNED SUPPLIERS TO PRIMARY PRODUCERS

Primary producers in farming, forestry and fishing have a lot in common. They are all involved in creating value in an uncertain encounter between humans and the natural world that depends on climate and topography, and that, because it is only partially under human agency, carries risks. They all need inputs to their production in the form of tools, seeds, feeds, fertilisers, nets, machinery and so on, and, because the transforming process takes time, they also need inputs of credit to provide cash flow. They also need insurance to lessen the risks, though some of the uncertainties they face are uninsurable. In all these respects, they can become customer-owners. Then, when the product has been created, they need to have it collected, put it through some basic processing and then marketed. If they are very well organised, instead of marketing their products right away they can extend their control along the value chain, transforming the product further and so capturing more of the realisable value. In these respects they can become producer-owners. The distinction is a fine one because in practice some agricultural and fishing cooperatives provide the links in the value chain at both sides of the farmer's own business. Only on the supply side can they be seen as consumers (Hansmann, 1996).

Like other types of customer-ownership, farm supply cooperatives were invented to help people survive in a new industrial society in which money values began to predominate and subsistence production gave way to production for the market. From the mid eighteenth century in Britain – later in other countries – the farming process became more intensive, more reliant on machinery and so on capital investment. It began to need regular inputs of fertilisers, seeds and livestock whose quality became more controlled (Smith, 1961). Supply co-ops ought to have been easy to set up; like consumer co-ops they involve joint purchase of a simple good that can be divided up. They began in 1865 in Switzerland for the supply of fertiliser (Birchall, 1997). However, their growth was inhibited by the way in which farmers relied on supply merchants for credit and could not easily break free. It took the development of the Raiffeisen banks to allow European farmers to supply themselves. First they purchased in bulk through their banks and then they formed separate supply societies. It was a rival group to Raiffeisen, the Hesse Union, that began this type; beginning in 1872, by 1886 they had formed a wholesale society, and by the end of the century were big enough to challenge the farm supply cartels.

We will leave the history of agricultural cooperatives at this point, because from then on supply, marketing and processing all became connected up, and it is difficult to separate out the role of farmers as consumers from their role as producers (a comprehensive treatment of the subject can be found in Birchall, 2010).

CUSTOMER-OWNED SUPPLIERS TO SMALL RETAILERS

When independent retailers began to face serious competition from consumer co-ops and saw the massive advantages their rivals were gaining from vertical integration, they began to organise their own wholesale supply co-ops. Like the Rochdale-type co-ops, they began in a small way: Unified Grocers in the USA was founded in 1922 by 15 retailers who shared out a carload of soap. This parallel movement has built up a formidable set of retailer-owned businesses that are now trying to match the buying power of a newer rival, the multiple chains such as Tesco and Walmart.

Retailer suppliers are strong in Western Europe. Rewe, based in Germany, is a group of independent retailers operating 7330 stores, and is the third largest player in the European food trade. Edeka is the fourth largest, with 4100 stores. In France, Leclerc has 17 per cent of the market, Intermarche 11.3 per cent and Systeme U 8.3 per cent (Baron, 2007). Pharmacy chains are also very strong; Noweda Apothek is the top pharmacy wholesaler in Germany, with 6000 member pharmacies, and Cooperativa Farmaceutica Espanola is the largest in Spain. They are also strong in Scandinavia; Kesko is the largest trading company in Finland, with 30 per cent of the market. It is the parent corporation of the

K-Group, comprising some 2400 independent retailer-shareholders who operate 2700 stores specialising in groceries, leisure goods and consumer durables. In the USA the Wakefern Food Corporation is the largest, with 43 members owning 200 Shoprite superstores, while Associated Wholesale Grocers, the second largest, serves 1900 stores in 21 states. In New Zealand, the cooperative buying group Foodstuffs is the largest grocery distributor.

There are interesting national variations; in the USA separate groups supply hardware stores, whereas in Europe the groups supply, and also own directly, a wide range of types of business. There are also complications in the type of ownership. The retailers own some groups, while wholesalers own others. Some have floated on the stock market and so have a mixed ownership structure, including independent storeowners, large retail chains and wholesalers. They tend to operate through franchises, and their members have to accept the discipline of the group. This raises the question of who holds the power in a franchise; it could be argued that because the relationship is unequal it is better if franchisees collectively own the franchisor. The retailer-owned wholesaler model has distinct advantages, as it creates an interesting mix of individual ownership of stores and group discipline that is self-imposed and, over time, can evolve quite sophisticated ways of aligning member interests and avoiding opportunistic behaviour. The Leclerc chain, for instance, has rules that enable the cooperative to control when stores can be sold and to negotiate the price, while allowing individual owners to own their own stores. This balances short-term gain against long-term benefits (Baron, 2007).

There are occasional demutualisations; in Britain, Londis used to be retailer-owned but sold out to a group of wholesalers. There is another interesting trend towards retailer ownership and consumer cooperatives coming together for joint supply. The Spar Group is the world's biggest retail chain, and its ownership varies from one country to another. In Finland, the consumer cooperative S-Group is now the majority shareholder in Spar, which means it can supply independent retailers as well as consumer cooperative stores. In contrast, Spar Scotland is wholly owned by a wholesaler, and retailers enter into a franchise agreement to gain access to the Spar brand. However, in 2006 the Co-operative Group and Spar entered into an alliance in which they agreed to pool their 'own label' volumes and jointly purchase from suppliers.

Here, the customer-owned type of business has demonstrated its effectiveness in shifting the balance decisively towards small businesses. Yet it is interesting to note that the retail buying groups are strongest in countries where there are few consumer co-ops: France, Germany and the USA. Faced with a strong consumer movement, Conad in Italy has become the country's second largest distributor but lags well behind Co-op Italia. Competition between different types of customer-owner can be just as serious as between them and the investor-owned businesses! Yet the future may be with strategic alliances between consumer-owned and retailer-owned businesses against the multiple chains.

CUSTOMER-OWNED SUPPLIERS TO SMALL BUSINESSES

The history of this type began as an offshoot of the cooperative banks in Germany, where Schulze-Delitzsch set up shared service co-ops to help small enterprises to compete; one of his first initiatives was a cooperative that supplied materials to shoemakers. As a result, they are a recognised category within the apex body, the German Co-operative and Raiffeisen Union, called 'small-scale industry commodity and service cooperatives'. There are over 1000 of them, providing economic support for their members who are described as 'traders, craftsmen and self-employed persons' in over 45 lines of business. They have set up two central in the retail sector and five in the trades and crafts sectors (Sudradjat, 2010). This type of business is also beginning to be recognised in other countries. In the UK, they are called cooperative consortia, and they have become common in locally produced food and drink, arts and crafts, tourism, market trading, provision of out of hours medical coverage, home care services, specialist teaching services, and actors' agencies, as well as in the longer-established sectors of taxi driving and consultancy services (Co-operatives UK, 2010).

The biggest individual shared service cooperative may be the UNIMED system in Brazil. Here, 109 000 doctors have banded together in 375 medical cooperatives to provide a complete system of healthcare to 83 per cent of the country. In Brazil the lack of basic infrastructure meant doctors were unable to find work, and so in 1967 they joined together in the city of Santos to found Unimed. In 1975 they founded a national federation, in 1983 they opened their first hospital and now they have 103 owned hospitals and 3244 accredited hospitals with which they have contracts. They also run their own ambulance and emergency services. They provide care to more than 16 million people who pay for the service through a user-owned health insurance cooperative called Usimed that has 34 per cent of the national market in health plans. This Brazilian model has been followed in Chile, Colombia, Costa Rica, Paraguay and Argentina.

Other very large shared service co-ops can be found in media services. The National Cable Television Co-operative is owned by 1100 cable companies and supplies 12 million subscribers in the USA. Associated Press supplies news from 243 offices in 97 countries to its owners, who are 1500 daily newspapers. At the other end of the scale, in developing countries there are some interesting examples such as cooperatives of shoe shiners and market stallholders, and the shared-ownership cooperative has been recognised as the only way of supporting workers in the informal economy (Birchall, 2004). This is exactly the kind of opportunity Schulze was creating 160 years ago in his supply cooperative for shoemakers.

THE ADVANTAGES AND DISADVANTAGES OF CUSTOMER-OWNERSHIP

The different varieties of customer-owned business grew up at a time when the needs of people on low incomes were not being met, either because of under supply or monopoly. Promoters stepped in who, by experiment and deliberate design, found a business model that worked and could easily be replicated. Underlying changes in society helped: industrialisation and urbanisation, the development of markets, the growth of a wage-earning working class, the struggle for political emancipation, the spread of literacy and so on. Emigration helped spread the business model around the world. Strong competition then grew up from investor-owned businesses that in some cases copied the methods of the cooperatives and in others found new ways of doing business that left the cooperatives disadvantaged. Government regulation also weakened the need for customer-ownership as investor-owned businesses were forced to behave responsibly. In the postwar period, in some cases the loyalty of members ebbed away along with the huge capital reserves built up. In other cases the customer-owned businesses were able to exploit their first mover advantage and remain competitive. Their task now is to realise the comparative advantages that come from having customer-members.

There are similar business advantages in each type of customer-ownership, such as the ability to cut out the profit-takers and return all the profits to the members, the focus on quality in the product, the lack of conflict between customers and shareholders (some of these are summarised in Table 11.2). There are also differences based on the nature of the product or service being provided (some of these are summarised in Table 11.3). If we shift the typology away from customer-ownership to member-ownership this allows us to theorise the advantages and disadvantages of a wider range that includes marketing and food processing cooperatives, and employee-owned businesses (Birchall, 2012d). However, the focus on customers produces a sharper picture when it comes to comparing

Finance in an age of austerity

Table 11.2   Some universal advantages of customer owned businesses

Derived from federation	Derived from ownership	Derived from control	Derived from benefits
Ability to balance localness and small scale with provision of a wide range of services at low cost	Prevents cartels or monopolies that damage consumer interests. Enables trust in long-term relationships under uncertain contracts	Focuses the business on what matters to consumer-members. Enables ethical choices to be made. Manages risk effectively	Patronage refund acts as a 'cost-price' mechanism providing consumers with goods at lowest possible cost

member-owned banks with similar businesses in other market sectors. It shows that there is nothing unusual in customers owning their own bank; they also own quite a lot of other businesses as well.

NOTE

1. In a recent book (Birchall, 2010) I classified customer-owned banks as part of a wider category of *member-owned businesses*. This made them part of a wider group that includes marketing cooperatives, worker co-ops, and other businesses whose members are producers rather than consumers. However, the idea of customer-ownership brings greater clarity in relation to banking.

Table 11.3   Some advantages of customer-owned businesses by type

Market sector	Type of business	Advantages to members	Advantages to wider society
Retailing	Consumer cooperative	Pure food, opportunity for fair trade, local food sourcing, dividend on purchases, consumer voice	Community engagement, social role, campaigning, ensuring competition and local presence
Insurance	Friendly society, mutual insurance company, consumer cooperative	Long-term trust, especially in pensions, low cost, reliability, ability to insure the less insurable	Ensuring competition, preventing cream skimming
Utilities	Utility cooperative	Spread of utilities to rural areas that investor-owners are not interested in, consumer monopoly ensures low prices	Prevention of monopolies, can be more efficient than public ownership, health and education benefits
Primary producer	Agricultural, fishery, forestry supply cooperative	Raising of incomes of primary producers through lower price and better quality of inputs	Strengthening of rural economies, increase in income impacting on education, health
Small business sector	Consortium cooperative, shared service co-op	Provision of at-cost services that give a competitive advantage, and ability of businesses to grow, competitive advantage against multiple chains	Helps local economies to grow, provides employment, ensures competition among different types of provider, preventing cartels

12. Conclusion: a cooperative counter-narrative

There are several prescriptions for putting right a banking system that has proved itself unfit for purpose. After the banking crisis of 2008, the first thing the regulators did was to tighten their rules so that banks have to hold more capital to cover potential losses. There were calls to break up the big banks described as 'too big to fail' and to separate out investment banking from commercial and retail banking, but these have stalled against resistance from the banks. After bankers began to divert public bailout money into massive bonuses, there were calls to change the incentive structure so that they would only be rewarded for longer-term success. As Vince Cable put it, 'Bank managers would be incentivised to be reliable, predictable and boring' (2010, p. 193). This is being done and the bankers' behaviour is changing as a result, though not as much as the public would like.

Another round of bank failures and bailouts within the European Union led to a plan to allow banks to fail in the future; the costs would fall on equity and bondholders rather than on taxpayers, and an explicit resolution regime would make the process orderly and predictable. A new tax on banking transactions is proposed that will recoup some of the losses to the taxpayer and build up a fund against future losses. Alternatively, an insurance scheme would do the same job by creating a rescue fund (Llewellyn, 2010).

There is a lingering fear among the public that tighter regulation on its own will not be enough – the banks have shown they can get round that. Calls for moral renewal meet with a cynical response from people who are so rich they do not seem to care what people think of them. The problem is that shareholder value will still drive the motivations of managers and boards, and this means taking risks, finding ways round the restrictions, and keeping a step ahead of other banks that are doing the same thing. John McFall (at the time Chair of the UK Parliament's Treasury Select Committee) wrote a foreword to the report arguing for remutualisation of Northern Rock. He captured the public mood when he said:

> What we need now is substantial change to the remuneration practices, corporate governance and culture of banking. I would hope that the nature of

banking would change of its own accord in response to the crisis, but I fear that as soon as public and media attention turns away we may see a return to 'business as usual'. This absolutely must not happen. We have a once in a generation opportunity to fix the financial system, which we ought to seize (Oxford Centre, 2009, p. 3).

Unfortunately, the plan to remutualise the 'Rock' and other banks that were in public ownership foundered on the simple fact that governments want their money back, and it is more profitable in the short term to sell the bank than to convert it back to a mutual.

The banking crisis has been followed by the 'Great Recession', the Eurozone crisis and a general slowdown in the world economy. There is profound uncertainty about when and if the world economy will recover. What is certain is that the rich are getting richer and more and more people are falling into poverty. This gloomy scenario has led to widespread protests by 'anti-capitalists' who are sceptical of all attempts at reform. However, theirs is an anti-narrative rather than a counter-narrative, and people need to oppose the damage the banks have done by supporting a realistic alternative.

This is why, if customer-owned banks did not exist, over the last few years they would probably have been invented. People need an alternative. This book has shown that there is an alternative that is well established, successful, sustainable and scalable. It has at its heart – we would now say coded into its DNA – a low-risk, ethical banking system that is just waiting to take over. The *Move your Money* campaign, that began in the USA and has recently been launched in the UK, has the great virtue of enabling people to do something about it. They can move their money to customer-owned banks wherever they are found, and they are doing so in their millions. As the book has shown, customer-owned banks can be found in most countries, in many of which they already have a significant market share. Ed Mayo, the Secretary General of Co-operatives UK, has put this argument eloquently:

> At an individual level, you can't do everything to put an unfair economy right – but you can do something. Move your money is the new fair trade. It is THE campaign for our time (Co-operatives UK, 2012).

Of course, the malaise in the Western banking system leaves people in the rest of the world unmoved. They have not suffered from the banking crisis but are suffering from its aftermath: a slowdown in growth and an upturn in poverty and unemployment (Birchall, 2012b). The book has shown how, despite enormous difficulties, credit unions have become established in most low-income countries and are out-competing other types of micro-finance institution. They are more democratic, more sustainable and more effective at reaching the poor. Through the development of federations they have demonstrated that they can grow into powerful financial systems that compete with investor-owned banks.

They can do this without needing support from governments or donors, though as we have seen such support can be useful if provided without undermining the autonomy and financial discipline of the bank. In particular, credit unions need a clear and reliable regulatory environment. One of the most inspiring stories to come out of the book is the way in which credit unions in the rich countries are helping to strengthen their counterparts in low-income countries. There is nothing like movement-to-movement support. This brings hope to people who are disturbed by the seemingly intractable problems of poverty in 'developing' countries but disillusioned with the aid industry. Again, we can move from an anti-narrative in which we are paralysed by disillusion, to a counter-narrative in which we regain the power to act.

Appendix – a note on terminology

Is there an umbrella term that can be used to include all member-owned financial businesses such as cooperative banks, credit unions, building societies, and savings and credit cooperatives? In a report for the World Bank, Cuevas and Fischer (2006) used the term *cooperative financial institutions* to cover cooperative banks, credit unions and savings and credit cooperatives. This follows a custom in financial economics of using the term 'financial institutions' to cover all financial intermediaries, including deposit-taking and loan-making institutions; insurance and pensions providers; and those concerned with investments. Other World Bank staff have used this term but it does not seem to have caught on elsewhere. The problem is that other disciplines use the term 'institution' very differently. Most social scientists, including institutional economists, see institutions as being the 'rules of the game'; both formal rules and social norms that govern individual behaviour and social interaction. They are not the same as organisations. The use of the term as a synonym for organisation means that we cannot then talk about institutions as being something distinct that is found in and among organisations.

If we drop the term institution we get *financial cooperatives*, which is used by Goglio and Alexopoulos in a recent edited book (2012). It is catching on; a forthcoming seminar organised by the International Co-operative Banking Association is titled 'Financial Co-operatives Contribute to a Better World'. This has two advantages; it has clarity, and emphasises the relationship between cooperative banks and credit unions and other types of cooperative. However, it does not include the word 'bank' and so cannot be contrasted directly with its two main competitors; investor-owned banks or savings banks.

The term *stakeholder-owned banks*, used by Ayadi et al. in two important reports on savings banks (2009) and cooperative banks (2010), does enable us to contrast different types of bank, but unfortunately it includes both cooperative and savings banks so for our purposes it is too big an umbrella.

The term *customer-owned banks* is used in this book because it captures all the types of financial organisation that make customers into members but then excludes all the rest, including the savings banks. It does not imply that all customers have to be members, because practice varies between cooperative banks and credit unions. Whether or not a customer-owned bank is fully mutual is a separate question. There is a relevant criticism of the use of the term 'customer'. In a study of Australian credit unions, Davis (2007) argues that their common bond is a safeguard against demutualisation. The common bond ensures that the community served is well delineated and common goals can be identified. When members are 'essentially customers who respond to competitive prices from other suppliers rather than member-owners exhibiting loyalty to the organisation', demutualisation is more likely (Davis, 2007, p. 290). This is an argument for traditional credit unions that will have resonance for many people. Yet in this book we are looking for an alternative that can compete with the big investor-owned banks, and customer-owned banks such as Bankmecu in Australia and the Co-operative Bank in the UK are demonstrating that they can do this.

It may be that both terms have their place. The term *financial cooperatives* might be used when the emphasis is on local, member-driven credit unions that still have a common bond and provide services for people on low incomes. The term *customer-owned banks* might be used when the emphasis is on alternatives to investor-ownership provided by larger, more sophisticated providers who see their members primarily as customers. However, there is a view that people on low incomes should not be treated differently than others. Even if a small credit union is the only provider they have access to, they also have the right to be treated as customers. It all depends whether one believes being a customer is an alienated status, or a normal way in which people buy services they need in a market.

Bibliography

Abacus (2012), *Australian Mutuals: Key Fact Sheet*, May.

ACDI/VOCA (2012), *Russia*, accessed 30 August 2012 at www.acdivoca. org.

AgFirst (2012), Website, accessed 6 July 2012 at www.agfirst.com.

Allen, E. and S. Maghimbi (2009), 'African co-operatives and the financial crisis', Coop Africa Working Paper No.3, Geneva: International Labour Organisation.

Allen, F. and D. Gale (2000), *Comparing Financial Systems*, Cambridge, MA: MIT Press.

All-Party Parliamentary Group for Building Societies and Financial Mutuals (2006), *Windfalls or Shortfalls: the True Cost of Demutualisation*, London: All-Party Parliamentary Group for Building Societies and Financial Mutuals.

Altunbas Y., S. Carbó Valverde and P. Molyneux (2003), 'Ownership and performance in European and US banking – a comparison of commercial, co-operative and savings banks', Fondacion de las Cajas de Ahorros Working Paper No. 180/2003.

Arbuckle, L. and D. Adams (2000), 'Reforming credit unions in Honduras', in G. Westley and B. Branch (eds), *Safe Money: Building Effective Credit Unions in Latin America*, Washington, DC: Inter-American Development Bank and World Council of Credit Unions, pp. 114–28.

Armitage, S. and P. Kirk (1994), 'The performance of proprietary compared with mutual life offices', *Service Industries Journal*, **14** (2), 238–61.

Association of British Credit Unions (2011), *Annual Report, 2010–11*, Manchester: Association of British Credit Unions.

Aubrun, R. (1915), *Mutual Aid Societies in France*, Paris: Exposition Universelle de San Francisco.

Axelrod, R. (1984), *The Evolution of Co-operation*, New York: Basic Books.

Ayadi, R., E. Arbak, S. Carbó Valverde, F. Rodriguez Fernandez and R.H. Schmidt (2009), *Investigating Diversity in the Banking Sector in Europe: the Performance and Role of Savings Banks*, Brussels: Centre for European Policy Studies.

Ayadi, R., D. Llewellyn, R.H. Schmidt, E. Arbak and W.P. de Groen

(2010), *Investigating Diversity in the Banking Sector in Europe: Key Developments, Performance and the Role of Co-operative Banks*, Brussels: Centre for European Policy Studies.

Bankmecu (2012), Website, accessed 21 September 2012 at www. Bankmecu.com.au.

Baron, M.-L. (2007), 'Defining the frontiers of the firm through property rights allocation: the case of the French retailer co-operative Leclerc', *Review of Social Economy*, **LXV** (3), 293–317.

Beito, D. (1990), 'Mutual aid for social welfare: the case of American fraternal societies', *Critical Review*, 4 (4), 709–36.

Birchall, J. (1987), *Save Our Shop: the Rise and Fall of the Small Co-operative Store*, Manchester: Holyoake Press.

Birchall, J. (1994), *Co-op: the People's Business*, Manchester: Manchester University Press.

Birchall, J. (1995), 'The Rochdale Pioneers', speech at the 150th Anniversary of the Co-operative Movement, Manchester: Co-operative Union.

Birchall, J. (1997), *The International Cooperative Movement*, Manchester: Manchester University Press.

Birchall, J. (2001), *The New Mutualism in Public Policy*, London: Routledge.

Birchall, J. (2002), *A Mutual Trend: How to Run Rail and Water in the Public Interest*, London: New Economics Foundation.

Birchall, J. (2003), *Rediscovering the Co-operative Advantage: Poverty Reduction Through Self-help*, Geneva: ILO.

Birchall, J. (2004), *Co-operatives and the Millennium Development Goals*, Geneva: ILO.

Birchall, J. (2005), 'Business ethics and the Co-operative Bank', in C. Tsuzuki (ed.), *The Emergence of Global Citizenship: Utopian Ideas, Co-operative Movements and the Third Sector*, Tokyo: Robert Owen Association of Japan, pp. 259–76.

Birchall, J. (2009), *A Comparative Study of Co-operatives in Scotland, Finland, Sweden and Switzerland*, Glasgow: Co-operative Development Scotland.

Birchall, J. (2010), *People-centred Businesses: Co-operatives, Mutuals and the Idea of Membership*, London: Palgrave Macmillan.

Birchall, J. (2012a), 'The potential of co-operatives during the current recession: theorizing comparative advantage', Keynote speech and conference paper for EURICSE/ICA conference 'Promoting the understanding of co-operatives for a better world', Venice San Servolo, 15–16 March.

Birchall, J. (2012b, forthcoming), 'The Big Society and the mutualisation of public services: a critical commentary', in J. Edwards (ed.), *Retrieving the Big Society*, Oxford: Wiley Blackwell.

Birchall, J. (2012c), *Common Cause, Collective Action*, London: Consumer Focus.

Birchall, J. (2012d), 'The comparative advantages of member-owned businesses', *Review of Social Economy* **LXX** (3), 263–94.

Birchall, J. (2012e, forthcoming), *Resilience in a Downturn: the Power of Financial Co-operatives*, Geneva: International Labour Organisation.

Birchall, J. and L. Hammond Ketilson (2009), *Resilience of the Co-operative Business Model in Times of Crisis*, Geneva: International Labour Organisation Responses to the Global Economic Crisis.

Birchall, J. and R. Simmons (2003), 'Motivating members: member participation on governance: a study of the Co-operative Group', Co-operative College Paper 3, Manchester.

Birchall, J. and R. Simmons (2004), 'What motivates members to participate in co-operative and mutual businesses: a theoretical model and some findings', *Annals of Public and Co-operative Economics*, **75** (3), 465–95.

Birchall, J. and R. Simmons (2007), *Our Say: User Voice and Public Service Culture*, London: National Consumer Council.

Birchall, J. and R. Simmons (2010), 'The co-operative reform process in Tanzania and Sri Lanka', *Annals of Public and Co-operative Economics*, **81** (3), 467–500.

Birchall, J. and R. Simmons (2013, forthcoming), 'The role and potential of co-operatives in the poverty reduction process', in J. Howell (ed.), *Non-governmental Public Action and Social Justice*, Basingstoke: Palgrave Macmillan.

Boddy, M. (1980), *The Building Societies*, London: Macmillan.

Bonner, A. (1970), *British Co-operation*, Manchester: Co-operative Union.

Boonstra, W.W. (2010), 'Banking in times of crisis: the case of Rabobank', in M. Balling, J.M. Berk and M.-O. Strauss-Kahn (eds), *The Quest for Stability: the View of Financial Institutions*, Vienna: SUERF, pp. 31–56.

Boscia, V., A. Carretta and P. Schwizer (eds) (2009), *Cooperative Banking: Innovations and Developments*, Basingstoke: Palgrave Macmillan.

Boscia, V., A. Carretta and P. Schwizer (eds) (2010), *Cooperative Banking in Europe: Case Studies*, Basingstoke: Palgrave Macmillan.

Bowles, S. and H. Gintis (2011), *A Co-operative Species: Human Reciprocity and its Evolution*, Princeton, NJ: Princeton University Press.

Brazda, J. (1989), 'The consumer co-operatives in Germany', in J. Brazda and R. Schediwy (eds), *Consumer Co-operatives in a Changing World*, Geneva: International Co-operative Alliance.

Brunner, A., J. Decressin, D. Hardy and B. Kudela (2004), *Germany's Three-pillar Banking System; Cross-country Perspectives in Europe*, Washington, DC: International Monetary Fund.

Building Societies Association (2010), *Conversations with Members; Member Engagement at Building Societies* (fourth edition), London: Building Societies Association.

Building Societies Association (2012), Statistics, accessed 4 May 2012 at www.bsa.org.uk.

Burnett, J. (1989), *Plenty and Want: a Social History of Food in England from 1815*, London: Routledge.

Bussoli, C. (2010), 'Credit co-operatives in Romania', in V. Boscia, A. Carretta and P. Schwizer (eds), *Co-operative Banking in Europe: Case Studies*, London: Palgrave Macmillan, 203–22.

Byrne, N., O. McCarthy, M. Ward and J. McMurtry (2012), 'Credit union restructuring: don't forget the member!', *International Journal of Co-operative Management*, **6** (1), 31–9.

Cable, V. (2010), *The Storm: the World Economic Crisis and What it Means*, London: Atlantic Books.

Carbó Valverde, S., E.P.M. Gardener and P. Molyneux (2005), *Financial Exclusion*, Basingstoke: Palgrave Macmillan.

Carroll, B., O. McCarthy and O. O'Shaughnessy (2012, forthcoming), 'Co-operatives: what relevance now?', in G. Doyle and T. Lalor (eds), *Social Enterprise in Ireland*, Dublin: Oak Tree Press.

Caudhill, J., S. Caudhill and D. Gropper (2001), 'Charter status, ownership type and efficiency in the thrift industry', *Applied Financial Economics*, **11**, 147–55.

Cebenoyan, A. (1993), 'The relative efficiency of stock versus mutual S&Ls: a stochastic cost frontier approach', *Journal of Financial Services Research*, **7** (2), 151–70.

Chaddad, F. and M. Cook (2004), 'The economics of organisational structure changes: a US perspective on demutualisation', *Annals of Public and Co-operative Economics*, **75** (4), 575–94.

CICOPA (2009), *The Impact of the Crisis on Worker and Social Co-operatives*, Brussels: International Organisation of Industrial, Artisanal and Service Producers' Co-operatives, accessed 19 May 2010 at www.cicopa.coop.

Cleary, E. (1965), *The Building Society Movement*, London: Elek.

Co-operative Commission (2001), *Report: the Cooperative Advantage*, London: Co-operative Commission.

Co-operatives UK (2010), Trading for mutual benefit: a guide to co-operative consortia, Manchester, accessed 19 May 2010 at www.cooperatives-uk.coop.

Co-operatives UK (2012), Website, accessed 29 August 2012 at www. cooperatives-uk.coop.

Cotugno, M. (2010), 'Co-operative banking in the ten newly admitted EU member countries', in V. Boscia, A. Carretta and P. Schwizer (eds), *Co-operative Banking in Europe: Case Studies*, London: Palgrave Macmillan, pp. 177–202.

Crear, S. (2009), 'Cooperative banks, credit unions and the financial crisis', paper presented to the *UN Expert Group Meeting on Cooperatives*, New York, April 28–30.

Credit Union Central of Canada (2010), 'The state of the system', System Brief no.2, Toronto: CUCC.

Credit Union Central of Canada (2012), Website, accessed 12 September 2012 at www.cucentral.ca.

Crespi, R., M.A. Garcia-Cestona and V. Salas (2004), 'Governance Mechanisms in Spanish Banks: Does Ownership Matter?', *Journal of Banking and Finance*, **28** (10), 2311–30.

Cuevas, C. and K. Fischer (2006), 'Cooperative financial institutions: issues in governance, regulation and supervision', Working Paper 82, Washington, DC: World Bank.

Davies, K. (2005), *Cooperative Principles and International Expansion: the Example of NTUC Fairprice*, Stirling: Stirling University Institute for Retail Studies.

Davis, D. (1966), *A History of Shopping*, London: Routledge and Kegan Paul.

Davis, K. (2007), 'Australian credit unions and the demutualisation agenda', *Annals of Public and Co-operative Economics*, **78** (2), 277–300.

Dawkins, R. (2006), *The Selfish Gene* (third edition), Oxford: Oxford University Press.

Delisted (2010), Website, accessed 18 May 2010 at www.delisted.com.au/ Demutualised.aspx.

Department for Work and Pensions (2012), *Credit Unions: Feasibility Study Report*, Credit Union Expansion Project, Westminster: UK Government.

Desjardins Group (2012a), *Annual Report 2011, Management's Discussion and Analysis*, Quebec: Desjardins Group.

Desjardins Group (2012b), Website, accessed 8–11 September 2012 at www.desjardins.com.

Desrochers, M. and K.P. Fischer (2005), 'The power of networks: integration and financial cooperative performance', *Annals of Public and Cooperative Economics*, **76** (3), 307–54.

De Waal, F. (2009), *Primates and Philosophers*, Princeton, NJ: Princeton University Press.

Develtere, P. (1994), *Co-operation and Development*, Leuven: ACCO.

Di Salvo, R. (2003), 'The governance of mutual and cooperative bank systems in Europe', *Cooperative Studies*, BCC/Federcasse.

Dowla, A. and D. Barua (2006), *The Poor Always Pay Back: the Grameen II Story*, Bloomfield: Kumarian Press.

Drake, L. and D.T. Llewellyn (2001), 'The economics of mutuality: a perspective on UK building societies', in J. Birchall (ed.), *The New Mutualism in Public Policy*, London: Routledge, pp. 14–40.

Emery, H. (2010), *Fraternal Sickness Insurance*, accessed 5 March 2010 at http://eh.net/encyclopaedia.

Empel, van, G. and L. Smit (2004), 'Development of sustainable credit co-operatives in China', in OECD (ed.), *Rural Finance and Credit Infrastructure in China*, Report No. 1, Paris: OECD.

Encyclopedia Americana (1920), *Friedrich Raiffeisen* (Vol. 29), Harvard: Encyclopedia Americana Corporation.

Encyclopedia Britannica (1911), *Schulze-Delitzsch, Franz Hermann* (11th edition), Cambridge: Cambridge University Press, accessed 8 March 2010 at en.wikisource.org/wiki/1911_Encyclopædia_Britannica/Schulze-Delitzsch,_Franz_Hermann.

Equitable Life (2010), The history of Equitable Life, accessed 8 March 2010 at www.equitable.co.uk.

Esty, B. (1997), 'Organisational form and risk-taking in the savings and loan industry', *Journal of Financial Economics*, **44** (1), 25–55.

European Association of Co-operative Banks (2008), *Statistics*, accessed 23 March 2010 at www.eurocoopbanks.coop.

European Association of Co-operative Banks (2012), *Statistics*, accessed 23 March 2012 at http://www.eurocoopbanks.coop.

European Savings Bank Group (2012), *Key ESBG Member Statistics at 1.1.2006*, accessed 6 August 2012 at www.esbg.eu.

Evans, A. and D. Richardson (1999), *Polish Credit Union Development: Building a Sustainable Network of Financial Services*, World Council of Credit Unions Research Monograph series, 17.

Expert Committee (2011), *Report on the Licensing of New Urban Co-operative Banks*, Delhi: Reserve Bank of India.

Fay, C.R. (1907), *Co-operation at Home and Abroad* (first edition), London: PS King.

Fay, C.R. (1938), *Co-operation at Home and Abroad* (fourth edition in two volumes), London: PS King.

Federal Deposit Insurance Corporation (1999), *History of the Eighties: Lessons for the Future* (Vol. 1), Washington, DC: FDIC.

Ferri, G. (2012), 'Credit cooperatives: challenges and opportunities in the global scenario', Euricse Working Paper No. 31/12, University of Trento.

Fisher, T. (2002), 'Emerging issues and challenges', in T. Fisher and M. Sriram (eds), *Beyond Micro-credit; Putting Development Back into Micro-finance*, New Delhi: Vistaar Publications, pp. 325–60.

Fonteyne, W. (2007), 'Cooperative banks in Europe: policy issues', IMF Working Paper WP/07/159, Washington, DC: International Monetary Fund.

Franklin, N. and W. Lee (1988), 'Demutualisation', *Journal of the Staple Inn Actuarial Society*, **31**, 89–125.

Fraser, D. and A. Zardkoohi (1996), 'Ownership structure, deregulation and risk in the savings and loan industry', *Journal of Business Research*, **37**, 63–9.

Garbaccio, R.F., B. Hermalin and N. Wallace (1994), 'A comparison of non-parametric methods to measure efficiency in the savings and loan industry', *Journal of American Real Estate and Urban Economics*, **22** (1), 169–93.

Girardone, G., J. Nankervis and E.-F. Velentza (2009), 'Efficiency, ownership and financial structure in European banking: a cross-country comparison', *Managerial Finance*, **35** (3), 227–45.

Global Finance (2012), *World's Biggest Banks*, accessed 12 April 2012 at www.gfmag.com.

Goglio, S. and Y. Alexopoulos (2012), *Financial Co-operatives and Local Development*, London: Routledge.

Gosden, P. (1973), *Self-help: Voluntary Associations in Nineteenth Century Britain*, London: Batsford.

Groeneveld, H. and B. de Vries (2009), 'European co-operative banks: first lessons of the subprime crisis', *International Journal of Co-operative Management*, **4** (2), 8–21.

Groeneveld, H. and D. Llewellyn (2012), 'Corporate governance in co-operative banks', Research Publication, Brussels: European Association of Co-operative Banks.

Gutiérrez, E. (2008), 'The reform of Italian cooperative banks: discussion of proposals', IMF Working Papers, No. 08/74, Washington, DC: International Monetary Fund.

Hall, P.A. and D.W. Soskice (2001), *Varieties of Capitalism: the Institutional Foundations of Comparative Advantage*, Oxford and New York: Oxford University Press.

Hannan, M. and J. Freeman (1989), *Organisational Ecology*, Cambridge, MA: Harvard University Press.

Hansmann, H. (1985), 'The organisation of insurance companies: mutual versus stock', *Journal of Law, Economics and Organisation*, **1** (1), 125–40.

Hansmann, H. (1996), *The Ownership of Enterprise*, Cambridge, MA: Harvard University Press.

Hardin, G. (1968), 'The tragedy of the commons', *Science*, **162**, 1243–8.

Heffernan, S. (2005), 'The effect of UK building society conversion on pricing behaviour', *Journal of Banking and Finance*, **29**, 779–97.

Hesse, H. and M. Cihak (2007), 'Co-operative banks and financial stability', IMF Working Paper WP/07/02, Washington, DC: IMF.

Hirschmann, A. (1970), *Exit, Voice and Loyalty*, Cambridge, MA: Harvard University Press.

Holyoake, G.J. (1857) *Self-help by the People: the History of the Rochdale Pioneers* (third edition 1907), London: Swan Sonnenschein.

Homans, G. (1974), *Social Behaviour, its Elementary Forms* (second edition), New York: Harcourt Brace Jovanovich.

Hopkins, E. (1995), *Working-class Self-help in Nineteenth Century England*, London: UCL Press.

Hulme, D., R. Montgomery and D. Bhattacharya (1996), 'Mutual finance and the poor: a study of SANASA in Sri Lanka', in. D. Hulme and P. Mosley (eds), *Finance Against Poverty* (Vol. 2), London: Routledge, pp. 159–221.

Huss, B. (1924), *People's Banks, or Use and Value of Co-operative Credit*, Natal: Mariannhill Mission Press.

Iannotta, G., G. Nocera and A. Sironi (2007), 'Ownership structure, risk and performance in the European banking industry', *Journal of Banking and Finance*, **31** (7), 2127–49.

International Co-operative Banking Association (2012), *Co-operative Banks Share as Core Tier One Capital: Basel II Impacts on the Co-operative Banking Model*, accessed 9 August 2012 at www.icba.coop.

International Co-operative and Mutual Insurance Federation (2010), *About Us*, accessed 8 March 2010 at www.icmif.org.

Jayaweera, P. (1987), 'The role of co-operatives in poverty alleviation', unpublished report.

Jeffreys, J.B. (1954), *Retail Trading in Britain 1850–1950*, Cambridge: University Press.

Jones, D. and P. Kalmi (2012), 'Economies of scale versus participation: a co-operative dilemma?', *Conference on Promoting the Understanding of Co-operatives for a Better World*, Venice.

Jones, P. (2012), 'Credit unions in Britain', unpublished working paper.

Kanther, M. and D. Petzina (2000), *Victor Aime Huber: Sozialreformer und Wegbereiter der sozialen Wohnungswirtshaft*, Berlin: Duncker and Humblot.

Kemp, T. (1985), *Industrialisation in Nineteenth Century Europe*, Harlow: Longman.

Kennedy, J. (1999), *Not by Chance: a History of the International*

Co-operative and Mutual Insurance Federation, Manchester: Holyoake Books.

Klandermans, B. and D. Oegema (1994), 'Why social movement sympathizers don't participate: erosion and nonconversion of support', *American Sociological Review*, **59**, 703–22.

Kropotkin, P. (1902, reprinted 2009), *Mutual Aid: a Factor in Evolution*, London: Dover Books.

Kurimoto, A. (2010), *Toward Contemporary Co-operative Studies: Perspectives from Japan's Consumer Co-ops*, Tokyo: Consumer Co-operative Institute of Japan.

Kurimoto, A. (2012), Personal communication on cooperative financial institutions in Japan.

Kuustera, A. (1999), *Niche of Co-operative Banking in Finland during the First Half of the Twentieth Century*, Helsinki: Pellervo.

Lakhani, K. and R. Wolf (2005), 'Why hackers do what they do: understanding motivation and effort in free/open source software projects', in J. Feller, B. Fitzgerald, S. Hissam and K. Lakhani (eds), *Perspectives on Free and Open Source Software*, Cambridge, MA: MIT Press, pp. 3–22.

Lee, J. (2012), 'Supersized savings banks dissolve in mismanagement', *Hankyoreh*, 7 May.

Lindenberg, S. (2001), 'Intrinsic motivation in a new light', *Kyklos*, **54** (2–3), 189–506.

Llewellyn, D. (2010), *The Global Banking Crisis and the Post-crisis Banking and Regulatory Scenario*, Topics in Corporate Finance 19, Amsterdam Centre for Law and Economics.

Lloyds TSB (2012), Website, accessed 9 May 2012 at www.savingsbanks-museum.co.uk.

MacPherson, I. (1999), *Hands Around the Globe: a History of the International Credit Union Movement*, Victoria, Canada: Horsdal and Schubart.

Malegam, Y. and Expert Committee (2011), *Report of the Expert Committee on Licensing of New Urban Co-operative Banks*, Delhi: Reserve Bank of India.

Manghetti, G. (2011), 'Do savings banks differ from traditional commercial banks?', in *200 Years of Savings Banks*, Brussels: World Savings Banks Institute/European Savings Bank Group, self-published.

Mansbridge, J. (ed.) (1990), *Beyond Self-interest*, Chicago, IL: University of Chicago Press.

Margolis, H. (1984), *Selfishness, Altruism and Rationality*, Chicago, IL: University of Chicago Press.

Mason, D. (2009), *From Buildings and Loans to Bail-outs: a History of the American Savings and Loan Industry, 1831–1995*, Cambridge: Cambridge University Press.

Masulis, R. (1987), 'Changes in ownership structure; conversion of mutual savings and loans to stock charter', *Journal of Financial Economics*, **18** (1), 29–59.

McCarthy, O., R. Briscoe and M. Ward (2000), 'Mutuality through credit unions', in J. Birchall (ed.), *The New Mutualism in Public Policy*, London: Routledge, pp. 41–59.

McGregor, P. (2005), 'Credit unions and the supply of insurance to low income households', *Annals of Public and Co-operative Economics*, **76** (3), 355–74.

McKillop, D. (2012), *Report of the Commission on Credit Unions*, Dublin: Dept of Finance, Irish Government.

Mester, L.J. (1993), 'Efficiency in the savings and loan industry', *Journal of Banking and Finance*, **17** (2–3), 267–86.

Michie, J. and D. Llewellyn (2009), 'Converting failed financial institutions into mutual organisations', Policy and Issue Reports, Kellogg College, University of Oxford.

Milne, A. (2009), *The Fall of the House of Credit: What Went Wrong in Banking and What can be Done to Repair the Damage?* Cambridge: Cambridge University Press.

Moody, J. and G. Fite (1984), *The Credit Union Movement: Origins and Development 1850 to 1980*, Duque, IA: Kendall Hunt.

Moss, M. (2011), 'Henry Duncan and the savings bank movement in the UK', in World Savings Banks Institute/European Savings Bank Group (ed.) *200 Years of Savings Banks*, self-published.

Munkner, H.-H. (ed.) (1989), *Comparative Study of Co-operative Law in Africa*, Marburg: Marburg Consult.

Murphy, N. and D. Salandro (1997), 'Form of ownership and risk-taking in banking: some evidence from Massachusetts savings banks', *Journal of Economics and Finance*, **21** (3), 19–28.

Murphy, S. (2010), *Life Insurance in the United States through World War 1*, accessed 7 March 2010 at www.eh.net/encyclopaedia.

Mutual Assurance (2010), Mutual assurance; its beginning in America, accessed 6 March 2010 at www.mutual-assurance.com.

Myners, P. (2004), *Final Report: Myners Review of the Governance of Life Mutuals*, London: HM Treasury.

National Council of Farmers Co-operatives (1996), *American Co-operation*, Washington, DC: National Council of Farmers Co-operatives.

National Credit Union Authority (2010), *Annual Report*, accessed 3 July 2012 at www.ncua.gov.

National Federation of State Co-operative Banks (2012), Website, accessed 9 August 2012 at www.nafscob.org.

National Rural Electricity Co-operative Association (2010), Website, accessed 12 April 2010 at www.nreca.org.

NCB (2012), Website, accessed 6 August 2012 at www.ncb.coop.

New Zealand Co-operative Bank (2012), Website, accessed 21 September 2012 at www.co-operativebank.co.nz.

Nickson, A. (2000), *Organizational Structure and Performance in Urban Water Supply: the Case of Saguapac Cooperative in Santa Cruz, Bolivia*, Birmingham: Birmingham University International Development Department.

Novak, M. (2011), *Super Cooperators*, Edinburgh: Canongate.

Olson, M. (1965), *The Logic of Collective Action*, Cambridge, MA: Harvard University Press.

Ong, L. (2006), 'Multiple principals and collective action: China's rural credit co-operatives and poor households' access to credit', *Journal of East Asian Studies*, **6**, 177–204.

Ory, J.-N. and Y. Lemzeri (2012), 'Efficiency and hybridisation in cooperative banking: the French case', *Annals of Public and Co-operative Economics*, **83** (2), 215–50.

Oxford Centre for Mutual and Employee-owned Businesses (2009), *Converting Failed Financial Institutions into Mutual Organisations*, London: Building Societies Association.

Planet Finance (2005), *Rural Credit Co-operatives in China*, background information, Paris: Planet Finance.

Power, C., R. O'Connor, O. McCarthy and M. Ward (2012), 'Credit unions and community in Ireland: towards optimising the principle of social responsibility', *International Journal of Co-operative Management*, **6** (1), 8–15.

Putnam, R. (2000), *Bowling Alone: the Collapse and Revival of American Community*, New York: Touchstone.

Rabobank (2009), 'Co-operative banks in the new financial system', self-published report.

Rabobank (2011). *Special Report: Co-operative Banks in the Spotlight*. Utrecht: Economic Research Department.

Raiffeisen Federation (2012), website, accessed 10 June 2012 at www.raiffeisen.ch.

Rajaguru, R.B. (1996), *Survival in the Open Market: a Critical Study on the Co-operative Movement of Sri Lanka within the Market Economy*, New Delhi: International Co-operative Alliance.

Rangarajan, C. (2008), *Report of the Committee on Financial Inclusion*, Mumbai: Nabard.

Rasmussen, E. (1988), 'Stock banks and mutual banks', *Journal of Law and Economics*, **31**, 395–422.

Redfern, P. (1913), *The Story of the CWS*, Manchester: Co-operative Wholesale Society.

Redfern, P. (1938), *The New History of the CWS*, London: JM Dent.

Richardson, D. (2000), 'Model credit unions into the twenty first century', in G. Westley and B. Branch (eds), *Safe Money: Building Effective Credit Unions in Latin America*, Washington, DC: Inter-American Development Bank and World Council of Credit Unions, pp. 91–114.

Ridley, M. (1997) *The Origins of Virtue*, London: Penguin.

Ridley, M. (2010), *The Rational Optimist*, London: 4th Estate.

Rosenthal, C. (2012), 'Credit unions, community development finance, and the great recession', Working Paper 01, San Francisco: Federal Reserve Bank of San Francisco.

Ryan, R. and E. Deci, (2000), 'Intrinsic and extrinsic motivations: classic definitions and new directions', *Contemporary Educational Psychology*, **25**, 54–67.

Sanasa Development Bank (2012), Website, accessed 19 September 2012 at www.sdb.lk.

Sasuman, L. (n.d.) *Credit Union Empowerment and Strengthening (CUES) Philippines*, Madison: World Council of Credit Unions.

Schediwy, R. (1989), 'The decline and fall of Konsum Austria', *Review of International Co-operation*, **89** (2), 62–8.

Seibel, H. (1998), 'Grameen replicators: do they reach the poor, and are they sustainable?', Working Paper 8, University of Cologne.

Seibel, H. (2009a), 'Restructuring a credit co-operative system: the People's Credit Funds of Vietnam', Working Paper, University of Cologne.

Seibel, H. (2009b) 'The rise and fall of the credit co-operative system in India', University of Cologne Working Paper.

Setzer, J. (1989), 'The consumer co-operatives in Italy', in J. Brazda and R. Schediwy (eds), *Consumer Co-operatives in a Changing World*, Geneva: International Co-operative Alliance.

Shah, T. (1996), *Catalysing Co-operation: Design of Self-governing Organisations*, New Delhi: Sage.

Sibbald, A., C. Ferguson and D. McKillop (2002), 'An examination of key factors of influence in the development process of credit union industries', *Annals of Public and Co-operative Economics*, **73** (3), 399–428.

Siddeley, L. (1992), 'The rise and fall of fraternal insurance organisations', *Humane Studies Review*, **7** (2), 13–16.

Simmons, R. and J. Birchall (2004), 'Creating and supporting co-op members in the West Midlands', *Journal of Co-operative Studies*, **37** (1).

Simmons, R. and J. Birchall (2005), 'A joined-up approach to user participation in public services: strengthening the participation chain', *Social Policy and Administration*, **39** (3), 260–83.

Smith, L. (1961), *The Evolution of Agricultural Co-operation*, Oxford: Blackwell.

Standard Life (2010), *Demutualisation*, accessed 8 March 2010 at www.standardlife.com.

Stefanetti, V. (2010), 'The co-operative banking system in Portugal', in V. Boscia, A. Carretta and P. Schwizer (eds), *Co-operative Banking in Europe: Case Studies*, London: Palgrave Macmillan, pp. 7–22.

Stiglitz, J. (2010), *Freefall: Free Markets and the Sinking of the Global Economy*, Harmondsworth: Penguin.

Strickland, C. (1922), *An Introduction to Co-operation in India*, London and Bombay: Oxford University Press.

Sudradjat, S. (2010), The German co-operative and Raiffeisen system; a brief overview, accessed 18 May 2012 at www.dgrv.de.

Swoboda, R. and Z. Ruibin (2007), 'The world's largest credit co-operative system: facing an uncertain future', *Journal of Co-operative Studies*, **40** (3), 47–51.

Thompson, E.P. (1968), *The Making of the English Working Class*, Harmondsworth: Penguin.

Tomasello, M. (2009), 'Why we co-operate', *Boston Review*, xiii.

Trivers, R.L. (1971), 'The evolution of reciprocal altruism', *Quarterly Review of Biology*, **46**, 35–57.

United Nations (2003), *World Development Report*, Geneva: UN.

Vacek, G. (1989), 'The consumer co-operatives in Japan', in J. Brazda and R. Schediwy (eds), *Consumer Co-operatives in a Changing World*, Geneva: International Co-operative Alliance.

Vaidyanathan, A. and Task Force (2004), *Revival of Co-operative Credit Institutions*, Draft Report, Delhi: Government of India.

Valnek, T. (1999), 'The comparative performance of mutual building societies and stock retail banks', *Journal of Banking and Finance*, **23** (6), 925–38.

Venice declaration (2012), 'Appeal on the importance of cooperative banks for Europe's economic recovery and growth', International Conference 'Promoting the Understanding of Cooperatives for a Better World', Venice, March 2012.

Verba, S., K.L. Schlozman and H.E. Brady (1995), *Voice and Equality: Civic Voluntarism in American Politics*, Cambridge, MA: Harvard University Press.

Vogelaar, N. (2009), 'Rabobank and the credit crisis', in J. Mooij and W.W. Boonstra (eds), *Een eigen koers, Coöperatief bankieren in turbulente tijden*, Amsterdam: VU University Press (English version downloaded from Rabobank.com).

Warbasse, J. (1936), *Co-operative Democracy*, New York: Harper.

Ward, A. and D. McKillop (2005), 'An investigation into the link between UK credit union characteristics, location and their success', *Annals of Public and Co-operative Economics*, **76** (3), 461–89.

Westley, G. and B. Branch (eds) (2000), *Safe Money: Building Effective Credit Unions in Latin America*, Washington, DC: Inter-American Development Bank and World Council of Credit Unions.

Westley, G. and S. Shaffer (1999), 'Credit union policies and performance in Latin America', *Journal of Banking and Finance*, 1303–29.

White, L. (1991), *The S&L Debacle: Public Policy Lessons for Bank and Thrift Regulation*, Oxford: Oxford University Press.

Wisconsin (2010), *User-owned comprehensive health insurance*, accessed 2 March 2010 at www.uwcc.wisc.edu.

Wolff (1893) *People's Banks: a record of social and economic success* (first edition), London: PS King.

Wolff, H. (1907), *Co-operative Banking: its Principles and Practice*, London: PS King.

Wolff, H. (1910), *People's Banks: a Record of Social and Economic Success*, London: PS King.

World Bank (2007a), *Strengthening India's Rural Credit Co-operatives*, Washington, DC: World Bank.

World Bank (2007b), 'World Bank approves US$600 million for Government of India to revitalise financial access for poorest farmers', Press Release no. 2007/494/SAR.

World Bank (2008), *Finance for All? Policies and Pitfalls in Expanding Access*, Washington, DC: World Bank.

World Council of Credit Unions (2012a), *2011 Statistical Report*, Madison, WI: World Council of Credit Unions.

World Council of Credit Unions (2012b), Information provided on website, accessed August 2012 at www.woccu.org.

World Savings Banks Institute (2012), Website, accessed 9 May 2012 at wsbi.org ac.

Wright, R. (1994), *The Moral Animal*, London: Abacus.

Xiao, Y. (2009), 'French banks amid the global financial crisis', IMF Working Paper, Washington, DC: International Monetary Fund.

Yunus, M. (1999), *Banker to the Poor: the Story of the Grameen Bank*, London: Aurum Press.

Yunus, M. (2008), *Creating a World Without Poverty: Social Business and the Future of Capitalism*, New York: Public Affairs.

Zamagni, S. (2012), 'The impact of co-operatives on civil and connective capital', *Conference on Promoting the Understanding of Co-operatives for a Better World*, Venice.

Index

ABACUS (Australia) 56, 86
Abbey National Building Society (UK) 82
ABCUL (Britain) 60
ACDI/VOCA 60
Afghanistan 51–2
Africa
    credit unions – current situation 48–9
    early history of credit unions 41
    impact of the banking crisis on credit unions 109
agricultural co-operative banks 88–9
All-Party Parliamentary Group Enquiry (UK) 101
Alliance and Leicester Building Society 83
America's Community Bankers 86
Asociation Espanola de Cajas Rurales (Spain) 29
Asia
    credit unions – current situation 49–55
    early history of credit unions 43
    impact of the banking crisis on credit unions 109
Associated Wholesale Grocers (USA) 205
Association of Co-operative Banks (Greece) 30
Australia
    credit unions – current situation 55–6
    demutualisation of building societies 85
    early history of credit unions 36
Austria
    current situation of co-operative banks 24–5
    history of co-operative banks 17

impact of the banking crisis on co-operative banks 106
Austrian Co-operative Union 24
Azerbaijan 51

Banche di Credito Cooperativo (BCC, Italy) 25
Banche popolari (BP, Italy) 25, 94, 106, 128
Bangladesh 39, 51
Bankmecu (Australia) 56
Bankrakyat (Indonesia) 146
banking crises (prior to 2007) 19, 29, 94, 99, 127–8
banking regulation 210–11
Banque Raiffeisen (Luxembourg) 30
Banques Populaires (France) 27, 103, 107
Barbados 57
Basel III regulations 157–8
Belarus 60
Belgium
    demutualisation 19
    history of co-operative banks 18
Belize 57
Benin 48
Bergengren, Roy 35–6
Bolivia 57
box societies 1–2, 191
BPCE Banking Group (France) 27, 107
Bradford and Bingley Building Society 83
Brazil 57
Britain
    current situation of credit unions 59–60
    early history of credit unions 42
    impact of the banking crisis on credit unions 111
Britannia Building Society 84, 90

building societies (*see also* savings and
     loans)
   demutualisation 82–4
   effects of the banking crisis 85
   impact of the crisis 114–15
   performance before the banking
     crisis 101–2
   their expansion during the 20th
     century 73–5
   their growth in Britain 68–71
   their invention in Britain 66–7
Building Societies Act (1836) 67
Building Societies Act (1874) 70

Building Societies Association (UK)
   75, 83
Burkina Faso 41
BVR (co-operative federation) 23

Caisses d'Epargne (France) 27
Caja Laboral Popular (Spain) 92
Caja Popular Mexicana 57
Cajas de Ahorras (Spain) 137
Cambodia 51–2
Cameroon 41
Canada
   credit unions – current situation
     61–3
   early history of credit unions 34–6
   impact of the banking crisis on
     credit unions 111
Canadian Co-operative Association
   48–9, 52
Caribbean
   credit unions – current situation
     57–8
   impact of the banking crisis on
     credit unions 109
Caribbean Confederation of Credit
   Unions 42
Casse di Risparmio (Savings banks,
   Italy) 25
Central Federal Credit Union (USA)
   61
Cheltenham and Gloucester Building
   Society (UK) 82
Chile 57
China
   credit unions – current situation
     54–5

early history of credit unions 40–1
   reform of rural credit co-operatives
     162
Coady, Moses 36
CoBank (USA) 88
Colombia 57
consumer co-operative banks 89–92
Co-op Italia 189
Co-op Schweiz 189
Co-operative Group (UK) 189, 205
Co-operative Wholesale Society (UK)
   185
Coopeuch (Chile) 57
co-operation – theories of 166–9
Cooperativa Farmaceutica Espanola
   (Spain) 204
Co-operative banks
   current situation (*see also* individual
     countries) 21–32
   early history in Germany 8–17
   impact of the crisis (*see also*
     individual countries) 102–8
   performance before the banking
     crisis 95–9
   recent history 19–20
   spread to other countries 17–18
Co-operative Central Bank (Cyprus)
   30
Co-operative Credit Societies Act
   (1904, India) 37
Co-operative principles 184
Costa Rica 57
Coventry Building Society 86
Credit Agricole (France) 26, 103, 107,
   158
Credit Mutuel (France) 27, 103, 107,
   158
Creditcoop (Romania) 32
Credito Agricola (Portugal) 30
credit unions
   classification systems 43–5
   current situation (*see also* individual
     regions/countries) 46–63
   early history in Canada, USA 34–6
   history in colonial countries 36–41
   impact of the crisis (*see also*
     individual regions/countries)
     109–113
   performance before the banking
     crisis 99

regulation and supervision 159–161
remittances 133
spread of the sector worldwide
     41–3
Credit Union Central of Canada 62
Credit Union National Association
     (USA) 35, 42
Credit Union National Extension
     Bureau (USA) 35
CUNA Mutual (USA) 35
customer-owned banks
     advantages derived from benefit
          123–4
     advantages derived from control
          121–3
     advantages derived from federation
          124–5
     advantages derived from ownership
          118–121
     benefits to the banking system
          130–2
     contribution to local economies
          132–4
definition of 1–3, 117–8
     disadvantages derived from diluted
          ownership 125–9
     disadvantages derived from
          federation 130
     disadvantages derived from lack of
          benefit 129–130
     disadvantages derived from lack of
          control 129
     regulation and supervision 149–150,
          156–8
customer-owned businesses
     advantages and disadvantages of
          customer-ownership 207–9
     definition 182
     insurance providers
     retailers 182–190
     suppliers to primary producers
          203–4
     suppliers to small businesses 206–7
     suppliers to small retailers 204–6
     utilities 198–203
Cyprus 30

demutualisation (also known as
     conversion) 4, 19, 25, 77, 85,
     101–2, 131, 196–7, 205

Denmark
     current situation of co-operative
          banks 30
     history of co-operative banks 18
design (of business organisations) 7–8
Desjardins, Alphonse 34–5
Desjardins, Dorimene 34
Desjardins Group (Canada) 61–2,
     111–2, 130
Developpement International
     Desjardins (Canada) 51
diversification and hybrid ownership
     forms 158–9
Dodson, Charles 194
Duncan, Henry 136
Dunfermline Building Society 85,
     114–15
DZ Bank (Germany) 21, 31, 94, 102–4

Ecuador 57, 99
Edeka Group (Germany) 204
El Salvador 57
electricity co-operatives 200–202
Equitable Life (UK) 194 (USA) 195–6
Ethiopia 48
Europe
     credit unions - current situation
          58–60
     impact of the banking crisis on
          credit unions 111
European Co-operative Banking
     Association 46
evolution (of business organisations)
     7–8
evolutionary theories of co-operation
     170–72

Farm Credit System Insurance
     Corporation (USA) 89
Fay, C.R. 13, 15, 17
Federal Home Loan Bank Board
     (USA) 76, 80–81
Federal Savings and Loans Insurance
     Corporation (USA) 76
Federcasse (Italy) 25
Fiji 55
Filene, Edward 3, 35
Finland
     current situation of co-operative
          banks 29

history of co-operative banks 18
impact of the banking crisis on
co-operative banks 108
Foodstuffs (New Zealand) 205
France
current situation of co-operative
banks 26–8
history of co-operative banks 18
impact of the banking crisis on
co-operative banks 106–7
friendly societies (in the USA known
as fraternal societies) 191–4

Gebhard, Dr 18
German Co- operative and Raiffeisen
Union 206
Germany
building societies 85
current situation of co-operative
banks 23
history of co-operative banks 8–17
impact of the banking crisis on
co-operative banks 105
landesbanks and *sparkassen* 137
Ghana 49
governance of customer-owned banks
151–3
Grameen Bank 5, 51, 143–5
Great Britain (*see* Britain)
Greece 30
Grenada 57
Guatemala 42, 57

Haiti 57–8
Halifax Building Society 83
Hesse Union of Co-operative Banks
(Germany) 204
Hevey, Monsignor 34
Honduras 42, 57
Hong Kong 50
Huber, Victor-Aime 10
Hungary 31

India
current situation/reform process
50–4
early history of credit co-operatives
36–9
reform of rural credit co-operatives
161–2

Indonesia 50
insurers owned by other types of
co-operative 195–7
Intermarche Group (France) 204
International Accounting Standards
Board 128, 158
International Co-operative Alliance
187
International Co-operative Banking
Association 157
International Co-operative and Mutual
Insurance Federation 196, 198
investor-owned banks with a
substantial cooperative ownership
stake 93
Ireland
current situation of credit unions 58
demutualisation of building societies
85
early co-operative banks 18
early history of credit unions 34–6
impact of the banking crisis on
credit unions 111
Islamic credit unions 52
Italy
current situation of co-operative
banks 25–6
history of co-operative banks 17–18
impact of the banking crisis on
co-operative banks 106

Jamaica 42, 57, 99
Japan 52, 162–3
Jay, Pierre 35

Kazakhstan 51
Kent Reliance Building Society 85,
114
Kenya 48
Kenya Co-operative Bank 92
Kesko Group (Finland) 204
Kyrgyzstan 51
Kiriwandeniya, P.A. 40

Landesbanks (Germany) 137, 140
Landshypotek (Sweden) 30
Laos 51
Latin America
credit unions – current situation
56–7

early history of credit unions 42
impact of the banking crisis on
   credit unions 111
Leclerc (France) 205
Leeds Building Society 86
legal framework for credit unions
   159–161
Lloyds Banking Group (UK) 138
Londis (UK and Ireland) 205
Luxembourg
   current situation of co-operative
      banks 30
Luzzatti, Luigi 11, 17–18, 34

Malaysia 39, 48, 51
Malawi 48
Mali 48
Massachusetts Credit Union Act 35
member participation in customer-
   owned banks 154–5
Metropolitan Equitable Building
   Society 68
Mexico 57
micro-finance institutions
   comparison with Sanasa movement
      145
   its adaptation (Grameen I and II)
      144–5
   origins of the idea 143–4
   other types of micro-finance
      institution 145–7
Migros (Switzerland) 188–9
Mondragon cooperative group 61,
   92
Mongolia 50
Motivation theories 164–6
Move your Money campaign 211
multi-purpose co-operative societies
   (Sri Lanka) 39, 92
multi-sectoral co-operative banks 92–3
mutual incentives theory
   evidence from case studies 176–81
   the theory explained 172–5
mutual insurance 194–5
mutualisation (ie conversion to mutual
   status) 196–7
Myanmar 51
Myners Review of Mutual Insurance
   (UK) 153

National Association of Co-operative
   Savings and Credit Unions
   (Poland) 59
National Bank for Agriculture and
   Rural Development (India) 53
National Cable Television Co-operative
   206
National Co-operative Bank (USA)
   92
National Credit Union Administration
   (USA) 112
National Federation of Savings
   Co-operatives (Hungary) 31
National Federation of State
   Co-operative Banks (India) 52
National Federation of Urban
   Co-operative Banks and Credit
   Societies (India) 50
National Rural Electric Co-operatives
   Association (USA) 201
National Union of Co-operative Banks
   (Poland) 31
Nationwide Building Society (UK)
   82–3, 86, 102
Nationwide Mutual Insurance
   Company (USA) 196
Navy Federal Credit Union (USA) 44,
   60
Nepal 50
Netherlands
   current situation of co-operative
      banks 28–9
   history of co-operative banks 17–18
   impact of the banking crisis on
      co-operative banks 107
New Zealand 55–6, 85
Nicaragua 57
Nicholson, Sir Frederick 37
Nongyup Bank (Korea) 89
Norinchukin Bank (Japan) 89, 94,
   113–4
North America
   current situation of credit unions
      60–3
   impact of the banking crisis on
      credit unions 111
Northern Rock Building Society 83,
   102, 210
Noweda Apothek (Germany) 204
NTUC Fair Price (Singapore) 190

Oceania
    credit unions – current situation
        55–6
    impact of the banking crisis on
        credit unions 113
Office of Thrift Supervision (USA) 81
Okobank (Finland) 18
OP Pohjola Group (Finland) 29, 108
OVAG Bank (Austria) 24, 106
Oxford Provident Building Society
    (USA) 68

Pakistan 39
Panama 57
Papua New Guinea 55
Paraguay 57
People's Credit Funds (Vietnam) 51
Philippines 49
Poland
    credit unions 59
    current situation of co-operative
        banks 31
    history of co-operative banks 17
    impact of the banking crisis on
        credit unions 111
Portugal
    current situation of co-operative
        banks 30
Public Service Investment Society
    (New Zealand) 56

Rabobank (Netherlands) 19, 21, 28,
    103, 107, 128, 158
Raiffeisen, Friedrich 3, 12–13, 34, 37
Raiffeisen Austria 24, 106, 158
Raiffeisen Switzerland 30, 94, 128
reform of government-controlled credit
    co-operatives 161–3
regional farm credit banks (USA) 89
Reserve Bank of India 38, 51
Rewe Group (Germany) 204
Rochdale Pioneers 182–5
Rochdale Savings Bank 185
Romania 32
Royal Commission of 1872 (into
    building societies) 69
rural credit co-operatives (China) 52
Rural credit societies (India) 52
Russell, A.E. 36
Russia 17, 60

Rwanda 41
RZB Bank (Austria) 24, 103

St Francis Xavier University
    (Extension Dept) 36
St Lucia 57
St Vincent 57
S-Bank (Finland) 90
S-Group (Finland) 189, 205
Saguapac (water co-operative, Bolivia)
    200
Sanasa movement (Sri Lanka) 40,
    49–50, 145–6
SaskCentral (Canada) 111
savings and loans (also known as
    S&Ls, thrifts)
    current situation 86
    demutualisation and financial crisis
        79–82
    performance before the banking
        crisis 99–100
    their expansion in the 20th century
        75–8
    their growth in the USA 71–3
    their invention in the USA 67–8
savings banks
    comparison with customer-owned
        banks 141–2
    conversion to other types 138–9
    current situation 137–8
    definition 135–6
    effects of the banking crisis
        139–141
    historical origins 136–7
Say, Leon 11
Schulze-Delitzsch, Hermann 3, 9–12,
    206–7
Schulze and Raiffeisen systems
    (comparison of) 14–16
Scratchley, Arthur 68
Senegal 48
Sicredi (Brazil) 57
Sierra Leone 49
Shinkin banks (Japan) 52
Singapore 39, 49
Skipton Building Society 86
Solomon Islands 55
South Korea 49, 140–1, 162
Spain
    Cajas de Ahorras 137

current situation of co-operative
banks 29–30
history of co-operative banks 17
impact of the banking crisis on
co-operative banks 108
Spar Group 205
Sparkassen (German savings banks)
137, 140
Sri Lanka (*see also* Sanasa movement)
history of co-operative savings and
credit 39–40
reform of rural co-operative banks
162
Sanasa movement 49–50
stakeholder banking model 5, 135
Standard Life (UK) 196
Starr-Bowkett building societies 70
Sweden
current situation of co-operative
banks 30
demutualisation 19
Switzerland
current situation of co-operative
banks 30
history of co-operative banks 17
Systeme U (France) 204

Taiwan 50
Tanzania 48, 49, 162
telecoms co-operatives 202
Thailand 49
Togo 41, 48
Tompkins, Jimmy 36
Tonga 55
transport co-operatives 202–3
Trinidad and Tobago 57
Trustee Savings Bank 139
types of bank 116–7

Uganda 48–9
UK Co-operative Bank 4, 23, 60, 85,
90–1, 123, 139, 189
UNIMED (Brazil) 206

Union Nacional de Cooperativas de
Credito (Spain) 29
United States of America
credit unions – current situation
60–1
early history of credit unions 34–6
United States Agency for International
Development (USAID) 42, 57–9
United States League of Local
Building and Loan Associations
73
United States League of Savings
Associations 77
Uruguay 57
US Central Corporate Credit Union
112

Vaidyanathan Report (India) 39,
53–4
Vietnam 41, 50
Volksbanken International (Austria)
24

Wakefern Food Corporation (USA)
204
water co-operatives 200
WGZ Bank 23
Wolff, Henry 11, 15–16, 31, 34, 66
Wollemborg, Dr 18
Women's Development Services
Co-operative Society 50
Woolwich Building Society (UK) 83
worker co-operative banks 92
World Council of Credit Unions
(WOCCU) 42, 43, 46, 49, 52,
57–9, 160
World Savings Banks Institute 137
Wrigley, Edmund 71

Yorkshire Building Society 86
Yunus, Mohammed 143

Zimbabwe 41